HELPING SINGLE PARENTS WITH TROUBLED KIDS

DR. GREG CYNAUMON

SINGLES *Ministry Resources*

DAVID C. COOK PUBLISHING CO.
ELGIN, ILLINOIS 60120

SINGLES MINISTRY RESOURCES is a division of Cook Communications Ministries. In fulfilling its mission to encourage the acceptance of Jesus Christ as personal Savior and to contribute to the teaching and putting into practice of His two great commandments, Cook Communications Ministries creates and disseminates Christian communication materials and services to people throughout the world. SINGLES MINISTRY RESOURCES provides training seminars, a national convention, a journal, and resource materials to assist churches in developing a ministry with single adults that will encourage growth in loving God and each other.

Helping Single Parents with Troubled Kids
by Dr. Greg Cynaumon

Unless otherwise noted, Scripture in this publication is from the Holy Bible: New International Version (NIV), copyright © 1973, 1978, 1984, International Bible Society, used by permission of Zondervan Bible Publishers. Other versions used include the New American Standard Bible (NASB), © The Lockman Foundation 1960, 1962, 1963, 1968, 1971, 1972, 1973, 1975, 1977; The Living Bible (TLB), © 1971, used by permission of Tyndale House Publishers, Inc., Wheaton, IL 60189, all rights reserved; and the King James Version (KJV).

Some of the anecdotal illustrations in this book are true to life and are included with the permission of the persons involved. All other illustrations are composites of real situations, and any resemblance to people living or dead is coincidental.

Those who assisted in the editing and production of this book are Donna Dare, Dan Jamison, Jerry Jones, Jean Stephens, Debby Weaver, Steve Webb, Thom Westergren, and Betty Wright.

Cover illustration by Tim Lewis.

Printed in the United States of America.

ISBN 0-7814-5043-8

CONTENTS

ACKNOWLEDGMENTS

To you pastors, singles' ministers, youth pastors, youth leaders, and lay counselors who have stepped forward and accepted the challenge to help the single-parent family, I give my deepest thanks and respect for rallying around the cause of the single-parent family. Your efforts demonstrate that we share a common belief, namely, that our churches are perhaps the final hope for truly helping the single-parent family.

Single moms and dads have perhaps the most underrated and underappreciated job of all time. In addition to being both a mom and a dad, they face daily parental challenges of being a friend when times are tough, a doctor when knees are skinned, and a counselor when feelings are hurt and spirits are low. They are the bread winner outside the home and the housekeeper inside the home. They care for their families with the selflessness of saints and the patience of Job.

Because of this, I give single moms and dads my respect, admiration, and commitment. I want to travel with them and help them along their journey. I pray God's continued blessings in their lives, and I pray that they will reap the benefits of every word of this book. I pray that God's Word will speak to them, either directly or indirectly, through the ministry of others, through these pages.

For the years of research writing that this project consumed, I thank my beautiful wife, Jan, for supporting and encouraging me in the pursuit of my ministry. You are the essence of grace. To my daughter Tracy Lynn and my son Matthew, I thank you for your love and support and your ability to keep balance and perspective in my life with your grace, love, and humor.

I thank my friends and colleagues at Minirth-Meier Clinic West—Dr. John Townsend, Dr. David Stoop, Dr. Henry Cloud, Bob Whiton, Guy Owen, and Gary Tash—for your support and encouragement. I thank Dr. Michael Kogutek, my friend and clinical mentor. I thank Jerry Jones at Singles Ministry Resources for your support of our shared vision, but most of all for your gift of encouragement and your great laugh.

Finally, I want to acknowledge and thank my parents, Ed and Myrna Cynaumon, and my brother and partner, Dana, for providing me with a loving and supportive family foundation on which to grow.

LIST OF FIGURES

FOREWORD

Throughout the United States of America, Minirth-Meier therapists see many thousands of children, teens, and adults who suffer from a variety of emotional pains stemming from single-parent family existence. Life can really be tough, even for two-parent "functional" families; but the difficulties multiply rapidly in single-parent situations.

That is why I am so thankful for this book by my good friend and fellow therapist Dr. Greg Cynaumon. Greg's experiences as a cop followed by a specialized career as a therapist and radio show personality focusing on single-parent problems have prepared him to give therapists, pastors, and single parents themselves the practical advice they need in dealing with single-parenting problems.

Throughout both the Old and New Testaments, God said that He measures our true spirituality by our loving concern and assistance for widows and orphans. As a psychiatrist, I can testify to the fact that, even if both parents are alive, single-parent families exist as functional widows and orphans. Over half of all children in America today will spend part or all of their lives in a single-parent family.

Those of us who are therapists, pastors, lay counselors, parents, or friends of loved ones who are tossed into single-parent family situations have a moral and ethical obligation—and a wonderful, rewarding opportunity—to reach out and touch someone in a meaningful way.

Studying the wise principles and advice in this book will be a great boost to our ability to fulfill this God-given commission more efficiently and meaningfully.

Paul Meier, M.D.
Co-director of the Minirth-Meier Clinics

INTRODUCTION

The last evening in August 1977 proved to be cruelly hot. Of course, a bullet-proof vest, wool long-sleeved uniform shirt, and a beat-up police car without air conditioning didn't help either.

Fresh out of the police academy, I had been radioed to investigate a possible child custody dispute. Although slightly disappointed that it wasn't something more exciting—say, armed robbery—I nonetheless proceeded to the scene with a rookie's enthusiasm.

As I neared the address in my smoldering patrol car (rookies always get a vehicle with one wheel in the junk yard), I was surprised by the tranquility of the neighborhood. No cars on blocks in the front yard. No dented garbage cans filled to overflowing. No toothy dogs tethered to trees by heavy rusted chains.

What I saw instead were shady evergreens presiding over even greener lawns; hedges that looked as if they had been sculpted by surveyors, they were so perfectly straight; and row after row of well-maintained homes. *Everybody must have the same gardener,* I thought. It was a Mr. Rogers kind of neighborhood, if you know what I mean.

So what is this bit about a child custody dispute? No way, I told myself, checking both sides of the well-illuminated street for the address. Not in a nice, middle-class neighborhood like this. After all, child custody disputes happen to other families, not to people who live in a place like this.

But the reality of the situation became apparent as I rounded the turn to the designated address. A well-dressed man in his mid-twenties was struggling desperately to wrench a child from a terrified woman's tight grasp. Although it played in my mind like a poorly acted scene from a second-rate movie, the situation was real. Unfortunately, nobody was acting.

The next few moments seemed like an eternity as I tried to persuade the man to release his son. The father was nearing panic. He closed his arm around his son's throat in a choke hold and demanded that I leave immediately or he would be forced to hurt his son. In his own terror, the boy screamed uncontrollably for his mother to help him.

After ten or fifteen minutes of negotiating, I was finally able to persuade the

- *How the author first developed an interest in single-parent families.*

- *How this book can be a practical resource for those in the church.*

father that *he* was placing his son's life in danger. Conceding that there was no good solution to this situation, the father quietly relinquished his son. "All I wanted was to be with my son," he said, losing the battle with his tears. "She won't let me see him, and I can't go on living like this anymore."

I had no way of knowing that those few minutes would influence my perception of life. Even though it was only the first of hundreds of similar cases I would handle, this routine child custody call served to direct my attention to the unique issues facing single-parent families.

Like other officers who are faced with similar situations on a day-to-day basis, I functioned with a legalistic mind-set. I found it difficult to resist the tendency to harden to life's problems. My colleagues and I often joked that it is easier to have a child than it is to get a driver's license.

Our response was that the problem was a governmental oversight. We imagined how much easier our jobs would be if the state would require prospective parents to achieve a passing grade on a parenting exam. We concluded that the exam would consist of a battery of psychological tests designed to rate the applicants' overall parenting skills.

We got very creative in thinking about the exam. It would start by rating levels of commitment and would end with a measure of how many years the applicant could endure Ninja Turtle reruns without becoming a mere shell (no pun intended). Of course, no exam worth its weight in fruit snacks would be complete without a take-home quiz. So, during this portion of the test (as we imagined designing it), the applicant would be loaned one or two "test kids" (one for the faint-hearted, two for those with strong stomachs), and the applicant would have to provide the normal parental stuff for a week or two. At the end of the exam period, the test kids would be returned to the exam place to rate the applicant. Needless to say, any bumps, bruises, or suspicious marks left by tire chains resulted in the automatic rejection of the applicant's permit. Also at this time, the test kids would be asked some questions about the applicant's ability to ensure they got at least eighteen hours of lively entertainment each day (as is customary in all normal homes). If the test kids didn't think the applicant was likely to be the next Bill Cosby, the applicant failed the test. Sorry, no kid permit this time. The applicant would then be required to take Remedial Parenting 101 and could apply again in three months.

Even with our enlightened sensitivity, we cops realized that this was a sarcastic and unreasonable (okay, silly) way to try to improve the conditions in which children are raised. But the one point our fantasy did serve to illustrate clearly was this: If it is the challenge of a lifetime to raise kids in a two-parent family, what must it be like to raise children alone? What could it possibly be like to stare straight into an eighteen-year commitment, without the assistance of a second parent, to raise children to become loving, responsible, and productive Christian adults?

How does one parent make up for the missing love, attention, guidance, role modeling, and sheer time that kids need and generally get (in varying degrees of success) from interaction with both parents? With the awesome responsibility of providing the basic necessities of food, clothing, and shelter, how do single

> "All I wanted was to be with my son," he said, losing the battle with his tears. "She won't let me see him and I can't go on living like this anymore."

parents cope with finding the time and inner strength to provide the emotional necessities such as love, morals, value systems, and self-esteem? Even in our most cynical moments, those of us on the police force knew that the questions facing single-parent families are complex and challenging.

ADDING NEW PERSPECTIVES

In an attempt to uncover clues to some of these questions, I accepted an opportunity to become a Big Brother to a teenager whose father had abandoned his family and had left behind a trail of emotional and physical abuse. I witnessed, firsthand, that even a family labeled as dysfunctional while together could become even further immobilized during the tumultuous months following a divorce.

From each experience, I gained insight into the lives of single-parent families which dramatically impacted the way I, as an officer, related to domestic violence and child custody disputes. I found myself becoming much more sensitive to the emotional welfare of the child rather than to that of the parents. I also became quite frustrated with parents who neglected to consider the impact of their behavior on their children, parents whose primary motives were their own pain, anger, frustration, and desire for revenge.

Tell Me How You Feel About This Ticket

After ten years on the force, I realized that police work was perhaps a poor personal choice for the next twenty-five years, so I decided to return to school. After receiving my undergraduate degree in psychology, another life lesson became apparent. That lesson was that sensitivity is to a policeman what a taste of wine is to an alcoholic: The two just don't go together. I found myself providing ten to fifteen minutes of roadside therapy with each traffic ticket I wrote. "So, sir, tell me how you are feeling about this traffic ticket. Have I taken on the role of a parental figure in your life?" Even though I loved helping people become law-abiding citizens, the idea of being everybody's dad grew less and less appealing.

However, leaving Winchell's Donuts was one of the most difficult steps in my decision to leave the police force. The kind folks there would forever be negatively impacted by my decision. As it happens, Winchell's stock took a turn for the worse in 1987, the year I gave up glazed donuts. Regrettably, part of my new career choice required that I give back the beeper Winchell's Donuts had given me to signal when the fresh donuts hit the oil.

Although I knew I would certainly miss the action and the camaraderie of my fellow officers (as well as the donuts), I realized it was time to move on to another profession that would allow me to concentrate more of my efforts on helping people before their lives reached a point of crisis. I wanted an opportunity to take a *proactive* rather than a *reactive* approach to helping people.

In search of additional direction, I contacted a friend whose company operated adolescent psychiatric hospitals in Southern California, and I accepted a position and set out on a new career. My hope was that I could be more *responsive* rather than *reactive* to people's needs. I also saw my new career as a way to continue my studies of single-parent families from a new and broader perspective.

You Mean There's More to Write About Than a Crime?

A few months into my new career, I decided to pursue a side interest in writing. (After all, ten years of polishing my skills by writing out police reports shouldn't go completely to waste.) After shedding the habit of writing everything in the third person ("While on patrol, the undersigned officer and officer Jones . . ."), I contacted a local newspaper editor to suggest an idea for a question and answer column focusing on adolescent psychological issues. From that contact, my column "Focus on Teens" was created.

The format for "Focus on Teens" was really a "Dear Abby" type column with a more psychological perspective. Another major difference was that I referred the readers' questions to a different psychologist, psychiatrist, or counselor each week. This allowed for literally hundreds of different opinions on hundreds of subjects. Using these clinicians also helped the reader understand that there are many different ways of looking at a problem as well as many workable solutions to the same problem.

After three years, "Focus on Teens" evolved into "Family Forum." In an effort to cover a wider variety of family issues, I used the column to respond to hundreds of teens, children, and parents. As these people wrote to me with their questions and problems, "Family Forum" allowed me to reach countless families and receive knowledge from professionals. The newspaper column also played an important role in helping me to process new facts about single-parent families. The importance of this issue was evident in the number of letters I received from adolescents as well as parents needing help with their own single-parent family issues.

I have been truly blessed with the luxury of perspective. I look back on my experiences as a police officer, newspaper columnist, and counselor, and I recognize that the Lord was leading me in directions that would enable me to minister to single-parent families. My challenge was to combine my varied perspectives to illuminate a new way of addressing the problems facing single-parent families.

THIS BOOK AS A RESOURCE

Helping Single Parents with Troubled Kids is intended to serve as a resource. I pray that it will provide hope, support, guidance, and a practical set of tools for those in the church who have been called to the ministry of helping others.

- *Pastors* oversee the church body and are often called upon by single parents and their children to provide counsel in emergency situations. Especially in smaller churches, it is the pastor who must have the best resources available—resources which will enable him or her to address individual needs of the parishioners in the most expedient manner.
- *Singles' pastors* quite often are the individuals who work most closely with the single parents and, therefore, know them best. The singles' pastors are in perhaps the best position to learn about the specific challenges facing single parents and about ways they can provide support and guidance.
- *Youth pastors and youth workers* have the children and teens from single-parent families in their groups, outings, and activities. Youth

pastors and workers are in the unique position to look for and proactively respond to the warning signs of crisis in young people.

● *Lay counselors* within the church often are called upon to provide ongoing counsel for single parents and their children if and when needs or problems arise.

Inter-Ministry Consultation

I can't stress enough the importance of frequent consultations between staff members. For instance, if the singles' pastor is counseling with a single mom who is experiencing emotional difficulties, it would be beneficial for that pastor to consult with the youth pastor. This process must be unilateral. Often the singles' pastor may not know a single mom is in need of help until the youth pastor reports a problem he or she is having with the child in youth group. Even though you are involved in busy ministries, you might try to set aside a few minutes at the end of staff meetings to discuss single-parent families within your various groups.

To the Task Before Us

Finally, before we begin the journey into the unique lives and emotions of single-parent families, it is imperative to make a statement about single-parent families. Years of interaction with this special population of parents, children, and teens have taught me that they can be incomparably healthy and resourceful people. I have often been in awe of the success that countless single parents have realized in raising their children with little and sometimes no help.

It is important to keep in perspective that millions of single-parent families make it through the tough times unscathed. This book is not intended to minimize in any way the accomplishments of these parents. It is intended, however, to illustrate, educate, and provide resource materials for those of us who work with single-parent families.

Helping Single Parents with Troubled Kids contains numerous case studies. Many of these cases came from the single-parent surveys themselves or from personal interviews. Others were discovered through interaction with other psychologists and marriage and family therapists. In all of the cases presented in the book, the patients' names and specific facts have been changed to protect their confidentiality.

It is important to keep in perspective that millions of single-parent families make it through the tough times unscathed. This book is not intended to minimize in any way the accomplishments of these parents.

AN OPPORTUNITY FOR TODAY'S CHURCH

Perhaps no people group better exemplifies the chance [the church has] to make a difference in people's lives. . . . Almost without exception, single parents hurt from their broken relationships, their economic hardships, and their bouts with self-doubt. And increasingly, we hear from single parents that the Church is not a place of healing but of condemnation. In what ways can we facilitate the Church becoming a reflection of God's values and love to the growing numbers of single parents?

— *GEORGE BARNA, author and researcher,* **Ministry Currents, April-June 1992**

⊰ 1 ⊱

THE SINGLE-PARENT FAMILY EPIDEMIC

Rebecca, age six, was brought into my office for counseling by her mom. The situation that her mother described to me over the phone involved the fact that Rebecca had recently begun wetting her bed, although she had originally stopped doing so almost four years earlier. Rebecca's mom grew even more concerned when Rebecca asked her to buy diapers during a subsequent trip to the grocery store. In addition, Rebecca was becoming very clingy. Whenever Mom dropped Rebecca off at school, Rebecca would cry and want to be held. Needless to say, these changes in behavior made life very difficult for both Rebecca and her mom.

During our first session, Rebecca clung to her mother's side and did not speak at all. Rebecca's mom talked about how Rebecca used to be very independent and outgoing until she and Rebecca's father had gone through a very unpleasant divorce. She also stated that Rebecca was very close to her father, who had moved a four-hour drive away.

After a few sessions, Rebecca began opening up. Slowly, I began asking her about her father, and I asked her to share with me how she felt about her parents' divorce. Rebecca did not respond immediately but just looked at her mother. I asked her if she would be all right if Mom waited in the outside room, to which she nodded her consent. After her mom left the room, Rebecca again looked anxious and began fidgeting in her seat. I asked, "Tell me about what kinds of things you and your dad used to do on weekends." As she stared at the floor, she softly answered, "We used to go to the park or to the zoo sometimes." "Do you get to see or talk to your father very often now that he has moved away?" I asked. Rebecca closed her eyes and began crying softly, "Why do Mom and Dad hate each other? Doesn't God want people to love each other and stay married forever?"

In subsequent sessions, Rebecca and I talked about how two people can start out in marriage being very much in love and how sometimes those feelings can change over time. She related stories of the anger that was present between her mom and dad prior to the divorce and how it got even worse after the breakup. Rebecca felt that she was at least partly to blame for the divorce. In her child-mind, her parents' frequent arguments about money and visitation revolved around her.

17

FIGURE 1.1
CHILDREN IN SINGLE-PARENT FAMILIES

How does your state compare? According to national research conducted by the Center for the Study of Social Policy,[1] the number of children living in single-parent homes drastically increased during the 1980s. In addition, the study found that one-fifth of all children are considered to be living in poverty—more than any other group in America. Below is a look at the percent of children in single-parent families by state as well as the increase or decrease (by percent) in each state from 1980 to 1991.

		National Rank (by State)	Percent Change Since 1980 NOTE: Black bar indicates average U.S. percent change (+13%) since 1980.	Percent of Children in Single-Parent Families	
			WORSE ◄——————► BETTER	1980	1991
	1	North Dakota	-28%	9.6	12.4
States	2	Idaho	-4%	14.2	14.7
with	3	Nebraska	+2%	15.2	14.8
LOWEST	4	Iowa	0	14.9	15.0
Percent	5	Utah	-30%	11.9	15.5
of	6	New Hampshire	+6%	17.4	16.3
Children	7	Wyoming	-26%	13.0	16.4
in	8	Wisconsin	-10%	15.8	17.5
Single-	9	Kansas	-13%	16.2	18.3
Parent	10	Connecticut	+13%	21.2	18.5
Families	11	Minnesota	-21%	15.6	18.9
	12	Rhode Island	+18%	23.0	19.0
	13	South Dakota	-52%	13.1	19.9
	13	Hawaii	-9%	18.3	19.9
	15	Montana	-49%	13.4	20.0
	16	Vermont	-52%	13.4	20.3
	16	Pennsylvania	-9%	18.7	20.3
	18	Alaska	-12%	18.7	21.0
	19	Maine	-27%	16.6	21.2
	20	West Virginia	-25%	17.2	21.5
	21	Ohio	-6%	20.6	21.7
	22	Texas	-12%	19.5	21.9
	23	Washington	-22%	18.1	22.0
	24	Missouri	-17%	19.2	22.5
	24	Oklahoma	-24%	18.2	22.5
	26	California	-4%	22.1	22.9
	26	New Jersey	0	22.8	22.9
	28	Indiana	-18%	19.4	23.0
	28	Oregon	-14%	20.3	23.0
	28	New Mexico	-33%	17.3	23.0
	31	Arizona	-18%	19.7	23.2
	32	Kentucky	-35%	17.6	23.7
	33	Virginia	-9%	22.5	24.5
	33	Massachusetts	-21%	20.3	24.5
	35	North Carolina	-13%	22.4	25.2
	36	Delaware	-32%	19.5	25.7
	37	Colorado	-46%	17.9	26.1
	38	Michigan	-19%	22.1	26.2
	38	Nevada	-33%	19.6	26.2
	40	South Carolina	-3%	25.5	26.3
States	41	Illinois	-16%	23.5	27.2
with	42	Arkansas	-35%	20.3	27.4
HIGHEST	43	Maryland	-17%	23.6	27.5
Percent	44	Tennessee	-24%	23.1	28.5
of	45	Florida	-1%	28.6	28.8
Children	46	New York	-15%	25.5	29.3
in	47	Georgia	-30%	22.9	29.7
Single-	48	Mississippi	-15%	26.8	30.8
Parent	49	Louisiana	-24%	25.3	31.3
Families	50	Alabama	-34%	24.3	32.6
	51	D.C.	0	55.0	54.9

A phone conversation I had between Rebecca's mom and dad resulted in the introduction of boundaries concerning the way her parents talked to each other around her. These rules included allowing Rebecca to visit her father more often and neither parent talking badly about the other. Within about six weeks, Rebecca's mom telephoned me and reported that Rebecca had stopped wetting her bed and was making great progress in demanding less attention from her mother.

For those who have not witnessed the unique situations facing single-parent families, Rebecca's story may seem unusual or even overstated. The fact is, Rebecca's experience following her parents' divorce is not at all unusual. In fact, by many standards her problems were quite mild. Pastors, youth workers, and therapists who have worked with parents and children of broken families understand the real-life trauma those families experience.

Those of us in the helping professions must come to terms with the fact that we are in the midst of an epidemic. This epidemic stems from the ever-increasing divorce rate and the rapid disintegration of the two-parent family. For quite some time now we in the U.S. have been faced with a divorce rate that hovers around 50 percent.[2] In other words, one-half of all marriages will end in divorce. A brief look into recent history also tells us that the number of single-parent families has increased by approximately *one million families* each year since 1971.[3] This increase takes into consideration three groups of single-parent families:

Nearly half of today's children will live in a single-parent family at some point during their childhood.

- Children of divorce
- Children whose parent is deceased
- Children born out of wedlock

According to research reported in *Single Adult Ministries Journal*, single-parent families were only 13 percent of all parent-child relationships in 1970. But today that number is almost 30 percent. Single-parent families grew by 32 percent during the 1980s.[4] Although there seem to be slight variances between government studies, the bottom line, according to the National Center for Health Statistics in 1988, is that nearly half of today's children will live in a single-parent family at some point during their childhood.

Although it is impossible to calculate the exact number of single-parent families who attend church, we do know from a 1989 Gallup Poll that 57 percent of all teens and 43 percent of all adults stated they had attended church within the previous week. I estimate the number of single parents and their children who attend church (both regularly and infrequently) to be at least fifty million.

The fact that we haven't developed adequate systems to help single-parent families first became clear to me as a young police officer. My continued experiences with single-parent families have only made this problem seem even more profound. We as a society have been collectively asleep at the wheel in addressing the needs of millions of single-parent families.

Those of us who have worked in the secular social service system know we can expect only so much in the way of help. Overcrowded and underfunded governmental offices and agencies are perhaps doing the best that they can; however, there is neither the manpower or funds available to address adequately these specialized areas. This is precisely why I see our churches as potentially the only remaining answer to the single-parent family epidemic.

OUR CHURCHES—THE FINAL HOPE FOR THE FAMILY

The obvious question, then, is, Have our churches adequately addressed the special needs of single-parent families? Sadly, in most cases (but certainly not all) the answer is no. In fact, although many churches offer groups and activities ranging from seniors to singles, relatively few churches offer parenting support groups. Even fewer offer consistent and organized support for single parents.

Perhaps the reason for the lack of single-parent family programs in churches is that, until recently, we haven't recognized the single-parent family as a significant enough part of our church population to warrant specialized classes. Perhaps the answer may simply be that we did not recognize there was a problem. Or maybe it was that single parents just didn't come forward to ask for help. But, whatever the reason, single parents and their children are a forgotten population in need of help.

Years of research have led me to the following conclusions:

- Literally millions of single-parent families attend church weekly.
- Millions of single-parent families are unchurched but could come to know Christ if they felt love and support through single-parent family programs.
- The number of single-parent families is increasing each year.
- Secular programs and agencies do not provide the necessary assistance to single-parent families.
- Our churches are the organizations most capable of addressing the single-parent family needs.

REASONS WHY THE CHURCH NEEDS TO REACH OUT TO CHILDREN FROM SINGLE-PARENT HOMES

- Approximately three out of four teenage suicides occur in households where a parent has been absent.[5]
- Children who grow up in fractured families are less likely to graduate from high school than children from intact families.[6]
- Young daughters of divorce often experience anxiety and guilt. In their teens, they are more likely to be sexually involved, become pregnant more often before marriage, marry younger, and be divorced or separated from their husbands.[7]

ParaParents, as discussed in chapter 7, can significantly help minimize these unfortunate and negative effects that many children experience when they are raised in a one-parent home.

⇥ **2** ⇤
OBSERVING
THE SINGLE-PARENT FAMILY

" 1 Alpha 23, respond with the paramedics to 3564 Flower Street regarding a teen suicide attempt. 1 Alpha 23, see the mother of the teenager, who states the boy has taken a drug overdose and is not breathing."

As I pulled up in front of the house, I saw the usual flurry of activity that accompanies the paramedics whenever they respond to a medical aid call. I stepped inside the neatly kept house to locate someone who could tell me what had happened. The boy's mother stood transfixed behind the paramedics, her hands cupped over her mouth and tears streaming down her cheeks. One of the most difficult aspects a policeman faces at the scene of an attempted suicide is being with the family while the paramedics try to resuscitate the victim. No matter how sensitive and empathetic I tried to be, there was never an easy way to gather information about the victim and the circumstances.

As the paramedics hooked the teenager up to an IV and monitors in an attempt to stabilize his shallow breathing and erratic heart rhythm, I was able to gather sketchy details from his mother. Jake, sixteen years old, had been very depressed. After spending the summer with his dad, he had recently returned to the home where he and his mother lived. His parents had been divorced almost two years, and the divorce had been particularly hard on Jake. Jake and his father had always been very close; but when his dad's company transferred him out of state, his father had no recourse but to go. Jake's mom said that, at the time, it seemed like the logical solution to their serious marital problems.

● *Thirteen common traits found in single-parent families.*

She went on to tell me that Jake had never talked about how depressed he was. But she could tell something was wrong. He had kept to himself since returning home from summer vacation. He had failed two classes during the first quarter of school and was doing poorly in three others, which was uncharacteristic for the unusually bright boy. "I put off calling his school to talk to a counselor because I didn't want to embarrass Jake. I thought it would get better if I just gave it time."

● *An overview of how this book will benefit you and your ministry.*

After what seemed like an eternity, Jake was loaded into the ambulance and transported to a nearby hospital where he died of a drug overdose. The lab report indicated he had taken a combination of pain medications, tranquilizers, and antidepressants—well in excess of 200 pills.

● *Three stated goals for this book.*

WHY RESEARCH SINGLE-PARENT FAMILIES?

Certainly, only a small portion of the research that went into *Helping Single Parents with Troubled Kids* was done to provide statistical data concerning the single-parenting problem. However, the much larger scope of the research focused on these goals:

1. To identify similarities (or characteristic traits) in single-parent families (parents, teens, and children).
2. To identify and address the specific problems facing single parents and their families.
3. To identify a Window of Opportunity (the time frame from the date of the divorce to a time of crisis) in which children are at highest risk.
4. To identify warning signs to watch for during the identifiable time frame.
5. To provide training for pastors, singles' ministry leaders, youth workers, and lay counselors on how to recognize and respond to these warning signs.

Characteristic Traits in Single-Parent Families

From my research, these traits (and their accompanying descriptions) were identified as being consistent between the hundreds of single-parent families who took part in the survey I conducted. The survey is further explained in chapter 3.

Unresolved anger. Frequently in single-parent families, the minds of those involved process feelings of frustration, victimization, jealousy, and blaming into anger. After a divorce, unresolved anger can be found in nearly everyone involved—in many forms and for many different reasons. These feelings remain unresolved until they are recognized, processed, and resolved.

Jane, a thirty-four-year-old divorced mother of two, came to my office in search of answers to her problem in getting along with the men she had dated since her divorce almost four years earlier. In our first few sessions, Jane related stories about her childhood, her marriage, and her fulfilling life as a wife and mother. She and her husband of eight years seemed to be getting along well. He made a good living as a salesman and provided well for her and the kids. She had not had to work a single day since getting married straight out of college. Then one day, Jane's husband told her that he had fallen in love with another woman and that he was leaving her and the kids to start a new life.

To say that Jane was shocked and devastated would be an understatement. To complicate her problems, she was not the type of person who could experience or talk about her pain. Even if she had had a support group where she could have talked about her anxiety and frustration in having to start over, she probably would not have done so. She never talked about the shattered dreams of her life and her marriage. Nor did she talk about her depression and her fears. In short, Jane lived in a state we call denial.

One reason Jane had such a difficult time establishing anything more than a casual relationship was because of her unresolved anger. On the surface, she had accepted her husband's departure and his abandonment of the children with the same resolve that most people accept a parking ticket: I don't like it, but what can I do? She felt some of the pain, anger, and victimization, but she never experienced it long enough to work through it. Subsequently, her anger was an open wound still present in her subconscious. As a result, she was not able to experience any of her new relationships without viewing them through her unresolved anger.

Ultimately, Jane realized that she had accepted her fate passively, almost like a victim. In one session, Jane finally was able to deal with the disappointments and insecurity in her life after the breakup of her marriage. After Jane had experienced some of her repressed anger, she began taking steps to regain her rightful power. One of these steps involved contacting an attorney to force her ex-husband to begin paying child support.

Parental stress/anxiety. Also consistent among single parents are feelings of some level of stress and anxiety ranging from minor to immobilizing. This anxiety can usually be traced to the common (yet sometimes overwhelming) adjustments that must be made when a parent becomes a single parent. A few of the most commonly discussed stressors include:

- The responsibility of raising a family alone
- Increased financial pressure
- Stressful problem(s) with a child
- Relocation
- Social pressures
- Over-concern for the opinions of others about the divorce or breakup

Anxiety due to these stressors often includes some common symptoms:

- Shortness of breath or a smothering sensation
- Palpitations, dizziness, chest pain, or accelerated heart rate
- Trembling or shaking
- Sweating
- Choking
- Nausea or abdominal distress
- Numbness or tingling sensations
- Flushes, "hot flashes," or chills
- Fear of dying
- Fear of going crazy or being out of control[1]

Don was a thirty-one-year-old father of one son. Don became a single parent when his wife died of cancer when Donny, Jr., was eight. For the first month or so following his wife's death, Don seemed to be getting along all right. He returned to work and to church and appeared to be adjusting to his role as a single father.

One morning while Don was getting ready for work, he felt himself becoming very anxious. His hand began to shake, and he felt dizzy. He called his office and told them he had the flu and would not be in. After getting Donny, Jr., off to school, Don returned to his room and got into bed, where he stayed for the entire day. He thought he might have a touch of the flu, even though he wasn't experiencing any symptoms. He just knew he didn't feel right and he couldn't go to work with his hands shaking so.

Don went on this way for almost ten days. During that time he had frequent chest pains, but passed them off as part of his virus. Finally, after a call from his boss, Don reluctantly made an appointment with the company medical group.

FIGURE 2.1
SIX CHARACTERISTIC TRAITS IN SINGLE-PARENT FAMILIES

1. Unresolved anger—feelings of frustration, victimization, jealousy, and blaming that turn into anger. After a divorce, unresolved anger can be found in nearly everyone involved. If not resolved, it will affect all future relationships in a negative way. These feelings remain harmful until they are recognized, processed, and resolved.

2. Parental stress/anxiety—brought on by the overwhelming sense of responsibility of being a single parent. This ranges from minor to immobilizing. It requires one to work through feelings of anger, frustration, hurt, and abandonment, and to learn to manage these new responsibilities in small increments (instead of viewing them as insurmountable obstacles).

3. Separation anxiety in children and teens—anxiety in the form of insecurity. This could include calling home from school several times a day (which is a way of asking, "Are you still here? Do you still want and love me? Will you go away just like my dad did?"). It can also include psychosomatic illness, an unrealistic fear that something bad may happen to a parent, fear of the dark, clinging, and repeated nightmares. Requires constant affirmation and assurance.

4. Transference—misdirected blame (such as a child being angry at the parent that stayed rather than the parent that left). This is a passive anger which is particularly difficult to identify and resolve. Once this transference of anger is brought out of the subconscious (the brain's storage area that often houses repressed anger and resentment) and into the conscious mind, then it can be resolved.

5. Owning responsibility—It is natural for a period of blaming to result; however, at some point, both spouses must accept their portion of the responsibility before resolutions can be found. Another dimension is seen when children, especially those under the age of ten, falsely assume responsibility for the breakup of the family. Because of this tendency, parents must repeatedly state that divorce can never be the child's fault.

6. A breakdown in communication—some ways include: Everyone assumes communication is okay and the child is doing fine; parents have a general misbelief that the child does not need to know or does not care what is happening; parents assume that the child is not old enough to understand or deal with what is going on; one or both parents may use the child as a messenger to send hurtful messages.

As he was preparing to leave the house, he experienced an overwhelming rushing sensation. His head started to pound, and the pressure was so intense he thought he might faint or even die. Very frightened, Don called the medical clinic to cancel his appointment, and he returned to bed.

The next day Don's boss called again and asked why he had not kept his appointment. When Don told him about his feelings of anxiety when he was leaving for his appointment, his boss was astute enough to realize that Don needed help. His boss rescheduled the appointment and went to Don's house to help him get ready.

After Don received a complete physical, the doctor told him that, although he was physically fine, he was suffering symptoms of a classic anxiety disorder with agoraphobic (afraid to go out of the house) symptoms. The doctor referred Don to a family therapist to begin a therapy program designed to help him manage his anxiety.

With the help of his boss and friends, Don kept his counseling appointments. After a few sessions, he was able to connect his anxious feelings with the addition of his new responsibility of raising his son alone following his wife's death.

Don didn't just get better after this discovery. Each day was a challenge, and he used a short-term medication to help him work through his crippling fear of leaving the house. But the more he talked about his fear and anxious feelings, the better he felt. Three weeks after beginning therapy, he returned to work and assumed his normal routines.

Don's case, although more severe than most, is still relatively common for new single parents. His anxiety over his new single-parent responsibilities overwhelmed him, causing him to shut-down involuntarily. He didn't make a conscious choice to withdraw and isolate himself from his work and parenting responsibilities; however, he was powerless, on his own, to correct his response. Once Don worked through his feelings of anger, frustration, hurt, and abandonment, he regained his control. He learned to manage his new responsibilities in small increments (instead of viewing them as large, insurmountable obstacles).

Separation anxiety in children and teens. One afternoon I received a phone call from a pastor who was doing some homework on behalf of a woman in his congregation. The pastor told me that the woman came to him because her sixteen-year-old daughter had been acting very strangely. The pastor related that, about three weeks earlier, the daughter began having problems with her health. She was fine when she left for school in the mornings; but then, at some point during the day, she would get sick and call her mom to come and pick her up. After her mom picked her up, the girl would change into her pajamas and lie on the couch. Often she would also want her mom to sit with her and watch television.

The mother finally took the daughter to the doctor for a physical. The doctor determined that her health was not the issue and suggested that a counselor might provide additional insight.

The first question I asked of the pastor was, "When were her parents divorced?" The pastor replied, "About three months ago." I then asked, "Has anything else been going on, prior to these sick spells, that might indicate they are a response

Many children transfer their anger at the parent who left to the parent who remains behind.

to her insecurity?" The pastor replied, "The girl is making two or three phone calls home during the day while she is at school. Is that what you mean?"

Cases such as these are not at all uncommon. Teenagers who have recently experienced the trauma of their parents' divorce often show their anxiety in the form of insecurity. In this instance, the girl had first shown her anxiety over her parents' divorce by calling home several times a day. This was her way of asking, "Are you still here? Do you still want and love me? Will you go away just like Dad did?" When her own anxiety became too intense to be satisfied by the phone calls alone, her methods altered to include sickness. For this daughter and others like her, this illness is real, not a faked excuse to go home early like all kids try at one time or another. This psychosomatic illness was her mind's way of making sure she still had a home and a parent who loved her.

Other common indications of separation anxiety in both children and teens include:

- An unrealistic fear that something bad may happen to a parent
- Fear of the dark
- Fears that something terrible will happen
- A reluctance or refusal to go to school
- A reluctance or refusal to sleep without being near Mom or Dad
- Avoidance of being alone
- Clinging to a parent
- Repeated nightmares involving separation themes
- Frequent complaints of physical symptoms on school or church days
- Problems that arise in anticipation of being away from Mom or Dad

Transference. In single-parent homes, what I refer to as passive anger, or transference of anger, is often passed around between parent and child like a bowl of popcorn. Often this anger is not based in the conscious awareness; therefore, it is particularly difficult to identify and resolve. Transference of anger usually goes unchecked until a major crisis erupts, at which time an outsider (generally a counselor, pastor, or youth leader) is called upon to intervene. Once this transference of anger is brought out of the subconscious (the brain's storage area that often houses repressed anger, resentment, and grudges) and into the conscious mind, then it can be resolved.

In single-parent families, transference of angry, unresolved feelings accompanies misdirected blame. Many children transfer their anger at the parent who left to the parent who remains behind. Also, in many cases, the parents misdirected their anger to the child. Anger transference from parent to child is sometimes a product of a child who looks like or has mannerisms reminiscent of the other parent. These reminders can arouse the single parent's unresolved feelings.

For example, seventeen-year-old Matt was having what his mother termed "uncontrollable temper outbursts." (Matt's mother and father were divorced when Matt was five; however, as we know, time does not heal all wounds in these situations.)

As I worked with Matt I realized that many of the family's problems could be traced to Matt's mother and her own anger. Over the course of several sessions, I learned from Matt that his father used to abuse his mother regularly and that she had called the police several times. She had finally worked up the courage to file for divorce.

At the time of our sessions, Matt's father sent child-support checks from another state. Even though he only occasionally talked to Matt's mother, the anger and victimization of her past were still fresh in her mind and surfaced with each reminder. Unresolved issues were less of a factor when Matt was young; however, as he matured, he began to look and act more and more like his father. With Matt as a constant reminder of her painful past, she began losing control of her temper and would lash out at Matt in her mistaken transference of anger at her ex-husband. Her feelings of anger and victimization resurfaced over and over again. Matt's defense became his own "uncontrollable temper outbursts."

In successful cases, once this unresolved anger is presented, it can be worked through effectively. In this case, however, Matt's mom was unwilling to admit that any portion of the problem could be the result of her transference of anger. She insisted that Matt was to blame and removed him from counseling.

Owning responsibility. When one member of the family is reluctant or refuses to acknowledge any part of a problem, it is unrealistic to expect much progress. I compare the process of parents owning their share of the responsibility to a doubles tennis match: If both of the players are on and they win, the credit is shared; if the doubles team plays poorly and loses the match, both players must accept some responsibility for the defeat.

In a marriage, when both partners are unable to keep the marriage together, both must accept some responsibility for the loss. This is especially difficult when either spouse betrays the trust of the other. It is natural for a period of blaming to result; however, at some point, both spouses must accept their portion of the responsibility. Unfortunately, the analogy of the tennis players and the married couple breaks down when emotional factors such as the ego, feelings of victimization, betrayal, pain, and stress enter into the match.

A couple who had been married for three years came to me for marriage counseling. The wife had had an affair with her boss; the husband was shocked, angry, and rightfully very hurt. Because he could focus on the act of her betrayal, the husband could not accept that he had even the slightest degree of responsibility for the situation.

Finally, after weeks of working through the wife's guilt and some of the husband's anger, he was able to admit that perhaps he had not shown his wife enough love and attention, and that this might have had a little something to do with her affair. In turn, she admitted that she had not been honest with him in communicating her needs so that he could at least have had a chance of meeting them.

In situations of marital infidelity, it is never *just* the husband's fault nor is it *just* the wife's fault. A feeling and acceptance of shared responsibility is necessary in order for the wounds to be healed so that the marriage has a chance of continuing. Any couple who is experiencing marital problems (or working through post-divorce emotions) must first own some responsibility for the problem before the solutions can be found.

Children (and sometimes teens) frequently exhibit a strange willingness to assume responsibility for the breakup of the family. Part of the reason for this is the innocently self-centered manner in which children view themselves and the world.

Still another dimension of owning responsibility is seen in children of divorce, especially in those under the age of ten. Children (and sometimes teens) frequently exhibit a strange willingness to assume responsibility for the breakup of the family.

Part of the reason for this is the innocently self-centered manner in which children view themselves and the world. Although a completely normal part of the developmental process, children believe they are immortal and the universe revolves around them. They think in terms of all black or all white, all good or all bad. Subsequently, when parents divorce, it is often the child who accepts personal responsibility.

Because of this tendency, parents must be as clear as possible about the true reasons for divorce. A divorce can never be a child's fault, and this fact must be reinforced regularly to the child. Don't assume that because the children have been told once or twice that the divorce is not their fault that they got the message. Parents—as well as pastors and teachers—need to reinforce this assertion often.

At a recent seminar I talked to a pastor who asked if I had any advice for him while he was working with a couple and their three children during a separation. My first response—controversial as it may be—was that short-term separation might be in the family's best interest. In most cases, except where there is severe dysfunction or the risk of harm to any member of the family, I believe in staying together, even if just for the sake of the kids. But occasionally, a separation will short-circuit an immediate or hasty divorce, which is longer term and has even more devastating results.

Second, I told him, the couple should call a truce during the time in which they are receiving counseling (both pastoral and psychological). Whether a couple is together or not, it is important to put aside hostilities in order to deal with their problems and to try to preserve the marriage. "Finally," I concluded in my advice to him, "if these efforts fail, please take the time to work with the children and the parents to ensure that the kids don't end up feeling responsible for the divorce." Divorce is never the fault of a child. Parents should make clear to their children that they own the responsibility for the divorce.

A breakdown in communication. During the separation or divorce process, it is common for both parents and kids to suffer a partial or complete breakdown in communication. When communication breaks down, kids frequently start feeling responsible for the marriage failure or start hearing things they don't necessarily need to hear.

Some ways that communication commonly breaks down are:

- Everyone assumes communication is okay and the child is doing fine.
- One or both parents get caught up in their own emotional pain and sense of loss, which can cause them to lose perspective.
- Parents have a general misbelief that the child does not need to know or does not care what is happening.
- Parents assume that the child is not old enough to understand or deal with what is going on.
- A parent may falsely assume that the child has been kept informed by the other parent.

- Parents interpret lack of questions as lack of interest or feeling.
- A parent may place the child in the middle by talking about the other parent.
- One or both parents may use the child as a messenger to send hurtful messages.

In chapters 5, 9, and 10 we will discuss some ways that these communication speed bumps can be minimized or avoided altogether.

Personality Problems

Children and teens who are subjected to any of the above communication breakdowns commonly develop some very problematic personality traits as they grow older. Studies have shown that dysfunctional styles of communication in the home can produce dysfunctional adult problems. As you read through the following personality disorders, you may be able to envision how childhood communication problems (especially during and after a divorce) can either bring about or complicate these problems.

The codependent personality. Although the term codependent is overused, it can certainly describe the adult who was exposed to dysfunctional communication. People with codependent personality types constantly try to be the peace-keepers in relationships at home, at work, or in social situations. They often will not make their needs or feelings known to those close to them and will accept emotional leftovers from people because of their own feelings of inadequacy.

Eve could have served as a poster girl for codependency when she came into therapy. She was married for sixteen years to a man who showed her little or no respect or attention. He reigned the household by intimidation, anger, and aggressiveness. Eve dared not speak up for fear that he would turn his wrath on her. She also surmised that her husband was an alcoholic; however, she did not dare approach him about his drinking. Instead, she minimized her marital dissatisfaction by telling her church friends what a hard-working, wonderful provider her husband was.

The narcissistic (or egotistic) personality. Adults and teenagers with narcissistic personality disorders typically display a pattern of grandiosity, a lack of empathy, and hypersensitivity to the evaluation of others. These individuals usually react to criticism with feelings of rage, shame, or humiliation. They may take advantage of others to further their own goals or position at work. They have an elevated sense of self-importance, which can be seen by exaggerating achievements and talents. They often expect to be noticed as special, even without the appropriate achievement. The narcissistic personality type may believe that his or her problems are unique and can be understood only by other special people. They may become preoccupied with fantasies of unlimited success, power, brilliance, beauty, or ideal love.

Gary, age twenty-two, entered therapy to work on his feelings of never being appreciated or understood. His mom and dad divorced when he was thirteen. Gary thought his boss, as well as his coworkers, did not understand how valuable he was to the company. He believed that he had single-handedly kept the company from bankruptcy by selling more computers than anyone else in his group except for two other salespersons. Gary was obsessed with the fact that they received more recognition than he did and feared that he would be passed over for a promotion because of their performances. Gary found himself hating his coworkers for their efforts.

As it turned out, Gary had deep-seated insecurities. These first became apparent when Gary believed his father left the home because he wasn't a good enough son. In his early teens, he had begun having a great deal of difficulty dealing with criticism because he ultimately equated it with the withholding of love.

The passive-aggressive personality. Adults and teens with this personality disorder often are procrastinators. They are commonly sulky, irritable, or argumentative when asked to do something they don't want to do. They frequently avoid obligations by claiming to have forgotten. They generally believe they are doing a much better job than others think they are doing, and they resent suggestions from others concerning how they could be more productive.

In work or school situations, they commonly obstruct or undermine the efforts of others by failing to do their share of the work. Passive-aggressive people frequently criticize or scorn others who are in positions of authority and have trouble relating to anyone of authority in their lives.

Taylor is an example of a passive-aggressive personality type. He grew up as a "momma's boy" after his parents divorced when he was only three years old. His mom was very aggressive and controlled his life. Following her divorce, her disdain for men was evident in all areas of her life.

Taylor left home when he was twenty-four and married a girl whose personality was similar to his mother's. When his wife would suggest things for him to do, he would do them without hesitation, but would later be angry at her for controlling him. He could not imagine confronting her with his feelings; so, instead, he would simply do a poor job at what she asked him to do. He would also leave messes everywhere and delay cleaning them up until the last minute or until she forced him to comply.

The histrionic personality. Adults and teens with this personality disorder are often seen as overly emotional and attention-seeking. Due to their insecurity, they constantly seek or demand reassurance, approval, or praise. They may be overly concerned with their own physical attractiveness and express their emotions with dramatic flair and inappropriate exaggeration. They are uncomfortable in situations in which they are not the center of attention, and they are generally self-centered.

Beth, an attractive twenty-year-old whose parents were divorced when she was eleven, had recently been diagnosed as having a histrionic personality disorder. Beth always chose to dress seductively on dates, at school, or even at church. She was constantly seeking approval from men, be it pastor, teacher, or fellow classmate. When asked why she needed to be the center of attention everywhere she went, Beth replied, "I guess I'm just a 'people person.'"

Post-Traumatic Stress Disorders

The single-parent family research clearly revealed the likelihood of a post-traumatic stress disorder (PTSD) following divorce. This disorder is just as likely to affect adults, teens, and children.

The single-parent family research clearly revealed the likelihood of a post-traumatic stress disorder (PTSD) following divorce. This disorder is just as likely to affect adults, teens, and children.

Jake, whose sad story I related at the beginning of this chapter, is a classic example of post-divorce PTSD. Consisting of depression, isolation, and poor school grades, his symptoms started about eight months after his mother and father divorced. These symptoms, although noticed, went unchecked until the time of his suicide, which occurred sixteen months after his parents divorced.

Some history of PTSD. PTSD is a relatively new area of psychological interest. Following the Korean War, soldiers returning home who had difficulty adjusting to a normal lifestyle were classified as having delayed stress syndrome. In the post-Vietnam War years, returning soldiers who have had psychological problems stemming from their combat experience were diagnosed as having PTSD, the "new and improved" version of delayed stress syndrome.

What we have found in studying PTSD is that soldiers have no exclusive rights to this disorder. In fact, PTSD is now found in the *Diagnostic and Statistical Manual of Mental Disorders* (DSM-III-R, an up-to-date diagnostic and statistical manual used for psychological research) and is becoming an increasingly used diagnosis for persons who are not adjusting to a traumatic experience such as a death in the family, an unusually serious traffic accident, or a disaster.[2]

PTSD plays a part in relation to children as well as parents during divorce and the disintegration of the family. A critical element of PTSD is that the symptoms must follow the trauma by at least six months: Otherwise the diagnosis is likely to be something different.

An example of post-divorce PTSD can be seen in Craig's case. Craig was six years old when his mom and dad finally decided to get a divorce, after several years of a rocky marriage. Loud arguments and often violent confrontations pervaded Craig's little world.

Craig was seven when his mom brought him to the counselor's office. According to her, whenever Craig would hear a loud male voice—even if it was just on the TV—he would begin crying and trembling. Craig was still suffering from the unresolved trauma of seeing his mother battered at the hands of his dad. Subsequently, a male's loud, angry voice was interpreted as a signal that physical violence was coming, which also triggered Craig's feelings of helplessness. Craig was diagnosed as having a post-traumatic stress disorder stemming from his early childhood traumatic observations of his mom and dad.

Children and adolescents who have been particularly traumatized by a divorce can display some or all of the following symptoms:

- Recurrent, troublesome, and distressing recollections of the traumatic event
- Distressing dreams or nightmares of the event
- Sudden feelings, similar to flashbacks, as if the traumatic event were recurring
- Feelings of intense distress when exposed to events, such as birthdays or anniversaries, that symbolize or resemble an aspect of the traumatic event; avoidance of thoughts or feelings associated with those events
- Efforts to avoid activities or situations that can cause the trauma to be remembered

- An inability to recall an important aspect of the trauma (psychogenic amnesia)
- A diminished interest in developmental activities (in young children, reversals in toilet training or language skills)
- A restricted range of effect (lack of emotions, responses, or personality manifestations) where before it existed
- Difficulty in falling or staying asleep
- Irritability or outbursts of anger (especially in children and teens)
- Difficulty concentrating
- An exaggerated startle response

Increased defense mechanisms. Commonly observed in single parent families were wide varieties of defense mechanisms. In many ways, it is logical that the symptoms listed for PTSD are part of the mind's defense system against further pain and trauma. The defense mechanisms that were more prevalent in children, adolescents, and adults of single-parent families often manifested themselves in more cautious or guarded natures.

Adolescents, for example, may find it very difficult to attach to a new adult. They commonly compare the new person (or parent) to the natural parent in an attempt to keep themselves from attaching and, sometimes, to keep the parent from attaching. If the new person becomes a step-parent, teens sometimes work diligently at keeping a distance, or they may try to sabotage the relationship, even if they like the new person. They are instinctively self-protective; they were hurt in their last relationship and will try to keep that from happening again.

An example of increased defense mechanisms can be seen in the case of seven-year-old Tanya. Tanya's mom and dad divorced when she was five. After that time, Tanya's mom dated very little. Each time her mom did invite a man over to the house, Tanya would cling to her mom. If the boyfriend tried to hold her mom's hand, Tanya would physically sit between them or do things to attract attention, even to the extent of having fits.

Younger children (generally five and under) are less entrenched in their defense motives and thus more open to new relationships. For whatever reasons, younger children seem to sense when people are good or bad for them and their family. They instinctively like or dislike certain people. If they sense that the new person in their life is good for them, then they will generally respond positively.

As a word of caution, however, parents who continually introduce a new adult into the family (e.g., a new boyfriend or girlfriend who is around and then is suddenly gone in favor of another relationship) are intensifying the child's tendency to develop defense mechanisms.

Emotional trauma. One similarity shared by many families during the emotional disputes associated with divorce involves the emotional trauma kids experience when they become the objects of a human tug-of-war. The trauma and isolation they feel generally starts during the early period of their parents' conflict and can continue long into the post-divorce years.

Evidence of this is chronicled in some of the work by Judith Wallerstein in her book *Second Chances: Men, Women and Children a Decade After Divorce.* She writes that a significant number of children are still dealing with the emotional aftermath as long as fifteen years after the divorce.[3] Her research clearly points out that the emotional fallout on children of divorce can last for many years.

Michelle was twelve when her mom and dad divorced. At age twenty-six, she found herself struggling to keep a dating relationship going for longer than a few months. During one session, Michelle stated, "It always seems to be the same old story. I meet a nice-looking guy who seems to have some class, but then I find that in a few weeks or months, he wants to break up."

It didn't take long to identify part of the cause for her short-term relationships. Michelle was very prone to find herself in bed with a new boyfriend on the first or second date. Sometimes she would hold off as long as she could, but that generally meant the third or fourth date. Over a period of time, Michelle came to understand that she was trying to solidify her relationships by sleeping with the men she dated. The longer she waited to become intimate, the more afraid she became that he would leave her. In truth, her feelings of being abandoned by her father were the source of her emotional trauma. In time, she was able to understand the connection between her feelings of abandonment and her yearning for intimacy, which compelled her to respond as she did—even at the expense of her personal morality.

CONCLUSIONS

In a majority of the families I studied, some evidences of emotional trauma were found, either alone or together in various combinations. Any one of these traumas is capable of causing tremendous stress within the family and can stall the healing process following a divorce.

While no easy solutions had yet been identified from my study of single-parent family traits, I was still convinced that there has to be an easier path for single-parent families. A road less traveled, if you will. A road with fewer detours, with less inherent pain. A road that can be frequented by families who recognize they are headed the wrong way and who are willing to stop for directions. In support of single-parent families, it was essential, then, that pastors, youth leaders, and counselors map out this road for future travel.

Literally hundreds of juvenile court judges, police and probation officers, psychologists, and counselors I have met over the years believe kids from single-parent families tend to get into trouble more frequently than kids living with both parents. Why, then, hasn't the social service system taken a more serious approach to this dilemma?

Years of research and years of exposure working within the social service system have only validated my assertion that our current system is capable of providing little support and direction for single-parent families. Somewhere in the system, there has been a terrible breakdown. Ironically, we spend millions of dollars trying to save redwood trees or exterminate fruit flies, but when it comes to helping millions of single-parent families, we have thus far been unable to develop effective programs.

Ironically, we spend millions of dollars trying to save redwood trees or exterminate fruit flies, but when it comes to helping millions of single-parent families, we have thus far been unable to develop effective programs.

We sat idly by throughout the sixties, seventies, and eighties, while our divorce rate reached 50 percent. We're afraid to confront an obvious fact that we recognized over three decades ago: The dual-parent family unit, as we know it, is disintegrating in epidemic proportions because of soaring divorce rates. We live in a disposable society where we throw away watches, cameras, and even cars when they get old or broken. Sadly, this disposable mentality has carried over into marriages.

Forget for a moment that 9 percent of all girls become mothers before turning eighteen[4] and that girls from single-parent families comprise the highest risk group in this category. Let's ignore the fact that my research shows that single-parent children who wind up addicted to drugs and alcohol compare to addicted children from dual-parent families at a rate of three to one. And, while we're at it, let's discount the fact that, according to my single-parent family survey, single-parent children make up 64 percent of all children and teenagers hospitalized for psychological disorders and chemical addictions.

What's more, no federal, state, or county social service agency has a clue how to slow down this epidemic. Just as ironically (if that's possible), even fewer psychiatrists, psychologists, and counselors have discovered other resources where single-parent families can find real assistance. Today, the most common concern expressed by our government officials toward single-parent families has been to acknowledge that a child-care problem exists for working moms. But our government has not yet been able even to address adequately this one small element of single-parenting concerns.

How This Book Can Help You in Your Ministry with Single-Parent Families

Fortunately, we are not without hope in helping single-parent families. You and your church can make a difference. The remainder of this book outlines strategies for providing assistance to this troubled group.

In the next chapter, you'll find information about how and why the single-parent family survey was conducted. Subsequent chapters detail the results of the survey from the perspective of both the parent and the child. Along with a discussion of each major subject is a message to pastors, singles' pastors, youth leaders, and lay counselors. These messages provide clinical and scriptural advice on ways to respond to a parent, child, or teen who needs support.

Chapter 3 deals with the Twenty-One Warning Signs of Crisis. Briefly, a crisis is any event that evokes a significant emotional reaction. These reactions may include depression, anxiety, terror, isolation, anger, or any number of other troublesome feelings. Learning these warning signs may allow you to know what the child's behavior means and how you can help. Each of the signs is accompanied by specific actions designed to avert a potential crisis.

Finally, *Helping Single Parents with Troubled Kids* concludes with lecture outlines. These lectures are divided into three categories. The first section (chapter 8) is a lecture outline designed for a senior pastor to give to the entire congregation. This outline provides a foundation to single-parenting issues on a local level; it also discusses how the staff may address these issues within the congregation. The outline is merely that and allows the pastor to personalize the message. This first lecture outline provides a suitable framework to kick off the new (or expanded) single-parenting ministry within the church.

Section two of the lecture outlines (chapter 9) includes twelve lectures for the pastor (or other staff members) to give at a rate of one each month. The goal is to form a single-parent support group within the church and to utilize these outlines to address and assist parents in key areas of interest. Integrating both clinical and scriptural advice, these lectures show parents the steps to take to correct some problem areas and avert others.

Section three (chapter 10) provides twelve months of lectures for both teens' and children's support groups. These lectures are designed to be given by the pastor, youth pastor, youth worker, or other staff.

Simply stated, my goal for you as you read *Helping Single Parents with Troubled Kids* is that you will be able to:

1. Recognize the single-parenting crisis in the United States, in your community, and within your congregation.
2. Come away with the knowledge, desire, and tools to impact the lives of single parents and children within your congregation in a significant way.
3. Understand how to use the book as a resource for helping single-parent families within your own ministry.

Helping Single Parents with Troubled Kids is capable of providing tools and insight that perhaps you did not possess prior to reading this resource guide. Although I feel this book is comprehensive, one element is essential for it to be considered effective: This element is *you*. Without your insight, talent, communication skills, and love, the book is powerless to help the millions of single-parent families.

I also want to encourage you to consult other professionals regularly. Remember, no two people are alike. People do not fit predictably into neat little categories. Whenever you are working with a difficult child or teen, utilize the many resources available to you. Talk to other pastors, staff, elders, and counselors for their observations and recommendations. Remember what Proverbs 11:14 tells us: "Where there is no guidance, the people fall, but in abundance of counselors there is victory" (NASB).

Without your insight, talent, communication skills, and love, this book is powerless to help the millions of single-parent families.

⊰ **3** ⊱
OH, NO!
NOT ANOTHER SURVEY

Surveys in general are boring. Some are less boring than others, but most of them are good reading material for bedtime. Yet daily we hear about this survey or that statistic. Gallup polls rate the popularity of politicians; Nielson polls try to determine top-rated TV shows. While surveys of these types are interesting and somewhat entertaining, they provide relatively little life-changing information. They don't tell us anything more than we already suppose; and most surveys certainly have no significant influence on the quality or the direction of our lives.

Survey Goals

From the start, the single-parent family's survey was designed to include parents, teens, and children in an attempt to provide answers to the following questions:

- Are children of single-parent families more likely than those from traditional families to have difficulty with alcohol and drugs, emotional problems, social problems, and premarital sexual activity?
- Are children of single-parent families more likely to require some type of counseling than children from two-parent families?
- If these answers are yes, are there any warning signs to look for prior to a crisis?
- What is the best way to respond to a warning sign in a child or adolescent?
- What advice do parents, teens, and children have to offer other single-parent families to help them avoid some of the problems they faced?
- How can the church prepare to be the resource of the nineties and beyond for single parents and their children?

Survey Method

As I was preparing my survey in December of 1986 I recalled being involved with a very expensive, multi-faceted scientific survey that we had commissioned for a hospital chain where I was working. We spent approximately $150,000 for a 300-page survey that appeared to have all the kinds of impressive bells, whistles, and graphs. It must have weighed in at around three pounds (or at least six pounds

**IN THIS
CHAPTER**

- *Information about those who participated in the survey.*

- *How the survey was administered and tabulated.*

37

soaking wet). We had only one problem: None of us could understand 90 percent of its contents. The 10 percent we could understand included the cover and the page numbers. My point is that, no matter how much money and time are involved in conducting a survey, it is of no practical value if it doesn't accomplish two goals: (1) It must provide information which can help to alter perceptions, and (2) it must present ideas or inspire change in a user-friendly manner.

With that experience fresh in my mind, I was determined to conduct my survey in such a manner that anyone could pick it up, look it over, and be able to determine if it had any personal relevance. That is how the single-parent family survey took its shape.

The predominance of males in the study reflects the fact that boys are generally more prone to become involved in activities that might call attention to their need for help.

Survey Size

The survey itself examined 1,000 parents, adolescents, and children, representing both two-parent and single-parent families. The questionnaires were distributed at various inpatient psychiatric hospitals and outpatient therapy clinics. Once the 1,000 questionnaires were completed, they were collected for the purpose of measuring the responses. From the distribution of the 1,000 surveys, a total of 640 respondents (or 64 percent) were found to be members of single-parent families. In no instances were the responses of two or three members of the same single-parent family added together, which would have skewed the responses.

In the past I have been aware of only a handful of single-parent surveys that examined children of divorce. These surveys focused on smaller groups of participants (10-100) and examined them over a longer period of time, sometimes over years. However, the scope of this survey was not to identify common long-term patterns among single-parent families, but rather to look at the short-term similarities and the warning signs of crisis.

Survey Participants

Out of the 1,000 families who took part in the survey, 640 single-parent family members were identified and subsequently interviewed. The 640 participants from single-parent families were comprised of the following groups: 288 single parents, 291 adolescents (ages thirteen to eighteen), and 61 children (ages eight to twelve). (See figure 3.1.)

The 352 adolescents and children who took part in the survey were further divided into males and females who were receiving some form of treatment or counseling. Interestingly enough, 68 percent of those children and adolescents surveyed were males.

The predominance of males in the study reflects the fact that boys are generally more prone to become involved in activities that might call attention to their need for help. The factors that illustrate this point will be covered in greater detail in following chapters.

Survey Locations

Like a forest ranger who needs to track the migration of the bears in his forest, I selected specific locations for tracking the information I needed. The ranger could hang out at the ranger station and tag each bear that rings his doorbell; or he could go out to the woods and frequent the places where his bears like to hang out.

For my purposes, the most logical locations for the surveys to be completed were at predominantly Christian outpatient counseling settings (therapist's office) and inpatient hospital programs for teens. I selected these locations because they provided an environment where families were learning about themselves. As a result, the participants were more open to sharing their life stories, including their successes and their failures.

The main thrust of this book is its message to pastors, singles' ministry leaders, youth pastors, and lay counselors, since they are in unique positions to deal with the numerous challenges facing single-parent families. Thus, Christian settings were selected so as to reflect an accurate representation of the Christian community. Additionally, Christian settings were selected to preclude the notion that single-parent families are primarily a secular problem.

Most of the families who participated in the survey resided in the counties of Los Angeles, Orange, Riverside, and San Diego. Occasionally, I encountered teenagers who were receiving inpatient hospital treatment outside these areas. However, due to their diverse cross-cultural, religious, and economic profiles, these regions should be considered a fairly accurate representation of national averages.

In the single-parent family survey, information from adolescents and children who participated in the survey was gathered from the following settings: 143 teens were interviewed while they were in hospital programs, and 209 teens and children were surveyed while receiving outpatient counseling.

Survey Administration

The 288 single parents who agreed to participate in the survey were given the survey by either their individual counselors or me. The adult participants were asked to complete the confidential survey (see appendix B) and to seal it in the envelope provided. All surveys were forwarded to my office on a weekly basis.

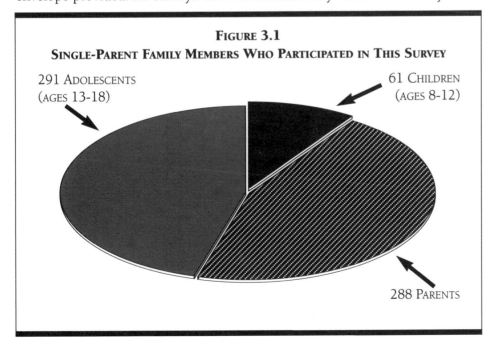

FIGURE 3.1
SINGLE-PARENT FAMILY MEMBERS WHO PARTICIPATED IN THIS SURVEY

291 ADOLESCENTS
(AGES 13-18)

61 CHILDREN
(AGES 8-12)

288 PARENTS

The 352 single-parent family teens and children who agreed to participate were also given a survey (see appendix C). This group, like the parent group, received the survey from either their individual counselors or me.

None of the participants were required or encouraged in any way to complete the survey. With each survey, a cover sheet was attached stating that the survey was voluntary and completely confidential and that refusing to participate had no consequences whatsoever. In each case, painstaking efforts were made to ensure confidentiality.

Survey Results

The questions in the surveys were of two styles. First, some of the questions asked for simple responses that could be easily tabulated. However, others asked for subjective and complex responses. These responses are presented throughout this resource book as specific advice to pastors, singles' ministry leaders, youth leaders, and lay counselors.

Sixteen Significant Findings About Single-Parent Families

Beginning with the first single-parent family interview in December 1986 and ending with the last survey in June 1988, I compiled months of research data to either prove or disprove the following theory:

> Children and teens from single-parent families are more inclined to suffer emotional problems, from the family's pre-divorce period through the post-divorce phase. As a result of adjusting to single-parent family situations, children and teens experience emotional transitions, which can result in a number of problematic behaviors affecting both parents and children.

SIGNIFICANT FINDINGS

The following information compiled from the parent surveys is summarized as significant findings. In most cases, the actual numbers have been left out so that the reader can focus less on statistics and more on the overall message. A full account of actual statistics is presented in appendix B.

FINDING 1

Three out of four single moms had custody of their children.

Eight out of ten of the parents who responded to the survey were moms, 6 percent were fathers, and 12 percent indicated they were either grandparents or other guardians. While some scientific purists may believe so many female respondents might skew the results, I must respond that, in the single-parent survey, the single mom's perspective is representative of the single-parent family culture. Following divorce, mothers most often have custody of their children.[1]

As an interesting side note, in nearly all cases the single mothers who participated in the survey were very compliant. Many made notes on the survey, indicated they were interested in the outcome, and asked how they might obtain information or advice that resulted from the study. On the other hand, single-parent

IN THIS CHAPTER

- *Children and teens most likely to need post-divorce counseling.*

- *Emotional problems most common among single-parent teens.*

- *The "window of opportunity" that exists for helping children of divorce.*

fathers, at least in some cases, seemed somewhat paranoid. Many of the fathers completed the survey without elaboration, while a few refused to complete the survey at all.

> **IMPLICATIONS FOR YOUR MINISTRY**

There is no hidden message here as it pertains to those of us in the helping profession. Most of the single-parent kids you have in your junior high, high school, and children's ministries live with their moms. Because of this fact, you may want to remember that these children may not be receiving the attention they need from male role models.

To illustrate this point, let me tell you about a call I received from a youth pastor. When Marty was six, her father and mother divorced. After that time, Marty had almost no contact with men. My conversation with Marty's youth pastor centered around his concern for her flirtatious nature. After providing me with some of Marty's history, it became apparent that she was flirting in an effort to seek approval from and relationships with men. Her need related to the relationship she missed with her own father.

Without the willingness to look past her surface behavior and try to understand reasons for her actions, we could have suspected only that she was a problem child. Instead, the advice I gave to Marty's youth pastor was to connect her with a man in the church who could represent a positive father figure. Marty needed a male in her life who could teach her that love and acceptance is unconditional and does not have to be earned by flirting or through other extra efforts. She needed to understand the principles behind God's unconditional love for her so that she could understand and seek unconditional love from the people in her life. (For further scriptural background, refer to 1 John 4:9-21.)

About six months later I ran into Marty's youth pastor at a convention. I asked him about Marty's progress and was pleased to learn that she had been "adopted" by one of the elders of the church. The elder had become quite involved in her life, and the two of them had been able to establish a healthy father-daughter type of relationship.

FINDING 2

Boys from single-parent families are at higher risk.
One of the common observations made by clinicians is that there seem to be more boys than girls in counseling programs. The single-parent family research validated that boys, at a ratio of almost three to one, are more likely to require counseling following their parents' divorce. One of the reasons can be seen by examining the following emotional problems, which much more commonly affect boys than girls. Given the nature of these disorders, it is understandable that boys are more prone to being identified as needing counseling.

Conduct disorders. The *Diagnostic and Statistical Manual of Mental Disorders* (DSM-III-R),[2] which is an essential reference book used by therapists, defines conduct disorders as:

- Two or more incidents of stealing
- Running away from home

- Frequent lying
- Deliberate fire-setting
- Frequent truancy
- Breaking into others' property
- Deliberate destruction of others' property
- Physical cruelty to animals
- Forced sexual activity
- Involvement in more than one fight in which a weapon has been used
- Frequent initiation of physical fights
- Stealing, with confrontation of the victim
- Physical cruelty to people

Alcohol and drug dependence. Although society has tried to see to it that we are all fairly well versed in what the alcohol- or drug-dependent person looks like, youth pastors and youth leaders should watch for specific signs of substance abuse within their youth groups. Some factors that determine if a child or teen is really drug- or alcohol-dependent are:

- The substance is taken in larger amounts or over a longer period of time than the user intended. ("I drink only on weekends; I'm in control.")
- A child or teen exhibits a persistent desire to cut down use or tries unsuccessfully to control the substance. ("I'm going to quit before school starts.")
- Frequent intoxication or withdrawal symptoms occur when the child or teen is required to fulfill major obligations at school or home. ("A little drink before a big test calms me down and helps me do better.")
- A great deal of time is spent getting the substance, taking the substance, or recovering from the substance.
- Important social, school, or recreational activities are given up or reduced because of substance use. ("Soccer is for kids anyway.")
- Continued substance use exists despite persistent emotional or physical problems caused by the substance.
- A child or teen displays a marked tolerance for the abused substance. ("It's no problem, I never get totally wasted.")
- Withdrawal symptoms occur on discontinuation or reduced consumption of the substance.
- A substance is taken to relieve or avoid symptoms of withdrawal.

The single-parent family research validated that boys, at a ratio of almost three to one, are more likely to require counseling following their parents' divorce.

Oppositional defiant disorders. A relatively common trait among post-divorce children and teens is what we call "oppositional defiant disorders." These are characterized by:

- Loss of temper
- Arguments with adults and authority figures
- Defiance of adult requests or rules
- Deliberate annoyance of other people

- Blaming of others for mistakes
- Behavior that seems to result from being touchy or easily annoyed
- Anger and resentment
- Spitefulness or vindictiveness
- Swearing or obscene language[3]

**IMPLICATIONS FOR
YOUR MINISTRY**

The important message here is that the post-divorce emotional problems usually found in boys are more easy to recognize than those affecting girls. Youth pastors and others who work with male children and teens should try to familiarize themselves with the above warning signs.

I should also point out an important fact about male children and teens with whom I have counseled for the above emotional problems. In all of these cases, some of these symptoms were at least present, even if they were not blatantly obvious. Teenage boys are not usually very sophisticated about hiding their problems for an extended period of time.

As youth workers, you should be willing to become detectives if you suspect that something might be wrong with one of the kids in your group. Don't be afraid to ask tough questions of parents, family, teachers, friends, or the child you suspect is having problems. For each parent who thinks you are being intrusive, a hundred others will thank you for your love, concern, and devotion to their child who is part of your ministry.

You may also find the "Single-Parent Family Wellness Checkup" located in appendix A helpful in determining if one of the kids in your group is having any of these emotional problems.

For those of you who work with children and teens in church groups or in counseling capacities, keep in mind that boys naturally follow a more aggressive course in life than girls. Thus, boys are more prone to doing things that are socially unacceptable (i.e., drugs, alcohol, fighting, shoplifting, and other behavior problems).

FINDING

3

Girls experience a less obvious variety of emotional problems.

Unlike boys, girls tend to act out in a more passive manner, which is less likely to be discovered easily. The reason for this can be seen in emotional problems that manifest themselves as eating disorders, depression, or teen pregnancies. These problems are considered to be more passive in nature than the more active, or aggressive, problems boys typically experience.

Eating disorders are emotional problems found predominantly in teenage girls and young female adults. It should be noted, however, that, for the first time since psychologists started exploring eating disorders, we are now starting to see teenage boys and young male adults with this problem.[4]

Anorexia nervosa. The first of the three major eating disorders, anorexia nervosa is characterized by the following tendencies:

- A refusal to maintain body weight above the minimum normal weight for the person's age and height; failure to gain weight routinely during periods of body growth, which leads to a body weight at least 15 percent below average

- An intense fear of gaining weight or becoming fat, even though the person is underweight
- A disturbance in the way the person reacts to his or her body weight, size, or shape (e.g., feeling "fat" even when emaciated or too thin)
- In female teens or adults, an absence of at least three consecutive menstrual cycles that would normally occur

Bulimia nervosa. This second of the major eating disorders is characterized by the following:

- Compulsive overeating in an effort to fill the missing love and relationships that have never been present or have been removed
- Recurrent binge-eating episodes (i.e., out of control eating)
- A feeling of lack of control over eating behavior during the binge cycles
- Self-induced vomiting as a regular practice (Also common are the use of laxatives or diuretics, strict dieting or fasting, or vigorous exercise in order to prevent weight gain.)
- A minimum of two binge-eating episodes per week, planned or impulsive, for at least three months
- Persistent overconcern with body shape and weight [5]

Compulsive overeating. This third of the typical eating disorders is characterized by:

- Compulsive overeating, especially when the person is under stressful conditions
- Out-of-control eating
- Hiding out to eat
- Feeling a sense of security, pleasure, or contentment while eating
- Obesity (a common but not essential element)
- Despondency or depression over a physical condition, generally accompanied by the individual feeling powerless to change behavior [6]

The subject of compulsive overeating brings to mind a teenage girl with whom I worked for over a year. Wendy was a bright sixteen-year-old, who was cute in spite of being almost forty-five pounds overweight. Her mom brought her to counseling for her weight problem at the urging of the family doctor, after he concluded there was nothing medically wrong with Wendy.

After a few sessions, Wendy began relating stories about her parents' divorce. For several years, Wendy's mom had been emotionally and physically abused. Although her mother had sheltered Wendy from much of this, Wendy was highly aware of the abuse. Instead of talking to her mom or others about the abusive home environment, Wendy would isolate herself in her room. During her times of fear, anxiety, and insecurity, she ate to comfort herself. Eating made Wendy feel good, mostly because it increased her blood sugar, which in turn took the edge off some of her depression. The sugar (like a drug) would wear off and leave Wendy feeling down and alone again. Without anyone to turn to for help, she continued her overeating cycle.

Once Wendy was able to see how she depended on food as a replacement for communication and relationships, she began feeling more in control. Through careful diet, exercise, and—most importantly—improved relationships (with God, her mom, and others), Wendy was able to overcome her eating disorder.

Depression. Another group of emotional problems affect girls more often than boys. Also known as dysthymia or depressive neurosis, these clinical terms are more broadly known simply as depression.

Although both boys and girls become depressed after their parents divorce, boys tend to act out their depression. Girls, on the other hand, mask their depression better. Here are some common signs of depression in girls:

- Poor appetite or overeating
- Inability to sleep, fitful sleep, nightmares, or sleeping too much
- Low energy, lack of motivation, or fatigue
- Low self-esteem or poor self-image
- Poor concentration or difficulty in making decisions
- Feelings of hopelessness and helplessness
- Tearfulness or sometimes uncontrollable emotions[7]

IMPLICATIONS FOR YOUR MINISTRY

As a youth pastor or someone who works with young people in your church, it is vitally important that you become familiar with these seven key symptoms of depression. Depression is, in nearly every case, a precursor to crisis or even suicide, which is the third leading cause of death among teens.[8] In fact, a recent survey by the U.S. Centers for Disease Control revealed that, out of 11,631 ninth through twelfth graders in this country, 27 percent had seriously thought about killing themselves in the preceding year. Sixteen percent stated they had made a specific plan, and one in twelve said they actually tried to commit suicide.

From my experience as a police officer and as a therapist, I can assert that at least one warning sign was present in every suicide case I had seen involving teens and children. Sadly, these warning signs usually were not seen or understood until after the child's death.

This is not to say that each child or teen you have in your class or group who is having trouble concentrating on his work is depressed. The concentration problems should simply signal that you need to take a closer look. If, at second glance, you notice the child or adolescent is also having motivation problems, then it is time to consider some one-to-one counseling. Your extra effort will enable you to get a clearer picture of what may be going on inside the child's private world and what type of support system the child has with friends and family. At that point, you can determine whether you can continue to assist the child or teen until the problems are relieved or if you should consider consulting another counselor.

Teen pregnancy. Of course, our list wouldn't be complete without discussing teen pregnancy. Teen pregnancy is obviously somewhat different from the other emotional problems that we have examined. I consider most teen pregnancies to be a symptom of a greater problem rather than an independent problem. For instance, I've often found that teen pregnancy is a result of low self-esteem, which can be a result of a girl's poor relationship with her father. Because of a girl's low self-esteem, she may feel she is unable to maintain a relationship with a boy unless she gives in to his sexual advances.

Support of this theory is found in a study by John Hopkins University where researchers found that "young," white teenage girls living in fatherless homes were 60 percent more likely to have premarital intercourse than those living in two-parent homes.[9] The article points out that teenage girls are becoming quite aggressive in their pursuit of love and acceptance from boys. The article attributes this need for male acceptance to the lack of a loving, consistent, and attached male figure (i.e., dad) in their lives. The result of this need for male acceptance has led many teenage girls into a lifestyle of premarital sexual relations, which they misinterpret to be a close male relationship. From my experience as a counselor, I believe this misinterpretation is based on the fact that most of these girls grew up without a healthy concept of how women act around men.

IMPLICATIONS FOR YOUR MINISTRY

The single-parent survey supported the Johns Hopkins University finding when it revealed that 67 percent of the teenagers and 18 percent of the children have had sexual relations following the divorce of their parents. The survey provides conclusive evidence that early sexual relations are related to self-esteem and insecurity in relationships. The more you can keep the young people in your church involved in relationships, the more likely their self-esteem will benefit. As a result, the more likely it is that these young people will learn about healthy relationships with God, with their parents, with you, and with others.

It would be reasonable to conclude that after divorce, although boys are three times more likely to end up in counseling, this does not mean that girls are not as emotionally disturbed by the divorce. What the survey does point out is that emotional problems in girls manifest themselves in different areas and have different consequences.

It is important for you as a pastor or youth worker to see teen pregnancy from a broad perspective. If you allow yourself to be caught up in a parent's feelings of embarrassment or shame, then you may miss the real problem. If a teen in your church or high school group becomes pregnant, try to look beyond the pregnancy. Attempt to find out what was going on in her mind before she became pregnant, then consider ways of helping her work through those problems. Remember, the pregnancy did not alleviate the underlying reason she may have become pregnant. In fact, it probably exacerbated the original problem. During the pregnancy, more than ever before, the girl will need an accepting friend.

Researchers found that "young," white teenage girls living in fatherless homes were 60 percent more likely to have premarital intercourse than those living in two-parent homes.

Because of the different ways in which boys and girls display their emotional problems, it is important for you to focus your attention on warning signs. You need to understand that boys work through their problems following divorce differently from girls. While everyone around you is criticizing a child's actions, you may be the only one who can see the warning signs. Through your efforts to identify warning signs that indicate deeper problems, you can intervene and avert potential crisis. The Twenty-One Warning Signs of Crisis are covered in greater detail in chapter 6. Figure 4.1 summarizes and compares similarities and differences between boys and girls that frequently manifest themselves in the aftermath of divorce.

FINDING

4

Teens ages sixteen and seventeen are at highest risk.
From a therapist's perspective, this was one of the more fascinating areas of the survey. I learned from examining the ages of the adolescents in various types of counseling that a definite high-risk group can be identified by age. The survey concluded that sixteen- and seventeen-year-old teens accounted for 53 percent of all adolescents who participated in the survey. Figure 4.2 provides a further breakdown of all teens surveyed.

> **IMPLICATIONS FOR YOUR MINISTRY**

Remember not the sins of my youth and my rebellious ways (Psalm 25:7). If you are responsible for the programs and groups that include teenage boys ages fifteen through seventeen, then you are responsible for the highest risk group in your church. The reasons for the higher risk factors are certainly multi-dimensional. A broad range of physical changes as well as an increase in social pressures can cause a myriad of problems for adolescents.

Hormonal changes. Ages fifteen through seventeen are often recognized as being the three most turbulent years due to physiological and hormonal changes.

Increased sexual pressures. These increased pressures are commonly brought about by a teen's increased sexual awareness. Even a cursory look at high school groups will point out the wide span of sexual awareness among individuals. Some kids just seem to act twenty-one even though they are only fifteen. These kids usually dress differently and talk differently; they typically associate less with younger teens and more with young adults and older people.

It is no secret in our society that premarital sex is becoming more prevalent among fifteen- through seventeen-year-olds. The increased awareness causes sexual pressures that often bring about emotional conflicts. Sometimes these conflicts involve personal, family, or religious morals and standards. The pressure, then, comes in the emotional struggles to either do the right thing or do what everyone else is doing.

This point seemed overstated to me before I became involved in what the Minirth-Meier Clinic West calls "Monday Night Solutions." "Solutions" is a weekly lecture that covers a wide range of mental health topics, such as forgiveness, needs and wishes, confronting anger, boundaries, and other topics. During these sessions we blend in biblical principles and sound psychological advice.

Due to the requests of many parents who regularly attended our program, we at the clinic decided to provide a similar format for their teenagers. "Teen Solutions," which is similar to junior high and high school church groups, got off to a great start. However, I quickly learned that the topics their parents were engrossed in in other rooms produced little or no interest to teens. Our sessions always began on the topic of the night, like "resolving conflict"; but once the teens began interacting, the topics quickly shifted to their real-to-life issues.

Invariably we would get on the subject of sex and dating, especially whenever the boys in the group felt like talking. To me, the most interesting aspect of their preoccupation with dating and sexual topics was that they were open enough to ask these questions (1) of a stranger acting as therapist, (2) in a large group, and (3) with teenage girls listening. Each week I conducted informal polls about with whom they discussed such issues. The polls revealed that most of them felt uneasy or rebuffed when trying to discuss these subjects with their parents. Some of these young people indicated they were able to talk about these issues with their church youth leaders; however, the teens frequently told me that in church settings there seemed to be boundaries that prevented an open discussion of sexually oriented topics.

During one evening, a sixteen-year-old girl in my group raised her hand and asked, "Why is it that when you go out with a boy and you don't let him at least make-out with you on the first date, he never calls you again?" Looking around

The teens frequently told me that in church settings there seemed to be boundaries that prevented an open discussion of sexually oriented topics.

FIGURE 4.1

WARNING SIGNALS:
SIMILARITIES AND DIFFERENCES BETWEEN BOYS AND GIRLS

TRAITS COMMON TO BOYS	TRAITS COMMON TO GIRLS
depression	depression
running away from home	running away from home
alcohol and drug use	alcohol and drug use
frequent loss of temper	frequent loss of temper
stealing/shoplifting	shoplifting
frequent lying	frequent lying
frequent use of profanity	frequent use of profanity
breaking into others' property	interruption in sleep patterns
frequent truancy	frequent truancy
deliberate fire-starting	poor concentration
destruction of property	decreased self-image
physical cruelty to animals	tearfulness
forced sexual activity	uncontrolled emotions
fighting/use of weapons	hopelessness/helplessness
poor school grades	eating disorders
likelihood of sexual activity	poor school grades
physical cruelty to others	likelihood of sexual activity

the room I noticed the nodding heads of many of the other girls and the down-cast eyes of many of the boys. We discussed this subject for about fifteen minutes until, fortunately for me and the boys in the group, we ran out of time. The last question I directed to the girls just prior to their leaving was, "Do you talk to your moms about these types of questions?" One girl replied, "Are you kidding? My mom hates men. My dad lives 500 miles away and yells at me whenever he hears that I'm dating. The people at my church won't let us talk about sex because they're afraid we'll get them sued or something."

I bring up the above situation to illustrate to those of you in youth ministries that Christian teenagers are just as preoccupied with sex and their increasing aware-ness of their sexual identities as secular kids are. There is perhaps an added dimen-sion with Christian children that puts them even a little more at risk, namely, the perceived reluctance on the part of parents and church leaders to address these issues. To make matters even worse, many Christian parents wrongly assume that their children are insulated from these issues just because they are part of a church youth group.

Ironically, as a footnote to this topic, a show of hands revealed that, week after week, about 60 percent of the teens in my group come from single-parent families. It makes me wonder where all the other single-parent family kids in the world are going to ask questions about dating and sex.

Awareness of the future. Somewhere between latency stages (preteen) and later teenage years, adolescents begin to realize they are not children any longer.

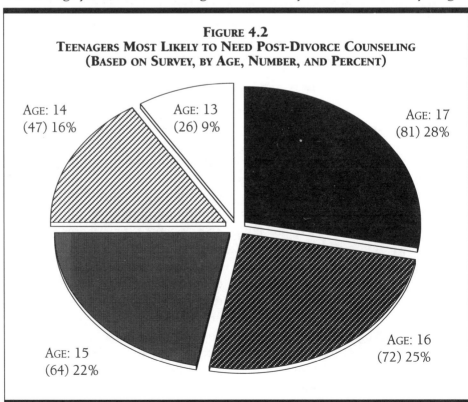

FIGURE 4.2
TEENAGERS MOST LIKELY TO NEED POST-DIVORCE COUNSELING
(BASED ON SURVEY, BY AGE, NUMBER, AND PERCENT)

AGE: 14
(47) 16%

AGE: 13
(26) 9%

AGE: 17
(81) 28%

AGE: 15
(64) 22%

AGE: 16
(72) 25%

As a result, they begin to feel anxiety about planning for their future. This planning process may include college, career, dating, or preparing to be out on their own, all of which can cause increased pressures. Most teens handle this increased pressure with the normal amount of adolescent chaos; however, others are not able to cope as well and require more help.

For this reason, I encourage churches to sponsor career and college counseling events. These sessions should include lectures from outside professionals who can assist teens in making tough decisions about their futures.

Separation and individuation. Probably the greatest influence on teenagers from ages thirteen to sixteen is the secondary phase of development. Most developmental experts agree that the primary stage of development takes place from birth through roughly thirty-six months.[10] In this secondary developmental phase, separation and individuation (growing up and becoming an individual) are perhaps at their strongest point since infancy, when children learn that they are separate people from their mothers.

Some amazing similarities exist between these two developmental phases. In developmental phase one, children begin to fulfill their need to establish themselves as separate from their mothers but still in need of a mother's attention and love. In phase two, teens experience a similar need to separate from the family (as they did from their mothers) and to establish again a separate identity.

It is at this stage of development that single parents, especially single mothers raising teenage boys, need to monitor their parenting styles and to consider outside male assistance. An enmeshed mom, one who is especially overly protective or smothering, will sometimes unknowingly inhibit a teenager's natural growth. These enmeshed mothers are often single parents who have their own need to feel attached. The mother's over-attachment generally will lead to even greater resistance from an older child or teen.

As youth workers, you can generally identify an overly enmeshed mom and child by the child's inability to answer questions independently from the parent. Even though children may resent the parent's authority and dominance, they often can't act independently and look to the parent for answers or approval.

It is easy to understand why the survey shows teens between the ages of sixteen and seventeen are in the highest risk group. It is at this age that most of the internal and external influences on their lives converge.

In spite of this focus on mid- to later-teen years, I want to be careful not to give elementary and junior high leaders the idea that you can relax. Don't forget for one second that a significant number of the children surveyed between the ages of nine and twelve were also struggling with serious emotional problems.

If you work with preteens and/or older children, you may consider that your ministry may, in some cases, be one of crisis intervention. Perhaps more than anyone else in the church, you have the opportunity to build self-confidence and communication skills in the children and teens you work with. Doing so may avert a problem before it becomes a crisis.

If you work with pre-teens and/or older children, you may consider that your ministry may, in some cases, be one of crisis intervention.

FINDING

5

Among children, eleven- and twelve-year-olds are at highest risk.

It is equally important to take a look at the high risk ages within the children's group. Interestingly, just as we saw that the highest number of teens in treatment were at the upper ages of adolescence, the same pattern holds true with children. Figure 4.3 includes the most common ages of children receiving counseling following a divorce.

It is important to note the disparities between the ages of teenagers in treatment and the ages of children in treatment. For instance, 9 percent of the teens surveyed were age thirteen, compared to 31 percent of the children surveyed who were age twelve. One possible reason that children between the ages of 10 and 12 are likely to experience more emotional struggles is because of their pre-puberty "transitional stage" in life. These changes during the pre-teen years can cause children to feel less stable and sometimes out of control.

> **IMPLICATIONS FOR YOUR MINISTRY**

Those who are actively involved in youth work should understand the messages behind the numbers. The most relevant point that can be made for the high number of children in counseling being ages twelve, eleven, and ten is that these kids are no longer children but are not yet teenagers; therefore, they are not accepted by or a real part of either group.

In addition, it is during this time that children start to have normal heterosexual thoughts. This natural development is part of the process called "individuation," which we looked at with regard to teenagers.

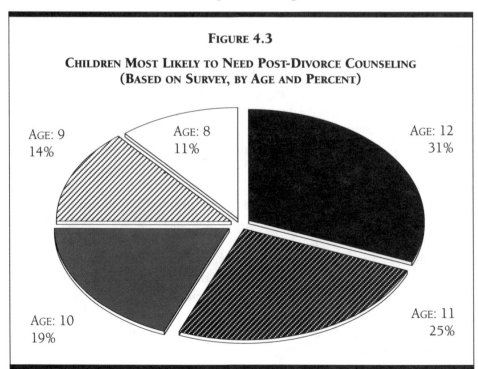

FIGURE 4.3

CHILDREN MOST LIKELY TO NEED POST-DIVORCE COUNSELING (BASED ON SURVEY, BY AGE AND PERCENT)

AGE: 9
14%

AGE: 8
11%

AGE: 12
31%

AGE: 10
19%

AGE: 11
25%

For instance, you can probably identify children in your youth groups who have no interest yet in the opposite sex. Typically, most eight-year-old boys will remind you that girls have cooties and are just plain stupid. But when they approach nine or ten years old, the boys begin noticing fewer cooties and the girls wise up a little. They begin to consider the opposite sex in a different light than even just a short time before.

Another factor in ten- to twelve-year-olds being in the highest risk group is that this age child frequently experiences increased pressure stemming from the divorce. This pressure, coupled with their own pressures in growing up, can cause quite a conflict in a child's mind.

As a result, the single-parent family kids between the ages of ten and twelve who attend your church should be recognized as being in the high risk group. As such, they should command a bit more of your attention.

What does that mean to you? It means very much the same thing that it meant regarding the teens with whom you work. You have to pay closer attention to these kids: you have to be on the lookout for the warning signs that can indicate serious underlying problems.

FINDING 6

Kids who live with their moms are more likely to be emotionally healthy.

Not surprisingly, the survey concluded that, following a divorce, 82 percent of teens and children live with their mothers, 6 percent of the children and teens reside with their fathers, and 12 percent live with someone else, usually their grandparents.

This area of the survey pointed out interesting facts when compared with the national statistics regarding where kids live after divorce. According to the U.S. Census Bureau, in 1989 only 2.8 percent of single-parent family children lived with their dads, compared to 6 percent in my survey. In addition, 12 percent of the children in the single-parent survey lived with someone other than one of their parents, while the national average was only 2.1 percent.

IMPLICATIONS FOR YOUR MINISTRY

Fortunately, this information further defines the high-risk group of kids, namely, those who don't live with their moms after the divorce. Although in your church youth groups you probably have fewer kids who live with their dads, it is a critical part of risk reduction to take the time to find out who they are. By identifying these kids, you have taken a major step in learning which kids need a little extra attention. Remember, not only are these kids working through their normal stages of growth and development, but they are also saddled with feelings of rejection and fears that they may not have been wanted by their moms and/or dads.

I want to be careful to point out that no data states that single moms, dads, or even grandparents are less capable of raising children. In no way are these statistics telling us that substitute parents are inadequate or doomed to failure. What the survey does say, however, is that kids who live with someone other than their moms after divorce have considerably greater pressure upon them, which often translates into greater risk. Remember, parenting is a tough two-person job even under the best of circumstances.

FINDING

7

Greater visitation increases emotional stability.

Results of the single-parent survey indicate that nearly one-half of the children and teens receiving treatment saw the other parent once a month or less. To most parents, the thought of seeing your child just once a month seems very hard to comprehend. But try to consider this from a child's perspective. Seeing your father (in most cases) only once a month or less would almost certainly feel like abandonment.

Many factors influence the frequency of visitation; however, the four most common factors are:

Kids who live with someone other than their moms after divorce have considerably greater pressure upon them, which often translates into greater risk.

- *Time and distance between parent and child.* Visitation is naturally influenced by the distance that the other parent lives from the family.
- *Financial considerations.* It is common for a parent to ask for joint custody (50 percent visitation) in order to keep child support payments at a minimum. In cases where one parent lives far away, flying or traveling back and forth for visits can become a financial hardship.
- *The other parent's desire to stay connected with his or her kids.* After divorce, parents often find it difficult to put the pieces of their lives back together and still find the time to spend with their children.
- *Cooperation between both parents.* Unfortunately for many children, parents sometimes use visitation as leverage or as a means of getting back at the other parent. In some cases, mothers refuse to allow the husband to visit the kids, even though the court papers indicate visitation is called for; in other instances, a father may refuse to bring the children home to the mom on time after a visit.

To obtain information concerning the average frequency of visitation, I interviewed two attorneys whose practices deal exclusively with large numbers of divorce and child custody cases. One attorney's practice was in Los Angeles County and the other was in Orange County. The composite information from both law firms provided some interesting facts. Nearly 65 percent of their combined custody cases called for the other parent to have visitation at least once a week. The most common settlements were those that called for visitation two days a week, while many cases called for as many as three to four days a week. This compares to the results of the single-parent survey, which showed that weekly visitation occurred in only 16 percent of the cases. Both attorneys also believe their figures to be representative nationally, regardless of the family's background or culture.

Prior to the single-parent study, I had often wondered to what degree frequency of visitation influenced a child's emotional health. Also prior to the survey, we weren't really able to identify how much of a hardship it would place on a child to have little or no visitation with a parent. In psychological terms, divorce interrupts what we call *object constancy*. This is a fancy psychological term, which means that, anytime you remove a parent from a child's life, it will have an impact on the child.

During certain ages, object constancy is more critical, such as between the ages of birth and three years. But this does not minimize the impact of divorce on a teenager. Remember, the research points to a second crucial period of a child's development, which occurs in pre-puberty adolescence. Even though volumes of studies look at the lack of object constancy mostly in infants and children, it is clear that the loss of a parent, at any age, is a potentially devastating life experience.

A second theory behind it being so difficult for children to adjust to limited or no visitation after divorce is post-traumatic stress disorder (PTSD), which is discussed at length in chapter 2. The application to visitation issues is that children who go through a divorce and see their other parent half of their lives or less are not as capable of processing their pain. As a result of the trauma of divorce, they feel a greater sense of loss than children who maintain frequent and consistent contact with both parents. How these children and adolescents deal with the stress and trauma of divorce is germane to how successful they will be in working through their pain and getting on with their lives.

IMPLICATIONS FOR YOUR MINISTRY

On the basis of the information supplied by the single-parent survey, I conclude that visitation between the absent parent and a child totaling less than one visit a week significantly increases the likelihood of emotional trauma. However, I would also point out that cases involving abusive parents or unfit homes are exceptions to this theory.

As the pastor, youth minister, or lay counselor to whom single-parent families come for support, you have a unique opportunity (and responsibility) to share these findings. One of the first things you might consider in familiarizing yourself with your single-parent families is, How often do the children see their other parent? If you find out that the child sees the father infrequently, try to understand why. If there is no logical reason for this policy, then you may even want to consider talking to the child's mom (or dad) about your concern for how this decision may affect the child involved. Remember, you are informing, not judging or condemning.

When you identify children who have infrequent visitation and there is no possibility of altering the situation, there is still hope. In these cases, I recommend introducing a ParaParent into the family system. This ParaParent can help fill the void left by the other parent. We'll talk more about ParaParenting in chapter 7.

FINDING

8

A quick response can avert serious emotional problems.
Several of the single-parent survey responses revealed that a problem must be addressed within a six-month time frame following the onset of the warning signs. Failure to notice or respond to the warning signs commonly resulted in the problem's escalating into a crisis. For further information, refer to the Twenty-One Warning Signs in chapter 6.

Christopher, a seventeen-year-old receiving inpatient treatment for depression, is an example of a teen whose symptoms preceded a crisis by approximately six months. Chris's parents went through a very difficult two-year separation process prior to deciding to get a divorce. During that time, Chris's dad moved in and out of the house several times, although he promised that each time would be his last.

Chris's grades started falling at school during the first month of the family crisis. During the second month, two of his teachers sent notices home that he was not completing his assignments, and he was failing in one of his classes. During the third and fourth months, his mom remembered that Chris began to isolate himself more and more from his family and friends. He would spend long hours by himself in his room. During the fifth month he got a one-day suspension from school for fighting, which was quite unusual considering Chris was a shy and passive boy.

During this fifth month, Chris also quit his baseball team because he thought his coach didn't like him and treated him differently from the other guys. During the sixth month after the breakup, Chris began shoplifting small items from the local department store. When he was finally caught, the police released him to his mom. Two weeks later, she found an undelivered note that Chris had written to one of his friends telling the friend that he didn't want to live anymore. Chris's story graphically illustrates how, in a span of six months, a young person's problems can turn into a suicidal crisis.

Another example of how response time is critical can be seen in the case of fourteen-year-old Mario. Mario lived in an up-scale beach community with his mother. His parents divorced when he was twelve, and his dad moved to another area of the state. At that time, Mario began having problems at school. First he cut classes infrequently, and then more often. He began failing classes for the first time. His mom talked to him once in a while about his problems but later stated, "I just thought it was a phase he was going through. I didn't want to overreact to him because he has a temper like his father's." Because of her passive nature, Mario's mother did not seek help for Mario until nearly six months later—after he was arrested for stealing beer from a store.

When I first met Mario, he was in a hospital program receiving treatment for depression and alcoholism. One of the questions I posed for Mario was, "Do you think you would have needed to be hospitalized if you had seen a counselor when your problems first started?" Without hesitation, he replied, "No. I thought someone would make me see a doctor or someone. I couldn't believe I pulled that stuff so long without getting busted."

IMPLICATIONS FOR YOUR MINISTRY

The results in this area of the survey have direct significance to pastors, youth workers, and lay counselors. The challenge for you comes after you have identified a child or teen whom you feel may be having some emotional difficulties. The easiest thing for you to do is to sit tight and watch, right along with everyone else in the child's life. Please, take the risk: Resist the temptations of passivity and apathy.

Your first step should be to talk to the child (as a friend) about the behavior you are seeing. If you are lucky, he or she will validate your concerns and agree to talk further, either with you or a counselor. You also need to consider bringing the situation to the attention of the parent(s). I generally request the child or teen talk to the parent before I do.

When you discuss your observations with parents, tell them clearly that you noticed some signs that sometimes indicate serious emotional problems. Express your concern. Suggest to the parent that the child might benefit from counseling.

Even if you are unsuccessful in getting the parent to see the warning signs you see, you have let the child or teen know that you care and are there to help. This places you in a position of trust and respect in the child's eyes and will make it easier for him or her to come to you in times of need.

Remember—time is of the essence!

FINDING 9

Trouble with police or school authorities indicates that the child or teen needs help.

This is a common warning sign. Nearly 70 percent of the parents surveyed stated their children had been in trouble with the police or school authorities prior to their needing formal counseling. I found this statistic particularly interesting considering my past experiences as a police officer, where I first surmised that children of single-parent families seem to have more contact with the police.

During a survey session at a hospital program, I had occasion to meet four teenagers who were just leaving a group therapy session. As we began talking, one of the boys and I realized we had first met almost four years earlier, while I was still a police officer.

I recalled the circumstances surrounding the first of our several encounters involving a chronic problem between the boy's parents. Nearly every week, his parents would have a knock-down, drag-out fight; and, invariably, I would be called to intervene. I always remembered the two boys: Mike (the boy in the hospital) and his brother Tom. Mike, who was about eleven years old at the time, used to get very upset during these arguments.

One Sunday afternoon, I had been called to the local mall to pick up a shoplifter that security had caught stealing clothing. You guessed it: The shoplifter was Mike. I was able to talk the security officer into letting Mike go and I took him home. (After all, taking a kid back home to that family was a stiffer sentence than any judge could have handed down.) I remember Mike telling me on the way home

Nearly 70 percent of the parents surveyed stated their children had been in trouble with the police or school authorities prior to their needing formal counseling.

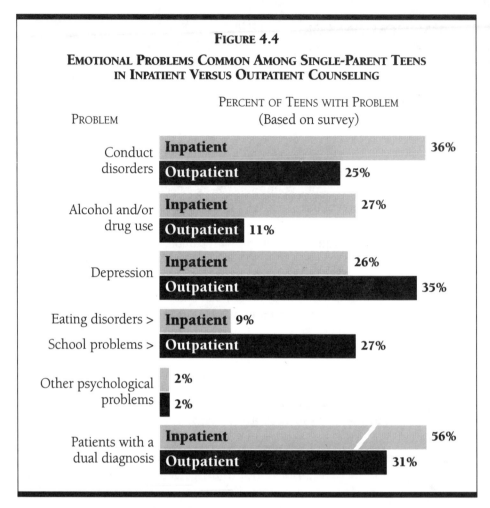

Figure 4.4

Emotional Problems Common Among Single-Parent Teens in Inpatient Versus Outpatient Counseling

Percent of Teens with Problem (Based on survey)

Problem

Conduct disorders
- Inpatient 36%
- Outpatient 25%

Alcohol and/or drug use
- Inpatient 27%
- Outpatient 11%

Depression
- Inpatient 26%
- Outpatient 35%

Eating disorders > Inpatient 9%
School problems > Outpatient 27%

Other psychological problems
- 2%
- 2%

Patients with a dual diagnosis
- Inpatient 56%
- Outpatient 31%

that his mom had finally left his dad and that they were getting a divorce. Until that day at the hospital, that was the last time I saw Mike.

After completing the patient survey for me, Mike and I were able to catch up on the last four years of his life. Mike went on to tell me how his mom, his brother, and he had moved into an apartment following the divorce. He hardly ever heard from his father, who had remarried and begun a new family. Mike's mom had had several boyfriends, two of whom had lived with the family for about a year each. Both men drank, and one used to hit the boys when he would come home drunk.

Finally, about six months prior to my running into Mike again, he had been expelled from school for poor grades and fighting. He had been having problems at home and was also arrested for breaking into a neighbor's house. Mike went on about how his life had fallen apart since his parents' divorce, but he was hopeful that he could turn it around since he learned how to talk about his problems while in the counseling program.

IMPLICATIONS FOR YOUR MINISTRY

I can understand how it could be difficult for youth leaders, pastors, and counselors to know if kids have been in trouble with the police or school authorities. Often, the only way of finding out this information is through the grapevine, which is better than not knowing at all.

It never hurts to discuss the biblical perspectives on stealing, particularly if you are working with single-parent kids in your groups. However, you should also use present-day examples to talk about stealing as well. Hit them where they live: Talk about the rising costs of goods, such as records, tapes, and CDs, which is partly the result of thefts and the need to offset those losses.

You may want to initiate a group discussion about stealing and find out what the other kids think. You will probably find that most of them have stolen something at some time in their lives. Discussing their indiscretions allows them to confess their sins, express their present feelings, and ask for forgiveness. It is also helpful to ask your group for their thoughts on why people steal.

If you have heard that someone in your group has been arrested or suspended from school for stealing, be aware that this is often a classic warning sign of greater problems. Be open and honest with the child or teen. Tell him or her that you heard the bad news and that you are available (and want) to talk about the incident. If you are unable to connect with the child or teen, try to ensure that he or she is receiving some form of counseling, either through the church or with a counselor.

FINDING 10

Three emotional problems are common among single-parent teens and children.

Of the teens who were receiving inpatient therapy (hospitalization), the most common emotional problems were *conduct disorders*, *alcohol and drug use*, and *depression*. The other problems are listed, along with relevant percentages, in figure 4.4.

Dual diagnosis reflects children and teens who are being treated for a psychological disorder (i.e., depression) and are also being treated for a chemical addiction. It is well documented that most kids with a chemical addiction in fact have an underlying psychological disorder that must be addressed at the same time. Failure to address both issues, by treating just the chemical addiction, generally results in the patient's relapse once he or she is back at home or around a peer group.

The second group surveyed included both teens and children. This group differed from the inpatient hospital group in that they were receiving outpatient therapy only. The reason school problems appear in the outpatient counseling group and not in the inpatient group is that school problems are not usually severe enough by themselves to warrant hospitalization. Figure 4.4 provides a breakdown of the most common diagnoses in the outpatient group.

In these cases, school problems included learning disabilities, attention-deficit disorders, failures, problems with IQ scoring, and other school-related difficulties that hindered the learning environment for the child or teen. Conduct disorders for this group were essentially the same problems as the ones experienced by those who were hospitalized, except that either the behavior for these children had not become dangerous or the parent had refused to consider hospitalizing the child.

It may be somewhat confusing to look at a heading like conduct disorders and determine what qualifies for hospitalization and what can be handled in outpatient counseling. Examples can be seen through the following two cases.

First, Jamie was a seventeen-year-old boy who was being treated for a conduct disorder as an inpatient. Jamie was brought into treatment by his mother, who found him in the back yard feeding meat containing rat poison to the neighbor's dog. When asked why he was trying to kill the dog, Jamie replied, "I don't know. He tried to bite me, and he barks at me all the time. I just hate him."

On the other hand, Tammy, a fifteen-year-old girl, was brought to a counselor's office because she refused to do what her mother asked her to do around the house. Challenging her mother's authority, she would argue and slam doors. These two cases represent two extremes of conduct disorders and how they can differ in severity but still be classified the same.

> *Children in single-parent families must acknowledge the fact that they are more prone to divorce than children from two-parent families.*

IMPLICATIONS FOR YOUR MINISTRY

Once you have a basic understanding of which emotional disorders you are most likely to encounter within your single-parent families, then you can begin to look for warning signs. Knowing which problems are the most prevalent is critical.

It is also important to remember that the majority of the surveys were conducted within Christian counseling centers and hospitals. I make this point to illustrate that, unlike many parents want to believe, Christian kids are as much at risk as their secular counterparts.

FINDING 11

Divorce rates climb from generation to generation within single-parent families.

Have you ever wondered if children from single-parent families are more likely to get divorced as adults? You can stop wondering. There was a 5 percent increase in the divorce rate of the parents who responded to the survey compared to the divorce rate of their parents.

To confirm the theory that divorce has some ongoing influences, further testing must be done in subsequent generations. We cannot just go back to our parents and ask if their parents went through a divorce. The answers would be shrouded in a mass of differences between our generation and that of our grandparents, and the numbers would not translate accurately to today's generation. Basic cultural differences between as few as two generations back and today indicate that predictions based on prior results would be inaccurate.

It is essential that we teach two extremely important messages. First, children in single-parent families must acknowledge the fact that they are more prone to divorce than children from two-parent families. Thus, they must learn how to avoid repeating the pattern in their own lives. Second, parents and children of single-parent families need to consider the church as the key to traditional Christian family values. Conversely, the church needs to consider single-parent families as a key area of ministry, where people are in great need of being loved and nurtured with the love of Christ. Through teaching and practicing scriptural perspectives, the church has the capability of reestablishing proper principles for life and family.

Margaret is a thirty-five-year-old divorced mother of two children. Her son Pete was one of the children who took part in the survey during an outpatient counseling visit with his therapist. During her son's session, Margaret told me that her parents were divorced when she was sixteen. She had very little contact with her father after the divorce; she and her mother were essentially alone.

Margaret promised herself that she would never marry, as she would never want to subject a child to the pain of going through a divorce. When she finally did marry, she waited until she was twenty-seven to have children because she wanted to be sure the marriage would last. But, much to her dismay, she and her family repeated the process that she had hated so much during her childhood.

Margaret's situation is similar to well over half of the parents who participated in the survey. On one hand, parents who have been through the pain of divorce as children should remember the trauma and somehow be able to avoid it in their marriages.

However, divorce significantly impacts children. Without good parental role models to emulate, people are naturally less likely to be equipped with the necessary skills to ensure that their own marriages will be good.

It would be fair to estimate that about 70 percent of our ability or inability to relate in a marriage comes from watching our parents. The other 30 percent includes outside influences such as relatives, friends, reading, television, and other observations.

IMPLICATIONS FOR YOUR MINISTRY

Through my years of research and experience with single-parent families, I am convinced that the best way to stem the tide of generational divorce within these families is for the church to intervene. When your church begins providing singles with alternatives such as parenting seminars, workshops, and support groups for parents as well as their children, a healthy change will begin to impact the families within the outreach of your ministry.

Communication problems are nearly always cited as a major contributing factor to divorce. Developing single-parent family ministries will significantly and positively impact this area. Children of single-parent families can grow up learning how to communicate more effectively through their church's single-parent family ministries. As a result, their relationships and marriages will be greatly enhanced.

FINDING

12

Crisis is most likely to occur during the twenty-four-month period following a divorce.

Yolinda, a sixteen-year-old girl, was brought to a Christian inpatient treatment center. Yoli was admitted for a number of problems, the most obvious being that she had gotten pregnant by her boyfriend of twelve weeks. She had also been failing in school and, according to her mom, had developed an eating disorder. She would eat very little at meal time and then disappear to the bathroom. She had gone from 135 pounds to 102 pounds in a span of three months. Because of the pregnancy, Yoli's mom knew that the eating disorder had to be treated.

Yoli's mother related to me that she and Yoli's dad had divorced when Yoli was a little over fourteen. Yoli's dad did not make any effort to visit Yoli or the other four children at home, and Yoli had taken the divorce the hardest.

Yoli's situation is not uncommon in single-parent families. Fathers play an incredibly important role in their children's lives, especially daughters. A parent who leaves the family unit disrupts object constancy, which is discussed earlier in this chapter. In effect, Yoli was modeling her mother's lifestyle in her own way. Since Yoli's mom was not in a healthy relationship with her father, Yoli had no base of knowledge for what healthy relationships were supposed to look like. The clue that Yoli was in emotional crisis came not so much from the fact that she was pregnant, but from her eating disorder.

The pregnancy was almost predictable in Yoli's situation. She was desperately seeking love and approval from male figures because she had known only rejection from her own father. In addition, she observed her mother as she dated several other men. Following the divorce, one of her mother's boyfriends moved in and also showed Yoli little or no attention. This compounded her perception that (1) men are emotionally unavailable (or abusive), and (2) the best you can expect is to get their attention through sexual intimacy.

Because the timing of Yoli's troubles can be traced to the divorce and to the absence of her father, her problems could be considered part of a post-traumatic stress disorder.

IMPLICATIONS FOR YOUR MINISTRY

Yoli's case is a good illustration of the Windows of Opportunity theory. Essentially, the single-parent family survey produced evidence of two separate and distinct windows. (See figure 4.5). The first and most critical window is established by logging the date of the divorce or separation and then projecting six months ahead. In Yoli's case, her school problems were the initial indication that something was going wrong. These problems occurred within the first six months of her parents' divorce and should definitely have been considered a warning sign of a potential crisis.

Remember, the first Window of Opportunity falls in the first six months following the divorce. Yoli did not come forward with her problems, nor did anyone notice she was having difficulty. Thus, her problems continued.

The second Window of Opportunity includes the length of time it took for Yoli to reach a point where she required counseling to avert a crisis. The point where many teens' and children's problems are finally discovered is referred to as the crisis point. In Yoli's case, her parents had been divorced eighteen months prior to her crisis. The total time—from the divorce to symptoms to crisis point—fell within the twenty-four-month Window of Opportunity.

For those who prefer a proactive approach to ministry, here are tips for you to pass along to parents in helping them through the twenty-four-month Window of Opportunity:

- Both parents should agree to keep arguments and differences of opinion between themselves.
- Parents should not use children as leverage for material things (e.g., property, more money).
- One parent should not try to influence the child against the other parent.
- Both parents should make visitation a priority (under appropriate circumstances).
- Both parents should be involved in making sure the child knows the divorce was not his or her fault.
- Both parents should spend quality time (as frequently as possible) with the child.
- The parent who does not live with the child should make frequent phone calls and send letters and cards whenever possible.
- Each parent should talk frequently to the child about that child's thoughts, feelings, and emotions about (1) the custodial parent, (2) the other parent, (3) the divorce, and (4) life in general.
- The parents should try to get the child to become active in church groups with other children and teens.
- Both parents should be consistent in watching for the warning signs of an impending crisis.
- Parents should not overindulge children because of their own feelings of sorrow or guilt.
- Neither parent should try to make up for the absence of the other parent. (It's better to be one good parent than two marginal parents.)

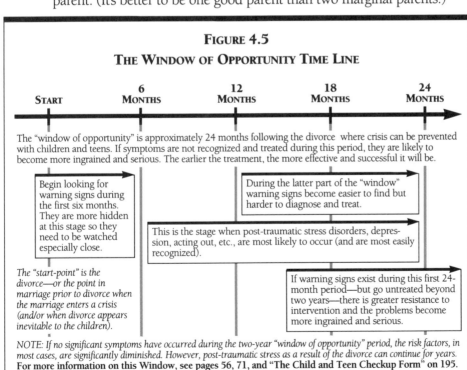

FIGURE 4.5

THE WINDOW OF OPPORTUNITY TIME LINE

| START | 6 MONTHS | 12 MONTHS | 18 MONTHS | 24 MONTHS |

The "window of opportunity" is approximately 24 months following the divorce where crisis can be prevented with children and teens. If symptoms are not recognized and treated during this period, they are likely to become more ingrained and serious. The earlier the treatment, the more effective and successful it will be.

Begin looking for warning signs during the first six months. They are more hidden at this stage so they need to be watched especially close.

During the latter part of the "window" warning signs become easier to find but harder to diagnose and treat.

This is the stage when post-traumatic stress disorders, depression, acting out, etc., are most likely to occur (and are most easily recognized).

The "start-point" is the divorce—or the point in marriage prior to divorce when the marriage enters a crisis (and/or when divorce appears inevitable to the children).

If warning signs exist during this first 24-month period—but go untreated beyond two years—there is greater resistance to intervention and the problems become more ingrained and serious.

NOTE: If no significant symptoms have occurred during the two-year "window of opportunity" period, the risk factors, in most cases, are significantly diminished. However, post-traumatic stress as a result of the divorce can continue for years. **For more information on this Window, see pages 56, 71, and "The Child and Teen Checkup Form" on 195.**

FINDING

13

Nearly three out of four parents believe the divorce led to their child's emotional problems.

When Lisa was being treated by a psychologist for her depression, her mother, Lenora, who had two other children, pondered a question typically asked by adults who have gone through a divorce: "I don't know 100 percent for sure if the divorce really caused Lisa's depression, but I feel it did. Her father and I were divorced almost two years ago when Lisa was only five."

She went on to explain, "Lisa currently sees her father nearly every other weekend but doesn't always want to go. At the time our marriage was falling apart, her father and I were in marriage counseling because of all our fighting, and I know that was hard on her. After about three months of counseling, we decided it would be worse on Lisa and our other children if we stayed together as we were than if we tried to part as friends. Actually, now that I think of it, I think Lisa is better off because of the divorce, although I feel very guilty for putting her through all that."

IMPLICATIONS FOR YOUR MINISTRY

As professionals who also work with parents following divorce, it is important for you to understand some of their post-divorce thinking. It is particularly important to understand how single parents connect the child's emotional problems with the breakup of their marriage. The survey concluded that almost three out of four parents believed (for whatever reasons) that their divorce significantly impacted their child and that it was a direct factor in the child's need for counseling.

I really cannot imagine (nor have I seen) a divorce that did not have a significant impact on the children involved. In fact, based on my counseling experience, I conclude that denial or rationalization played a major part in the thinking of one in four parents who did not believe their divorce had an impact on their children.

FINDING

14

Three out of four parents saw changes in their children but did not recognize the warning signs.

Specific areas of the survey that led me to this conclusion pointed out a very important fact to those of us in the helping profession. Almost 80 percent of the parents noticed changes in their children following the divorce, which tells us that the warning signs of impending crisis are observable.

A second thing the survey tells us is that, following a divorce, the alertness or level of awareness of some parents can be quite low. This reality is understandable due to the numerous distractions going on during a divorce.

IMPLICATIONS FOR YOUR MINISTRY

You will need to provide two important areas of training to single parents in your church:

1. The Windows of Opportunity theory, which was charted under finding 12 of this chapter and will be elaborated on in greater detail in the

group session outlines in chapters 9 and 10.

2. The Twenty-One Warning Signs of Crisis, which are referred to throughout this book, discussed in detail in chapter 6, and presented in figure 4.6 on page 66.

This training will help parents not only see the warning signs but also interpret those signs.

THE TWENTY-ONE MOST COMMON WARNING SIGNS OF CRISIS AFTER DIVORCE

Two survey questions in particular were designed to help discover the most common warning signs prior to crisis. Learning these warning signs should be considered "preventative medicine" for those who work with teens and children from divorced families. Before we take a look at the warning signs, let me tell you about Bennie's sad but all too typical situation.

Bennie, age sixteen, was a junior in high school. For three years he had excelled and lettered in three sports: football, baseball, and track. At the majority of the games and track meets, Bennie's dad cheered his son on from the stands. Then after the games, he would take Bennie out for a soda or ice cream.

In addition to his athletic prowess, Bennie was quite popular at school and carried a 3.0 grade point average. He was generally considered a shoe-in for a college scholarship. He was a generally outstanding young man.

One night during his junior year, Bennie and his dad went out for pizza after a baseball game. This particular evening with his dad was different, and Bennie sensed there was bad news coming. His dad started the evening's conversation by asking Bennie if he had noticed that he and Bennie's mother had been arguing more often lately and that the arguments had become violent on a few occasions. Sadly, Bennie nodded his head.

His father continued, "I just don't think I can stay with your mother any longer. Things have changed between us. I know you've noticed that all we do is fight and argue. And I suppose you could say we don't love each other anymore. Not only that, but the company has offered me a promotion to general manager at the East Coast office, and I just don't see how I can turn it down."

Bennie sat motionless and stared numbly at the table as his father spoke. "I know it's going to be rough on you and your sister, but you can spend summers with me, and we'll do the things we always have. You'll see. It will be okay."

Bennie helped his father move out of the house a few weeks later and stood at the curb as the large moving van lumbered down the street enroute to his father's new house, across the country.

The ensuing weeks were not particularly noteworthy for Bennie. He maintained his busy schedule but found himself becoming less and less interested in playing baseball. One afternoon, he got into a fight with a teammate; and after a confrontation with the coach, Bennie quit the team. Bennie didn't want to tell his mother that he had quit; so after school, instead of going to baseball practice, Bennie started going to the mall to be with classmates who hung out there regularly. His new routine included wasting his afternoons until 6:00 or 6:30 p.m., then he would go home, have dinner with his mother and sister, and go back out.

Bennie's grades began dropping, which was unknown to his mom until a progress report was sent home indicating he was failing algebra and English. When Bennie's mom approached him demanding to know why his grades had fallen from Bs to Fs, Bennie just looked at her and said, "You don't care anyway," and walked to his room.

In many ways, Bennie typifies a teenager who has not been able to cope with his feelings following the separation of his parents. Bennie never became suicidal and never stole anything or hurt anyone. In many ways, though, the impact of his new pattern was just as negative. He had lost his purpose and motivation. He had lost the direction that had been pointing him toward a scholarship, a good education, and a chance to play college ball.

Fortunately for Bennie, his youth pastor identified some of the symptoms as warning signals and associated them with the changes he had been noticing in Bennie. His observations resulted in a few counseling sessions between Bennie and

FIGURE 4.6
TWENTY-ONE WARNING SIGNS OF CRISIS

SIGN NUMBER	DESCRIPTION OF WARNING SIGN
❑ 1	My child became lonely, quiet, or moody.
❑ 2	My child just seemed depressed.
❑ 3	My child's self-esteem was very low.
❑ 4	My child began having difficulty sleeping.
❑ 5	My child seemed so negative about everything.
❑ 6	My child began to isolate himself or herself.
❑ 7	My child was often very angry and abusive.
❑ 8	My child's eating habits changed.
❑ 9	My child became argumentative and lied to me.
❑ 10	My child began fighting at school and at home.
❑ 11	My child's school grades began to fall.
❑ 12	My child began violating curfew times.
❑ 13	My child was arrested for shoplifting.
❑ 14	My child dropped out of once-loved activities.
❑ 15	I caught my child drinking or taking drugs.
❑ 16	My child refused to go to church anymore.
❑ 17	My child became lazy and procrastinated regularly.
❑ 18	My child dated/befriended kids against my wishes.
❑ 19	My child became sexually active.
❑ 20	My child's appearance really changed.
❑ 21	My child stopped making eye contact.

the senior pastor, who recommended that Bennie see a Christian counselor who works mostly with teens.

| IMPLICATIONS FOR YOUR MINISTRY |

On page 66 is a list of the most common warning signs that parents indicated they observed (or missed and later remembered) as preceding their child's crisis. You may notice that many of these signs seem to fit children in general and not just those of single-parent families. While these warning signs are general in nature, they are specific in many areas. A doctor cannot treat a stomachache by means of a phone call, even if he or she knows the symptoms indicate a stomachache. In the same way, you will need to identify *specific* warning signs in order to determine the source of the problem and, more importantly, to look for solutions that will lead to emotional health.

As people in the helping profession, it is important for you to be familiar with these warning signs. The more familiar you are with them, the easier it will be to recognize them in individuals who are part of your various church ministries. In this immediate context, it is important to see them as parental responses.

FINDING 15

In terms of how they handle divorce, little difference was noted between Christian kids and secular kids.

I specifically wanted the survey to evaluate differences between the way secular single-parent children and Christian single-parent children handle divorce. The reason for exploring this area was in part to dispel the false sense of security that Christian parents feel because their children are involved in church activities and have Christian friends.

The survey concluded that 72 percent of the parents stated they attend church on a fairly regular basis, i.e., about twice a month. This statistic is somewhat higher than the national average of 60 percent,[11] possibly because many of the families surveyed were receiving treatment or counseling from Christian therapists.

In order to determine if there were any significant differences between the two groups in the way in which the children and teens responded to divorce, I separated the results of the Christian group (460 responses) from the secular group (180 responses). The results were *virtually identical* in each category, except for questions specifically regarding church.

Conclusively, I found that the Christian children and adolescents were no better equipped than their secular counterparts to handle the emotional impact of divorce. Logically, I wonder why we should ever consider that Christian children would suffer any less emotional trauma going through a divorce than secular children. The impact, in either case, is inherently profound.

I found that the Christian children and adolescents were no better equipped than their secular counterparts to handle the emotional impact of divorce.

| IMPLICATIONS FOR YOUR MINISTRY |

A January 1990 Gallup Poll showed that 43 percent of adults and 57 percent of teens in the United States go to church weekly. A second report tells us that three out of ten households are nontraditional families (e.g., single parents, adopted children, children living with grandparents).[12]

Together, these figures should be alerting us to the fact that a large portion of the Christian population is comprised of single-parent families. The relevant question, then, is, Are our churches meeting the needs of this significant population?

Perhaps for us as Christian counselors, the important message is that many of the children we see in our church youth groups are the same children we must be ready and able to counsel in our offices.

FINDING

16

Kids feel they have no one to talk to about the divorce.
Sadly, 45 percent of the single parents surveyed said that their children essentially had nobody (other than them) to talk to. Only 5 percent of the single moms said their children talked to the youth pastors at church, and only 3 percent said that they took their child to a counselor immediately after the divorce. A surprising 13 percent of single moms said that their children talked to their ex-husband throughout the divorce process and afterward.

**IMPLICATIONS FOR
YOUR MINISTRY**

Generally speaking, parents are poorly prepared to help their children cope after divorce. As you can see, very few parents (actually only twenty out of 288) turned to their church pastors or youth leaders for assistance.

An informal inquiry as to why more parents did not look to their churches for support produced surprising responses. The most common response given was that parents thought no one in the church was trained to help in this area. The second most common response was that they felt embarrassed to discuss their family failures with their pastors.

Their responses should be teaching us a crucial lesson. Accurate or not, if their perception is that pastors and youth leaders have not been adequately trained to help out in these specialized areas, then we have a problem. Additionally, we also need to work on the problem that, because they feel embarrassed, troubled families fail to look to their church families for help at a time when they really need it. While this misconception is not always the fault of pastors, singles' pastors, youth leaders, or lay counselors, the burden of changing this perception clearly lies with the leadership of our churches.

EXPERT ADVICE—FROM SINGLE PARENTS TO SINGLE PARENTS

Penny stared blankly out the window of the waiting room office as she considered her response to what advice she might be able to give to other single parents. Her daughter PJ had been seeing a therapist for about six months, and life had only recently started to return to normal for her family.

I continued observing Penny as she began making a few notes on the two blank lines that followed question 18 on the parent survey and then as she turned the paper over and began filling up the page with her thoughts and emotions. Penny began wiping back tears as she wrote about PJ and the pain she had been through since the breakup of the marriage nearly two years earlier.

"You see," Penny wrote, "PJ is one of those kids who is very sensitive. When Jack and I got divorced, I made the mistake of letting PJ know how angry I was that Jack had had an affair. I told PJ that he was a bad father and a bad husband. I told her that Jack was a bad influence on PJ and that any man who would destroy his family like he had didn't deserve our love and respect. I manipulated PJ to the point where she would not talk to her father any longer. When he would call, I would tell him that PJ wasn't interested in talking to him anymore and just to prove it I would hold the phone up and ask, 'Do you want to talk to the man who abandoned us?'

"I look back on those two years now and realize that I did the wrong thing. I was angry and extremely hurt by what Jack did; however, that didn't excuse what I was doing out of anger and revenge. Now that PJ and I have been through therapy, I am able to see that I was partially to blame for the breakup of my marriage and that I shouldn't have tried to ruin PJ's relationship with her father because of our problems. After all, Jack does love PJ and he is a good father, even if he failed as a husband."

Do's and Dont's

Here are the remaining responses listed in the order of the frequency in which they appeared in the survey. The response is followed by the percentage of those surveyed who offered a similar response. (*Note:* Each of these responses is explained in detail in chapters 9 and 10, which provide lecture materials for pastors and youth leaders.)

- Don't take your anger at your ex-spouse out on your kids. The divorce is not their fault. (88%)
- Make sure your kids don't think the divorce was their fault. (78%)
- Don't do what I did and miss the signs that things are going wrong with your kids. (73%)
- Don't try to get your kids to dislike your ex. If you do, it will backfire on you and only make things worse. (72%)
- Let the kids visit with their other parent as much as they want. Don't punish the kids by trying to get back at your ex. (67%)
- Don't let your kids stop talking and hide. (64%)
- Begin socializing (and dating) as soon as possible. Make some time to spend with friends so you don't sit around getting depressed. (63%)
- Don't try to be both parents to your kids; just do your best at being a mom (or dad). (61%)
- Ask for help from friends and family while you are putting your life back together. (58%)
- Pay attention to your kids' friends. See if they are hanging around with a different crowd. (51%)
- Get active in your church right away. Don't be afraid they won't accept you just because you're divorced. (47%)
- Encourage your kids to make friends with other kids of divorced families. The support will help them. (44%)

- Get your kids involved in church youth activities right away. (43%)
- Don't let your kids make you feel guilty for the divorce. Don't beat yourself up over it. (43%)
- Don't get buried in the feeling that your life is ruined because of the divorce. It will get better. (41%)
- Don't start backing off the discipline with your kids because you are afraid of being too tough or you are feeling guilty. (32%)
- Try to find a man who will talk to your boys about "guy stuff." (32%)
- Go to divorce recovery workshops and support groups. They are a good means of support. (27%)

I think we'd all agree that, when you want specialized information, you go to an experienced specialist. The advice provided *by* single parents *for* other single parents should be regarded as expert advice.

FIGURE 4.7
SUMMARY OF THE FINDINGS IN CHAPTER FOUR

1. Three out of four single moms had custody of their children.
2. Boys from single-parent families are at higher risk.
3. Girls experience a less obvious variety of emotional problems.
4. Teens ages sixteen and seventeen are at highest risk.
5. Among children, eleven- and twelve-year-olds are at highest risk.
6. Kids who live with their moms are more likely to be emotionally healthy.
7. Greater visitation increases emotional stability.
8. A quick response can avert serious emotional problems.
9. Trouble with police or school authorities indicates that the child or teen needs help.
10. Three emotional problems are common among single-parent teens and children: conduct disorders, alcohol and drug use, and depression.
11. Divorce rates climb from generation to generation within single-parent families.
12. Crisis is most likely to occur during the twenty-four-month period following a divorce.
13. Nearly three out of four parents believe the divorce led to their child's emotional problems.
14. Three out of four parents saw changes in their children but did not recognize the warning signs.
15. In terms of how they handle divorce, little difference was noted between Christian kids and secular kids.
16. Kids feel they have no one to talk to about the divorce.

⊰ 5 ⊱

WHAT YOU NEED TO KNOW ABOUT CHILDREN AND TEENS OF DIVORCE

If the survey had stopped with only the information from the parent survey, that information would still have proven to be quite a valuable resource tool from which we all could learn. However, I wanted as broad a perspective as possible, since a common limitation to many surveys is that they utilize only one dimension of research. In this case, for a more complete view of single-parent family issues, the responses of the children and teens had to be factored in.

The child and adolescent surveys took place within two treatment settings: inpatient hospitals and outpatient counseling offices. Inpatient hospitals treated children and adolescents who needed twenty-four-hour psychological care. Outpatient counseling sessions usually included one regularly scheduled, hour-long counseling session per week.

The sixty-one children who took part in the survey were found solely in out-patient counseling offices, whereas the 291 teens surveyed represented a cross-section of both inpatient and outpatient programs. The reason for this difference is that often children who are involved in inpatient hospital programs tend to be more chronic patients. They usually have been more seriously disturbed over a longer period of time than the children who have a short-term crisis over a particular event such as divorce. These inpatient children are often on heavier dosages of medications, which can make it difficult to administer tests like the single-parent survey.

Another interesting facet of the survey was how children's and teens' responses compared to the responses of parents. Questions such as, "Do you feel you would be in treatment or counseling now if your parents had stayed together?" provided significant insights when contrasted with the parent responses.

FINDING 1

The child and adolescent survey verified the Windows of Opportunity theory.

You may recall my initial identification of the Windows of Opportunity theory from the parent's survey (pages 62-63). This theory was further tested and validated in the child and adolescent surveys. The survey provided evidence that the average age of a child at the time of divorce is between ten and eleven. I subsequently

71

compared this statistic to the average age of all children receiving counseling, which was twelve. Case after case (irrespective of the child's age) verified a time frame of two years or less from divorce to crisis, thus validating the Windows of Opportunity theory.

A similar window was discovered in relation to teenagers. Among teens, the most common age at the time of their parents' divorce was fifteen. The parent's survey indicated that the most common age of an adolescent receiving counseling or treatment was seventeen. Again, the time frame, or window, between divorce and crisis among teens was under two years.

| **IMPLICATIONS FOR YOUR MINISTRY** | For us to pass these windows off as coincidence is irresponsible. Several possible theories could serve to explain why there |

is consistently a two-year lapse between the time of the trauma (divorce) and the time of crisis (therapy or some form of treatment.)

The theory that makes the most sense is that children and teenagers experience PTSD, or post-traumatic stress disorder, which is explained in detail in chapter 2. As discussed earlier, one essential element of PTSD is that the onset of a problem does not usually begin until at least six months after the trauma—in this case, the divorce. Since children and teenagers from our surveys frequently went into some form of crisis within two years after the divorce, the survey information is consistent with the theory concerning PTSD, which suggests that a waiting period exists between trauma and crisis.

I also considered a second factor in the two-year gap between crisis and treatment. The first two years following divorce are extremely stressful for parents as well as their children. Conflicts and issues run the gamut from financial survival to meeting their own (as well as their children's) emotional needs, and these all consume much of the adults' attention. During this survival period, while lives are being put back together, it is common for the emotional needs of both the parent and child to be under-served. Therefore, it seems quite logical that it would take a period of at least a year or two for a parent to begin what I call "damage control." Thus, during these two extremely critical years, the church needs to actively encourage single-parent family participation in its programs.

FINDING 2

Children and teens view parental arguments differently.
Essentially, the survey revealed that children, more than teenagers, tended to view life in extremes (i.e., fighting all the time or never fighting). Younger children quite naturally tend to see things as either all good or all bad. Their ability to discriminate typically doesn't develop until later childhood, generally around seven or eight years of age. I should include, however, that many adults have just as difficult a time differentiating between things (and people) as being either all good or all bad.

Children tend to be more engrossed in their own worlds than teens. When this logic is carried out, divorce could be more of a shock on children than on teens, since the children have observed fewer problems and arguments. Instead, observing fewer of these warning signs left them less prepared for something bad to happen to their parents.

On the other hand, due to their sharper (more mature) observation skills, teenagers had a more life-like view of their parents' conflicts. Teens' survey responses often reported that their parents argued "pretty often," which indicated they were less apt to see problems in extremes.

IMPLICATIONS FOR
YOUR MINISTRY

For those of you who work consistently with the same kids and teens, you can look for a few signs that might indicate rough times at home. These signs were derived from the symptoms that kids demonstrated when there was a lot of conflict between their parents. I call these the P.A.I.N. symptoms.

- Passive-aggressiveness (talking behind others' backs, being afraid to confront, undermining projects/activities, being non-compliant)
- Anger (arguing, refusing to follow instructions, talking back)
- Increased aggressiveness (being short-tempered, having trouble sitting still, fighting, pushing, playing too roughly, exhibiting poor concentration)
- Negativity (not liking anything or anybody, revealing a bad attitude)

FINDING 3

Domestic violence is prevalent prior to divorce.
Wendy, a church youth leader, approached me following a weekend retreat for the seven- through twelve-year-old children. Wendy was faced with a dilemma when she found out from a child that one of the eight-year-old boys at camp had bad bruises on the backs of his legs and arms. When Wendy asked him about the bruises, the boy became quiet and muttered, "I got in trouble and my dad spanked me." Wendy knew that the boy's parents were going through a trial separation and that things had been pretty rough for the whole family.

Using good judgment, Wendy decided to bring the incident to the attention of the church staff. On the following day, I met with the boy and his parents and learned that things had been quite tumultuous at home during the very emotional separation period. The boy's father admitted that he had lost his temper and "over-corrected" his son.

Unfortunately, after examining the marks on the boy's legs, I was bound by law to report the case to the Department of Youth Services. But, fortunately, the father agreed to enter counseling for his problem with managing his anger. The silver lining was that both parents decided to begin marriage counseling.

This situation, like many others, simply illustrates the fact that we are more prone to lose our tempers and resort to physical violence, with each other as well as with our children, during a stressful separation or divorce process. The best way to minimize this risk is to recognize this tendency and to face it head on. The time to begin addressing these increased pressures is prior to there ever being a potential situation where physical violence could take place in the home.

IMPLICATIONS FOR YOUR MINISTRY

Domestic violence is a very sensitive area to all of us who work with children and teens. Many states have passed laws requiring mandatory reporting of any violence against children. Many have also enacted similar laws protecting wives from physical abuse from husbands. Since these laws vary from state to state, I encourage you to check with your local department of social services or police agency to determine what reporting requirements affect you.

Children and teens of divorce often believe they were the cause of the divorce.

The single-parent family survey revealed that domestic violence occurred between husbands and wives in well over one-half of the cases. Perhaps an even more startling discovery was the high number of children and teens who stated they were the target of violence (69 percent of the teens and 45 percent of the children). These statistics should confirm for us that we need to pay particular attention to families in these situations, as emotions are raw and tempers are more likely to flare during divorce.

Characteristics of victims of domestic violence. Individual members of families who are victimized by domestic violence consistently exhibit certain identifiable personality traits.

Protective. In the families I interviewed regarding domestic violence, I learned of an interesting correlation between the violence and the child's behavior at church, school, or social settings. This correlation concerned the child's or teen's unwillingness to divulge any information about the abuse or violence. Even when good relationships existed between the therapist or the pastor and the child, the child still seemed trapped in a mode of protection.

Codependent. From further research I've concluded that this tendency is related to codependency and often exists in abused or battered children and teens. Often the abusive parent threatens the child and warns him or her not to tell about the violence at home. Abusive parents often play additional mind games, such as threatening more violence for telling or intimidating children by telling them they will be taken from the home.

Ashamed. Receiving abuse is also very difficult for children and teens because it adds to their feelings of shame over the divorce. Victimization of a child by an abusive parent often causes the child to feel insignificant, insecure, and unlovable. As dysfunctional as it sounds, abused children resist reporting the incident out of fear that the victimizing parent will be taken from their lives.

Needing attention. In families such as these, often the only attention the child receives is in the form of punishment. Sad but true, for many children this form of attention is one step above emotional abandonment.

Self-blaming. We also need to understand another side of this complex issue of domestic violence. Children and teens of divorce often believe they were the cause of the divorce. These feelings can be brought on by angry statements made from parents to children.

I also found that many children and teens simply assumed they were to blame for the marriage. During the weeks, months, and years preceding divorce, arguments and domestic violence are much more prevalent. Often children saw this anger as cyclic—from the father to the mother and back to the father again. Once the father left the house, the mother and children were often left at home to deal with their feelings of abandonment. In a child's mind, since the mother was blamed by the father for the marriage failure and the father left her with the children, then the children themselves must also be to blame.

Unresolved anger. Unresolved anger typically stems from marital problems prior to the divorce coupled with anger and anxiety caused by the many aspects of the divorce. Alimony, child support, visitation, community property, and many other issues factor into this equation.

Because we tend to hurt the ones who are closest to us because they are "safe," children tend to receive more than their share of anger. This anger is often misdirected from the ex-spouse to the children and can be seen in the form of emotional as well as physical abuse.

This anguish can sometimes be distributed to children in double doses when they visit the other parent who also has not resolved his or her anger at the ex-spouse. So, in essence, children can and often do become carriers of bad feelings between parents. Parents need to learn not to export their anger through their children.

Detecting abuse. A few signs indicate children and teens who may be on the receiving end of abuse during or following a divorce. They may exhibit some of the following traits:

- Anger
- Failure to make eye contact with authority figures (i.e., pastor, youth leaders, adults)
- Denial of anything being wrong
- Avoidance (i.e., a child will not want to go home or will stall around the church when being picked up by a parent)

If you notice any of these signs, you should talk to the child about your concerns. Remember, you are offering love and acceptance, which the child may not be getting at home. A consistent message of support should eventually break down the child's defenses and allow him or her to come to you for help. For instance, you might consider saying something like, "I really know how tough it has been for you the past few months, and I just want you to know how much we appreciate you here and how hard I know you are trying."

If you see evidence of physical abuse, don't hesitate to call the authorities in your area for assistance. As painful as it is for any of us to report child abuse cases, it is much more painful for the child to receive it.

FINDING
4

Marital problems are seldom a surprise to children or teens. I recently conducted an assessment of a sixteen-year-old boy whose parents had filed for divorce, although they were still living together. The boy came to me after he told his mom that, during one of his parents' recent violent arguments, he had gone into the garage, found one of his dad's handguns, pointed the gun at his head, and pulled the trigger back. He had no idea when he pulled the trigger that the gun was unloaded. He was simply desperate. During our session, the boy stated that he was at the breaking point from listening to his parents fight. He didn't know how to cope with his life in any other way. He described his emotional dilemma this way: "On one hand I want my dad to leave the house and to quit hurting my mom and me, but I feel terrible that he may be gone forever."

In a more rare case involving an eight-year-old child whose parents were filing for divorce, I learned from the boy that he never saw or heard his parents fight. As a result, when the boy was told his father was leaving the house, he went into a state of shock. For all he knew, his world was fine and secure because he was not aware of any trouble between his parents.

IMPLICATIONS FOR YOUR MINISTRY

Understanding that 87 percent of the teens surveyed knew of their parents' marital problems tells us that we need to deal with these problems openly. This information also leads to a valid concern; namely, if the vast majority of children and teens know their parents are not getting along well prior to the divorce, who can they talk to about it? The current answer is probably nobody, with the possible exception of friends.

It is imperative that we provide a forum for the single-parent family children and teens in our church groups to talk about their observations and their problems at home. They need feedback from trained professionals as well as from their peers. See chapters 9 and 10 for information on establishing support groups to provide a forum for the open discussion of these problems.

FINDING 5

Girls tend to feel post-divorce stress more than boys—or do they?

My personal theory had always been that girls (both teens and children) are more in touch with the stress of divorce. This is not to say that they are more affected by the divorce than boys, but rather that they are more honest and aware of their feelings. The survey seemed to support this theory in the following manner:

- On a scale from 1 to 10, female adolescents rated their stress during the divorce as an "8" while males rated their stress as a "6."
- On a scale from 1 to 10, female children rated their stress during the divorce as a "9" while males rated their stress as an "8."

This survey tells us a few other important pieces of information. First, boys are probably in stages of greater denial of their feelings than girls. This means simply that boys are more likely to hide from their feelings or will try not to talk about them. Additionally, children of both sexes feel greater levels of stress during divorce than teens.

Some important warning signs of stress in children and teens (especially girls) after divorce are:

- An inclination to vegetate (i.e., excessive sleep, low motivation, lethargic appearance, slothfulness about grooming and personal hygiene)
- An inclination to isolate

- A decline in performance at school or work
- Changes in affect (quiet, sullen, moody, somber, unresponsive)

FINDING

6

Most teens and children have nobody to talk to about divorce.

I had just finished a lecture on the subject of communication to a group of teenagers in a hospital program when Stacy, a thirteen-year-old girl, approached me. Stacy told me that, perhaps for the first time, she was beginning to recognize the terrible communication problems in her family. She went on to tell me about how her mom and dad used to argue constantly over everything. These arguments would become heated, violent confrontations often ending with her father leaving the house, sometimes for days.

Stacy related that this pattern went on from the time she was old enough to notice to the time her parents divorced, when she was eleven. Stacy said she realized after my discussion how this led to her inability to talk about her feelings, which eventually led to her emotional problems.

What Stacy was telling me, in effect, was that she learned at a young age that it wasn't okay to be honest. Communication was not part of her family life; and therefore, when she had personal problems, she didn't feel there was any safe place to talk about them.

What do you think might have happened if Stacy had been a member of a church youth group that actively encouraged communication through group support? Stacy likely would have found a safe place to talk about her feelings. She could have seen that poor communication was a problem in her family but that the problem did not have to be the same in other families or other relationships.

IMPLICATIONS FOR YOUR MINISTRY

For whatever reason, the number of children and teens who either sought or found help within the church is low.

After their parents' divorce, six out ten children (and almost seven out of ten teenagers) said there was nobody around for them to talk to about their problems. Unfortunately, these kids, just like Stacy, tend to keep their problems inside until they finally explode from all the pressure. Sadly, at that point these feelings often come out in self-destructive attitudes or behaviors such as suicidal feelings, depression, eating disorders, substance abuse, or other physical problems. Inpatient hospital programs and counseling offices are filled with children and teens who feel they have nobody to talk to about their problems.

Remember that, in the parent survey, 72 percent of the parents reported they attend church, and 66 percent stated that their children also attend. Why is it, then, that only 4 percent of the teens and 2 percent of the children said they were able to talk to a pastor or youth leader? Logic would seem to dictate that children, as well as single parents, are not seeking and/or not finding the support they need at church. For whatever reason, the number of children and teens who either sought or found help within the church is low.

A note of encouragement. I hope those of you in the helping professions recognize that you have been blessed with the spiritual gifts of helps and teaching.

Personally, whenever I am having a tough day (or sometimes several of them) or when I am dealing with some particularly tough cases, I like to review 1 Corinthians 12:28, which helps to restore my faith in what I am doing: "God has appointed in the church" (notice Paul didn't say the therapist's office) "first apostles, second prophets, third teachers, then miracles, then gifts of healing, helps, administrations, various kinds of tongues." In verses 29-31, he continues: "All are not apostles, are they? All are not prophets, are they? All are not teachers, are they? All are not workers of miracles, are they? All do not have gifts of healing, do they? All do not speak with tongues, do they? All do not interpret, do they? But earnestly desire the greater gifts. And I show you a still more excellent way" (NASB).

This message should be very clear to all of us who have an opportunity and responsibility to help children in need. You have been given a spiritual gift and, along with it, the ability to carry out God's wishes. But as verse 29 points out, it is our responsibility to utilize our gifts. If not us, then who?

FINDING 7

Over two-thirds of teens and children believed divorce led to their serious problems.

I watched quietly as Courtney finished filling out her survey. Courtney was a very bright twelve-year-old who was receiving outpatient counseling for her problems with anxiety.

After she completed the survey, she handed it to me with a bright smile, and (I must confess) I questioned in my mind, "What kind of father could leave behind such a beautiful child? Could a marriage really be so bad as to force a parent to walk away from a child like Courtney?"

After stuffing my own feelings of anger (remember, nobody's perfect), I had the opportunity to chat with Courtney about the circumstances that led up to her parents' divorce and how her anxiety attacks came about. Courtney stated she knew her parents weren't getting along for quite some time before the divorce. Her father would come home from work (usually after stopping off for a few beers) and immediately begin complaining about the meal, the condition of the house, Courtney's school work, and anything else he could think of.

To make a long story short, I was beginning to understand what type of dad leaves a daughter like Courtney. She related a few incidents when her dad had pushed her mom down or slapped her. After the divorce, Courtney learned that her father had received partial custody consisting of every other weekend and some holidays.

At the time, Courtney felt this arrangement would be okay; however, the more time she spent with her father, the greater the conflict she felt. Her discomfort centered around her feelings of abandonment, fear, and intimidation by her father and conflicted with her love for him and her codependent thoughts regarding how she should act. These feelings went on for the first year after the divorce until she began having stomach ulcers and problems sleeping.

Courtney went on to tell me that she and her therapist had discovered the reasons for her troubles. She found she was really afraid of her father's rage and that her stomach problems came about because she really didn't want to see him but felt she couldn't tell anyone. Courtney couldn't tell her mother, who was showing her own codependent traits. She knew her mom would only tell her to go visit dad and she would be okay.

Even if Courtney's parents had stayed together, odds are she would have needed counseling at some point in time to help her work through her fear of and anger at her father. Because of her strong objections to visiting her father after the divorce, I conclude that the divorce was a major factor in accelerating her need for counseling.

IMPLICATIONS FOR YOUR MINISTRY

Of the non-adults surveyed, 61 percent of the adolescents and 64 percent of the children felt the divorce was responsible for their emotional problems. Add to this the 72 percent of the parents who believed likewise, and what does this tell us? It should tell us that divorce seriously impacts a child's emotional stability.

If you know of a family in your congregation who is having serious marital problems, consider offering your assistance. You can refer them to a counselor or work with them yourself. As you are working with them, share with them stories like Courtney's, and let them know about the risk they are taking with their children's mental health. Share other stories you can draw from that will help to illustrate the ramifications of their actions.

FINDING 8

Three out of four teens shoplifted after their parents' divorce.

To me, this number was perhaps the most predictable of all considering the experience I had with adolescent and child shoplifters while I worked as a police officer. Shoplifting differs from other types of thefts in that it is a crime of impulse. About one-half of the young people I have interviewed after they were caught stated that they weren't thinking of shoplifting when they entered the store. As they were walking around and looking at all the merchandise, they were overcome with the desire to take something. These kids are likely to be one-time shoplifters who never steal again.

On the other hand, another population of shoplifters premeditate their thefts. These kids are more likely to graduate from shoplifting to other types of crimes and antisocial behaviors.

IMPLICATIONS FOR YOUR MINISTRY

Shoplifting is undeniably one of the warning signs of child and adolescent crisis. This is not to say that all kids who shoplift are in crisis or will shortly go into crisis. The important aspect of shoplifting to take notice of is if it follows divorce. Shoplifting alone, or coupled with other warning signs, must not be trivialized as just something all kids do. Be cautious, too, of the parent who rationalizes the theft by thinking their child was just with a friend who was shoplifting.

If a parent brings a child to you for counseling after the child has been caught shoplifting, consider the following:

- Is something going on at home that could have influenced the child to steal (i.e., divorce, marital problems, money problems)?
- Is the child or teen trivializing the theft, or does he or she understand the seriousness of the act? (Trivialization generally leads to further thefts.)
- What other warning signs may be present? (Additional warning signs are covered in depth in chapter 6.)

FINDING

9

More than half of the teens and children used drugs or alcohol during or after their parents' divorce.

Jonathan's mom brought him into my office after she discovered a marijuana pipe hidden in one of his drawers. As they took their seats, Jonathan's mom began to cry. As Jonathan slouched in his chair, his mom started by saying she didn't know anything about drugs and that ever since her divorce eight months earlier she had been noticing a change in Jonathan. First she noticed that he was not going to church activities as often as he used to. His friends changed from those in the church group to some kids who had longer hair and went to his school. His taste in music changed from Christian rock to heavy metal and rap. A couple of weeks earlier, she had left forty dollars out for the housekeeper, but somehow the money was missing.

Jonathan's mother found the final clue while inventorying his socks to see if he needed more. As she moved the socks around inside the drawer, she came across a metal pipe that resembled a crude-looking homemade tobacco pipe. Next to the pipe were matches and a small plastic bag containing some green substance.

At this point in her explanation to me, she produced the pipe and baggie from her purse as Jonathan sank a little deeper in his chair. I asked Jonathan some questions about the pipe and marijuana, but he was obviously uncomfortable and finally asked his mom if she would mind leaving the room for a minute. After she had left, he told me that he had been smoking marijuana nearly every day for about six months. He had tried cocaine on a few occasions but didn't like the way it made him feel. Jonathan admitted he had a problem, but he did not feel he would be able, nor did he want, to stop smoking marijuana. The times he had tried to cut back, he ended up just using more. He realized he needed professional help in quitting and decided he would enter a drug and alcohol treatment program.

Information gathered from children and teens who participated in the survey provides the following statistics:

- Fifty-seven percent of the teenagers and 37 percent of the children stated they had smoked marijuana around the time of the divorce.
- Thirty-four percent of the teens and 11 percent of the children said they had used cocaine around the time of the divorce.
- Ninety-three percent of the teens and 69 percent of the children and teens reported they drank alcohol around the time of the divorce.

FIGURE 5.1
INDICATIONS OF DRUG AND ALCOHOL USE

INDICATIONS OF
MARIJUANA USE

- Redness of eyes, droopy eyelids, watery and itchy eyes
- Decreased level of activity, laziness, slow or slurred speech
- Increased sleep (10-12 hours a day is not unusual)
- Truancy from or tardiness to school
- Declining grades
- Change in friends
- Overall slow and subtle change in appearance (i.e., hair, cleanliness, clothing, jewelry)
- Increase in weight from inactivity
- Isolation from family
- Trouble making eye contact with adults (shame response)
- Marijuana paraphernalia (pipes, roach clips, rolling papers, baggies)

INDICATIONS OF
COCAINE USE

- Extreme paranoia (particularly right after use and for approximately two hours following)
- Intense denial of an ongoing problem
- Occasional violent behavior
- Hallucinations (with persistent use)
- Irritability (ongoing)
- Agitation (hyper-activity)
- Sleeplessness (immediately after use and for several hours)
- Anxiety (immediately after use and for several hours)
- Physical addiction as well as psychological addiction
- Depression or suicidal thoughts with overuse
- Isolation from family
- Trouble making eye contact with adults (shame response)
- Change in friends
- Change in appetite (generally loses weight)
- Cocaine paraphernalia (water pipes [bongs], small amber-colored glass vials, straws, small mirrors, single-edge razor blades, small spoons)

INDICATIONS OF
ALCOHOL ABUSE

- Decreased activity
- Change in sleeping patterns (i.e., going to sleep late at night, waking late in the morning, difficulty waking in morning)
- Moodiness (i.e., depressed, sensitive, argumentative, angry)
- Social problems
- Fighting or aggressive behavior
- Staying away from home (staying out later, ignoring curfew, hanging out at mall)
- Isolation from family
- Trouble making eye contact with adults, especially with authority figures (shame response)
- Change in appetite (generally a weight loss)
- Change in friends
- Tardiness or absenteeism from school
- Decreased function in class; dropping grades; lethargic appearance; bad attitude; nodding off in class; daydreaming

On a national average, in 1989, 10.3 percent of all high school students used cocaine,[1] compared to 34 percent of the teens in the single-parent survey. This same government study revealed 43.7 percent of high school students used marijuana, compared to a 57 percent of the teens in the single-parent survey. Thus, teens from single-parent families are more likely to use cocaine at a ratio of three to one.

FINDING

10

Running away from home is prevalent in single-parent families.

According to the survey responses, two out of ten teenagers and almost one out of ten children ran away from home during or after their parents' divorce. Unfortunately, there are no figures available for the average number of children who run away from home each year. The only means of comparing rates of runaway children and teens would be to examine police records, which is a virtually impossible task on a national level.

An examination of the police logs from three cities within Los Angeles and Orange County during three randomly selected months (June 1987, November 1987, and March 1988) revealed that an average of fourteen teen and child runaway reports were taken each month. Based on the entire populations of each city, this number is less than 1 percent of the adolescent and child populations. Thus, according to this comparison, children of single-parent families are considerably more likely to run away, especially during the tough divorce period.

FINDING

11

Fighting is often a sign of emotional struggles.

Six out of ten teens and three out of ten children surveyed stated they had gotten into fights. Fighting is one of the predominant warning signs of children and teens who develop conduct disorders. Conduct disorders, as discussed in chapter 2, involve many elements of acting-out behaviors; however, fighting is usually present.

The general theory behind this increased aggression is that the child does not have any other outlet available in which to work through his anger, fear, frustration, and anxiety. These pressures and problems are commonly brought on by the parents' marital conflicts and their subsequent divorce.

IMPLICATIONS FOR YOUR MINISTRY

Many experts agree that fighting (after a divorce) is a child's way of releasing anger and frustration at being so powerless. It can also be seen as a defense mechanism. Don't be misled by these kids. They are usually acting in this fashion because they don't know how to ask for attention.

Here again, as with kids and teens who shoplift, fighting is sometimes considered a normal part of growing up. It is important to evaluate the circumstances surrounding the fight as well as to look for any additional warning signs of crisis.

If you are working with a child or teen in your church who is getting into fights, it would be wise to take a closer look. If other warning signs are present, you may want to sit down with the child and discuss your observations. If you feel you haven't gotten through, you may want to talk to the parents about referring the child to a counselor to try to avert a crisis.

FINDING 12

Suicidal thoughts are common among children and teens following the parents' divorce.

The survey revealed an alarming statistic: Seven out of ten teenagers and four out of ten children had suicidal thoughts during and after their parents' divorce.

Several factors should be considered in evaluating that surprising trend. First, we must consider that teenage suicide is the highest cause of death, after traffic accidents, in the United States. Also, you may want to factor in that all of the kids in the single-parent family survey were receiving some form of psychological care. Some were even in a hospital to be treated for suicidal thoughts or attempts. With those other pieces of information, perhaps the high rate of single-parent family kids who have had suicidal thoughts doesn't seem quite so alarming and incomprehensible.

In the course of my work, I meet hundreds of adolescents each year, most of whom are at conferences or seminars. Oftentimes I ask for a show of hands of anyone who knows someone who has talked about, attempted, or even committed suicide. Invariably, I see about 70 percent of the hands go up. I then ask for a show of hands of those who have ever thought about suicide. The number usually reaches 20 to 30 percent.

Girls are "significantly more likely" to have suicidal thoughts or to attempt suicide than boys.

IMPLICATIONS FOR YOUR MINISTRY

An interesting survey came out during the time I was writing this chapter. In 1991, the U.S. Centers for Disease Control studied 11,631 high school students from every state. The study focused on the suicide rate for teens and provided the following data related to stress among teens and children:[2]

- Twenty-seven percent of all high school students have had suicidal thoughts.
- One in twelve said they had actually attempted suicide.
- Sixteen percent said they had made a specific suicide plan.
- Eight percent said they had tried suicide within the last year.
- Girls (34 percent) are "significantly more likely" to have suicidal thoughts or to attempt suicide than boys (21 percent).
- Ten percent of the girls had actually attempted suicide, while only 6 percent of the boys had attempted it.

This government study would certainly support the single-parent family survey, which found that girls are more prone to stressful feelings including depression and suicidal thoughts.

The fact that teenagers and children consider suicide at the rate they do illustrates that they are not connected and grounded with others. Ephesians 3:17 tells us that we are to be "rooted and grounded in love" (NASB), and throughout the Bible, God is telling us that he has made us to be relational, to be connected to others.

When children go through the pain of divorce, much of their feeling of being connected, or "rooted and grounded in love," is pulled out from under them. The single most valuable thing you can do for these kids is to love them and to make sure they know that God loves them also.

This message of love is powerful coming from a single mom or dad, but children usually expect to hear this from their parents. This same message coming from a pastor, singles' pastor, youth pastor, or lay counselor takes on a whole new significance. The vast majority of the suicide cases I have seen, both as a police officer and as a counselor, involved teenagers and children who were not particularly connected with others.

FINDING

13

Anger toward self and others is normal in kids during and after divorce.

Several questions were asked of the teens and children in order to learn more about their feelings of anger, hopelessness, and helplessness during and after the divorce. The survey concluded that over seven out of ten teens and six out of ten children felt as if they hated everybody in their lives during and after their parents' divorce.

Children from divorce often feel angry at both parents and sometimes at God for allowing the family to break up. Because the children have no power over the decision that has been made, they often turn their anger and frustration inward toward themselves (suicidal thoughts) or outward toward others (angry, hurtful thoughts). This is the time when children typically begin to feel as if they hate everybody.

IMPLICATIONS FOR YOUR MINISTRY

While the following case is an extreme example, it illustrates how this pervasive feeling of anger at everyone can turn violent. You may recall the serial murder case of Jeffrey Dahmer out of Milwaukee in 1991. In this case, the suspect was found to be responsible for the murder and mutilation of at least fourteen people. When the detective handling the case was interviewed, he stated he believed that the suspect blamed his problems on the divorce of his parents when he was a youngster. This detective was convinced, after weeks of investigation and hours of interviewing the suspect, that the parents' divorce played a major role in the crimes, at least in the suspect's troubled mind.

When you work with children, teach them that anger is probably the single most self-destructive emotion they have. Ask them how much sleep the person they are angry at is losing; and then ask them how much sleep they are losing by being angry. Teach the child that angry feelings need to be worked through by talking about the anger. As Colossians 3:8 tells us, we must learn to "rid [ourselves] of . . . anger, rage, malice, slander, and filthy language from [our] lips."

You can initiate conversation with children or teens about their anger by means of what psychologists call *empathic listening*. For instance, you may start by asking a teenager, "I noticed that you didn't look very happy this week. Is there something bugging you?" If the teen replies, "Yeah, my mom has been on my case about my wanting to spend a couple weeks with my dad," empathic listening comes into play when you repeat back something like, "So what you are telling me is that your mom doesn't understand why you are wanting to visit your dad; is that it?" By simply repeating portions of their statement in the form of a question, you allow for greater disclosure of feelings and at the same time minimize the child's fear that you don't understand.

FINDING 14

Sleeping problems were present in most cases after the parents' divorce.

One little girl whom I saw in an outpatient counseling session told me about some of the problems she was having getting to sleep. For reasons unknown to her, Suzie would often lie in bed unable to get to sleep for hours. In addition, once she finally went to sleep, she would often awaken with a recurring nightmare.

Suzie told me that her mom and dad had divorced about a year prior to the time I was counseling her and that she had been going to see her dad about once a month since then. Her dad, who has a disease, had been very sick and was confined to a wheelchair. In this particular recurring dream, she was walking around a big zoo and looking at all the animals. She came to a cage and saw her father inside seated in his wheelchair. He looked helpless and called to her to come to him. She tried to help him but the zoo keepers pulled her away from his cage. Suzie was quite disturbed by her dream for several months, and her lack of quality sleep was beginning to impact her school work and emotional well-being.

After some time, Suzie came to understand that her dream was her way of experiencing her feelings of loss for her dad. The fact that he was caged in a zoo was a visualization of her helpless feelings of being unable to change her parents' divorce. His being confined behind bars not only reflected her feelings about his handicap and confinement, but also his being kept away from her by the divorce. The fact that the zoo keepers would not let her take care of him illustrates the conflict in her mind over wanting to be with him and take care of him. However, due to geographic constraints and visitation laws, she could not.

Once Suzie understood what her dream was all about, I encouraged her to talk to her counselor, her mom, and her dad about these feelings. At last report, she had not been bothered by this dream again.

IMPLICATIONS FOR YOUR MINISTRY

Whenever a symptom appears in 76 percent of teenagers and 83 percent of children, you know it is a subject that demands consideration. While there are those who think that dream interpretation is of the New Age or just weird psychology, the fact is that interpreting and understanding our dreams is biblical. In fact, the words *dream*, *dreams*, or *dreaming* are seen at least 114 times in the *New International Version* of the Bible.

Dreams and sleep patterns are undeniably an integral part of recognizing warning signs in children and teens. We know from studies that we are more prone to dream when we are under a great deal of stress or feel depressed. Dreams are the mind's way of allowing us to experience thoughts in our subconscious that we are unable to access during our waking hours. As we saw with Suzie, taking the time to examine and to work through dreams not only provides us with valuable insight but also allows us to understand our subconscious feelings.

Many books on the subject of dream interpretation are available at the public library or bookstores. As a word of caution, it's interesting to read up on this subject, but be cautious about interpreting dreams as a matter of course. Additionally, I am unfamiliar with any dream interpretation books written from a Christian perspective, so I urge you to view the secular books on this topic as just another potential tool. Remember, the mind is releasing powerful and personal information through dreams and not everyone, especially children, will have the mental strength to deal with it.

As an interesting footnote, sleeping problems (and dreams) was the first of only four areas where the children outscored the adolescents. A possible theory for this is that children are less capable of denying or hiding from their fears and feelings, especially in their sleep. Children also have a greater fear of the dark than adolescents. Thus, when a child is fearful or anxious prior to going to bed, the sleeping experience can be much more anxiety-producing.

Additionally, we can all identify with the thought process that goes on just prior to going to sleep. We tend to dwell on our day, or on things that are going wrong in our lives. For the child, these thoughts can become consuming and can disrupt normal sleep patterns.

Once again, we also find another characteristic symptom of PTSD (post-traumatic stress disorder). Sleep problems or nightmares are symptomatic of this disorder.

FINDING
15

After parents divorce, one in ten girls develops troublesome eating habits that can lead to an eating disorder.
In chapter 2 of this book, we saw that 9 percent of the adolescents surveyed were being treated for an eating disorder. The slightly higher number seen here (11 percent) represents teens who were not currently being treated for eating disorders, but who had them in the past.

An interesting statistic turned up in the survey that, to my knowledge, has not been addressed previously: Teenagers of divorced parents are nearly three times more likely to develop troublesome eating habits or disorders than kids from two-parent families. These habits can range from troublesome under- or overeating problems all the way to life-threatening eating disorders. Although there have been no recent studies as to exactly how many teenagers have eating disorders, Dr. Paul Meier of the Minirth-Meier Clinic states that "approximately 3 percent of all teenage girls have such disorders."

The most common theory behind this alarming rate is that during and after the divorce, the teenager feels helpless and out of control. In fact, the only thing in her life that she is able to control is what she eats. As a result, she discovers that by controlling her diet, she has control over her weight, her overall appearance, her perception of herself, and her perception of what others think of her.

Sometimes her newfound control allows her to get even more attention from friends who tell her how thin she looks, which is of paramount importance to teenage girls. She may also get attention from well-meaning friends and relatives who see her pale or frail appearance and ask, "Are you feeling okay?"

IMPLICATIONS FOR YOUR MINISTRY

For many reasons, eating disorders among teenagers and children are considered "closet" addictions. Most therapists agree that this is due to the unpleasant ritual eating disorder sufferers go through. Eating disorders are dangerous and can ultimately lead to serious health problems and even death.

For those who work with teens, and especially with girls, it is difficult to pick up on the signs of eating disorders. Here are a few things you can look for:

- Does she refuse to eat with a group?
- Does she talk about her weight a lot, even though she may be thin?
- Does she disappear after meals or excuse herself to the rest room?
- Does she bring her own food to group dinners or social events?
- Does her skin have a pale or yellowish appearance?
- Has she gained or lost a significant amount of weight in the last four to six months?
- Is she having problems with her teeth (caused by the constant exposure to stomach acid)?
- Does she look frail and gaunt?
- Does she wear baggy clothing in an attempt to hide her weight loss?
- Is she having stomach problems (i.e., stomach ulcers and stomachaches)?

FINDING 16

One in three teens commit theft after divorce.
There is a psychological difference between teens and children who shoplift and those who steal from other people. The difference can be seen in the depersonalization of the act itself.

When I interview young people who have been arrested for shoplifting, invariably one of their remarks is, "I didn't think I was hurting anybody." A key reason shoplifting is so easy is that it is a theft from a nameless, faceless company and has no identification with a person. On the other hand, when kids steal from other people, it is usually a more defiant, premeditated act. Young people, especially teenagers, who deliberately steal from others often are categorized as having a rather serious psychological disorder called *oppositional* or *antisocial behavior*. Children and teens who exhibit these behaviors commonly can't stop themselves until they have received counseling or legal supervision.

IMPLICATIONS FOR YOUR MINISTRY

Just around Christmas a few years ago I received a call from a pastor who was quite distraught about a twelve-year-old boy in his congregation. The pastor related a specific incident when he had come into the church office and found the boy taking some cash from a fund which was to be donated to homeless children. After a lengthy conversation, the pastor realized the boy was sorry he had been caught but felt no remorse for his deed. The pastor correctly understood this to be a serious indication of a deeper problem, in this case, an oppositional behavior disorder. I suggested the pastor meet with the boy's mom and include the boy in the conversation. I advised the pastor to look deeper into the child's recent past and try to understand what might have transpired to lead the boy to commit a theft.

About three weeks later the pastor called and told me that the boy's father, a policeman, had all but abandoned him since his parents' divorce about two years earlier. He learned that the divorce was particularly unpleasant and that the boy had taken the transition very poorly.

In this case, the pastor did an excellent job in drawing out the motive behind the actions. The pastor concluded that, since the dad was a policeman, the son knew he could hurt his dad the most if he committed a criminal act. In addition, since his mom was such a committed Christian, he could show his anger toward her by stealing from the church—sort of the proverbial killing two birds with one stone. The pastor concluded our conversation by telling me that he was meeting with the mom and son once a week and that he had already seen positive changes in the boy.

I relate this particular story to illustrate that pastors and church leaders do some remarkable counseling work. I am consistently amazed at the skills they demonstrate in some of the toughest situations.

If you have children or teens in your congregation who you hear are stealing or shoplifting, take the time to do a little detective work. You will find that a theft is seldom just a theft. More frequently, it is a cry of a deeper need.

FINDING 17 — Many teens and children drank alcohol after their parents' divorce.

Phillip, age fifteen, is one of the adolescents who took part in the teen survey. Phillip was brought into outpatient therapy by his mother, who came home unexpectedly from work one afternoon to find Phillip and another boy drinking beer and looking at his father's old *Playboy* magazines. The fact that Phillip had cut school and was interested in the magazines did not bother her nearly as much as the fact that he was drinking. In therapy, he related that he didn't really see the seriousness of what he had done. After all, his father used to drink beer nearly every day after work before he divorced Phillip's mom.

Any number of messages can be learned as to why so many adolescents and children in the survey have used alcohol. Perhaps the number is so large because drinking is an acting out behavior, much like shoplifting and cutting school. An additional attraction to drinking is that it allows the consumer a temporary escape from painful situations (i.e., divorce, separation, loneliness, anger, etc.).

This is how chemical addictions generally begin with children and adolescents. The temporary feeling of relief that was acquired through the consumption of alcohol (or a drug) wears off and reality once again sets in. When reality returns, so does the pain and the desire to escape again. Many young people get caught up in this addictive cycle.

| IMPLICATIONS FOR YOUR MINISTRY |

As elementary as it seems, it is important to familiarize yourself with the obvious warning signs of alcoholism and alcohol abuse in teens and children. They are listed in figure 5.1 on page 81.

FINDING 18

A majority of teenagers and nearly 20 percent of children got sexually involved during and after their parents' divorce.

Johns Hopkins University researchers found that teenage girls living in single-parent families (without a father) were 60 percent more likely to have premarital sex than those living in two-parent homes.[3] The single-parent family survey verified that teenage girls from homes where the father is gone (and no close relationship with him exists) are at the highest risk of becoming sexually involved.

Girls who grow up without a father's presence don't learn that real love (especially from men) is unconditional and isn't related to sexual performance or intimacy. Therefore, teenage girls from single-parent families often find themselves looking for approval and for relationships with men—two things that were missing in their lives. Unfortunately, many teenage boys will take advantage of this vulnerability.

Another factor involving teenage boys and premarital sex is often ignored, possibly because the consequences (i.e, pregnancy, stigma, etc.) are more limited for boys than for girls. Most therapists assume that many boys who grow up in homes without a father (or close male role models) do not learn how to relate to girls or women. Many have not seen their fathers and mothers together, except—in many cases—in an abusive relationship. Oftentimes, this inadequate modeling creates an interpersonal conflict. The young person knows that he wants to be in a pleasant emotional relationship (free of pain) with a girl, but he doesn't know how to establish it without including the sexual aspects. Emotional closeness or intimacy has not been learned through proper observation with adult role models.

Perhaps the most important thing you can do for children and teens of divorce is to get them involved in a ParaParenting program. We will be discussing this subject in chapter 7.

FINDING 19

Cruelty to animals often reflects past child abuse.

Jeremy, age fourteen, was admitted to an inpatient Christian treatment hospital after a neighbor saw him and two of his friends torturing a rabbit with rocks and sticks. When I asked Jeremy about the incident, he calmly related how he and his friends had been talking about animal sacrifices and how they were going to leave various parts of a rabbit at the houses of the neighborhood kids he didn't like.

A brief look into Jeremy's past revealed that his parents divorced when he was eight. Prior to the divorce, Jeremy's dad was physically and sexually abusive to Jeremy and had put his mom in the hospital on two occasions.

Further conversations with other teenagers and children who responded that they have hurt animals revealed that all of them, with the exception of one girl, had been either sexually, emotionally, or physically abused by their fathers or others prior to the divorce.

Conversely, I don't want to leave the impression that all abused children will grow up to abuse animals. That's clearly not the case. It is noteworthy, however, that all the respondents except one shared a common history.

IMPLICATIONS FOR YOUR MINISTRY

You may recall that we looked earlier at a type of behavior called *oppositional behavior* in teens and children or *antisocial personality disorders* in adults. Of the 288 adolescents surveyed, fourteen stated they have hurt animals. Perhaps that doesn't seem like such a significant number until you understand the ramifications of a case like Jeremy's.

I can tell you very little to watch for when trying to spot these kids. For the most part, their behavior takes place in private, and you will probably never know about it. One thing you can look for in these kids is a marked change in their attitude. Children and teens who find it emotionally uplifting to hurt animals can often be quite cruel to other kids at school or church. They may say or do mean or violent things to others and then appear to have no remorse for their actions.

FINDING 20

After divorce, more than half of the teens and one-third of the children feel like hurting others.

When I began reviewing the responses in this area, I was surprised by the high number of those who responded that they have wanted to hurt others. Subsequently, I reinterviewed several of these teens and children in order to learn more of what they had thought and felt when they had wanted to hurt others.

Brian, age seventeen, responded that he thinks about hurting others "all the time," although he was receiving only outpatient counseling for a learning disability. When asked about how he envisioned hurting others, Brian stated, "I want to hurt other kids who have things I don't have." When pressed to be more specific, Brian admitted his anger was directed to teens with both parents.

Christina, age thirteen, stated that she hasn't hurt anybody, although she finds herself becoming very angry and sometimes thinks about hurting her teachers or some of the adults she knows. Christina's anger is what we term *transference*. In other words, her pent-up anger at her parents is transferred to other adults. Most often, these will be people in positions of authority, like a school teacher.

The ways that teens and children feel anger toward others covers a wide range of emotions. I have even talked to children as young as six who have convinced me they are willing and able to commit murder. The common link between all these children and teens was a general feeling of anger. Violence was seen as a viable option, as they didn't have the knowledge of how to diffuse or dispense of their emotions by talking or through passive expressions.

As a professional who works with children and teens individually and in groups, you should be aware of the warning signs of anger. Some of the more common signs are listed in figure 5.2 below.

FINDING

21

Following a divorce, few teens or children talk to parents about their real problems.

When I think about children who didn't talk to their parents about their problems, I always think first of thirteen-year-old Terri. Terri's parents got a divorce when she was eleven. After the divorce, her mom began working two jobs, and Terri stayed with a neighbor after school until around 7:00 p.m. when her mom came home.

Terri's problems included an eating disorder, which she developed when she was around twelve years old. Her routine would include skipping breakfast, having yogurt or nothing at lunch, and then eating a small salad at dinner before her mom got home. When her mother asked if she wanted dinner, Terri stated she had already eaten. Terri also began exercising compulsively. She began long-distance running; and although she lost almost thirty-five pounds, Terri's mom thought Terri was healthy because she was running.

It wasn't until Terri missed three of her periods and thought she might be pregnant that she went to her mother for help. A trip to the family doctor for a pregnancy exam revealed the eating disorder, which in turn led to her psychological treatment.

IMPLICATIONS FOR YOUR MINISTRY

I don't think it comes as a shock to any of us who work with children or teens that few of them talk about problems with their parents. To make matters worse, many single moms and dads like Terri's get so caught up in trying to earn a living and adjusting to a life alone that they get too busy to see the warning signs. It is very easy for single parents to become distracted from their most important full-time job, parenting.

You can help by being there for the kids in your groups. Provide an atmosphere of openness and honesty where kids and teens will feel safe in relating their secrets and problems. You can do this by letting them know from the outset that you are their advocate. State clearly that you are on their side and that you will be

---

FIGURE 5.2
WARNING SIGNS OF ANGER IN TEENS AND CHILDREN

- Hostile feelings
- Lack of regard for the property of others, or damaging property
- No sense of caring for others' boundaries or feelings
- A lack of self-control
- Poor self-image
- Signs of a temper increasing
- Use of profanity, vulgarity, or other means of shocking others
- Restlessness, fidgeting, disrupting class
- Inability to own responsibility for anything

there for them when they need to talk. If at all possible, share with them stories of your childhood and teen years; help them to see that you weren't always a pastor and that you have a life, too.

When you work with these kids following a divorce, you may want to keep in mind that insecurity plays a major role in why kids don't reveal their bad sides to a parent. All the time they are wrestling with their problems they may be thinking, "What if this is too bad for mom or dad to deal with? What if 'I'm sorry' isn't good enough? What if he leaves me like he left Mom?"

FINDING

22

Nearly two in ten teens and one in ten kids are arrested after their parents' divorce.

Allison, a pretty fifteen-year-old high school cheerleader and member of the student council, related the following account of her life to me. At age thirteen, two years after her mother and father divorced, she began sneaking alcohol from her mother's refrigerator and liquor cupboard. She did this for almost a year before she realized that she wanted more but couldn't risk being caught.

She began attending friends' parties on the weekends so that she could drink. She would even take several bottles of beer or wine home and hide them in her bedroom or backyard so she could drink them later. Finally, at one party, the police showed up and called all the parents. When Allison's mom arrived, Allison was drunk and ended up telling her the truth about her drinking problem.

In addition to being arrested for drinking, it is also common for children and teens to be arrested for misdemeanor crimes such as shoplifting, auto thefts, truancy, or other miscellaneous troubles with the law.

IMPLICATIONS FOR YOUR MINISTRY

Many experts agree that children and teens will intentionally do things to get caught, even if it means getting into trouble. The most common explanation for their behavior is that they may be feeling out of control. By getting caught by the police (or others), it is possible for children and teens to regain control without appearing weak or having to ask for help. It is a shame that, in many cases, the police are the first ones to inform parents of their child's problems. By becoming active and responsive to the needs of the children and teens of divorced families, you have an opportunity to recognize and respond to warning signs before they reach the point of crisis.

FINDING

23

Only 2 percent of those surveyed reported their problems were observed by church staff.

Before we take a look at some of the reasons behind this relatively low figure, you may recall that 119 out of the 352 children and teens stated they attend church. So, what we are really talking about is that there were only two kids out of 119 whose problems were noticed by church staff.

Let's take a look at some of the possible reasons why so few children's and teens' problems were discovered by church staff members:

- One-to-one contact between children, teens, and church youth workers is often limited.
- The teens and children who generally have psychological issues like the ones this book discusses are not typically the kids who are active in extended church programs such as youth groups and activities.
- Pastors and youth leaders have not been trained to look for the warning signs that may indicate a child or teen is in crisis.
- Many of our churches have not developed programs that create an environment where these children and teens can openly disclose their personal problems.
- Considerably fewer church-related programs are available for children than for teens.
- There is usually a desperate shortage of church staff and volunteers to help out with teens' and children's ministries.

FINDING

24

Most problems are discovered by teachers and school officials.

The survey indicated teachers and school officials as being the most likely to learn of a child's or teen's problems. Although this is cause for concern, it is also understandable since teachers are with our children throughout much of their day.

The vast majority of the children in the survey attended public schools, where they were just one student in a class of at least thirty-five others. Given this number multiplied by six to eight class periods each day, it is incredible that teachers have the time to notice individual problems at all. Yet, unfortunately, many parents are depending on their children's teachers, principals, school counselors, and report cards to let them know how their child is doing emotionally.

According to the survey, the primary areas in which teachers and other school officials noticed problems were:

- Grades (e.g., poor tests, poor performance, or refusal to complete homework assignments)
- Tardiness
- Absenteeism
- Acting out in class (disrupting others)
- Cutting classes
- Fighting at school
- Stealing from classmates

Three case examples may better illustrate this point. The first case was thirteen-year-old Kati, whose parents had recently separated and were in the process of filing for divorce. Kati was referred to me by a nurse at the school she attended. After Kati had missed the equivalent of one day of school each week over a span of ten weeks, the nurse called Kati's mother to discuss possible health problems. At that point, the mother realized, even though her daughter had been home sick several days, that didn't explain the other absences. When confronted, Kati admitted she had been cutting school. However, she could offer no reasons, nor did she seem to understand her actions.

After a couple of sessions, Kati told me that she felt anxious and panicky whenever she left for school. Some days she would tell her mom she was feeling ill, and other days she would leave for school and then return home after her mom went to work. We were able to isolate her feelings of anxiety, which centered around her fear of further abandonment. On days Kati was able to convince her mom she was sick, her mom would stay home and take care of her. On other days, she would have a panic attack on her way to school, at which time she would turn around and go home. Even though she was alone at home, Kati still felt safer there and closer to her mom. Through our counseling together, Kati was able to understand that the trauma of her parent's divorce created her anxiety. As a result of that anxiety, Kati felt unwanted, unloved, and afraid that she would someday also be separated from her mom.

In another case study, Van, a fifteen-year-old high school sophomore, was sent to the principal's office for smoking in the bathroom. When I talked to Van, along with his outpatient therapist, he told me that he was not only smoking at school, but also cutting classes, writing on walls with marking pens, and breaking into other kids' lockers for money. The only act he had ever been caught doing was smoking. Van admitted that he would still be doing the same things if he had not been caught by one of the teachers.

The third case involves a high school junior named Jana who told me that she had intercepted two deficiency notices, had signed them both in her mom's name, and had taken them back to school. When Jana's final report card of the year came home indicating she had gone from Bs to Ds and Fs, she hid it from her mother for most of the summer without so much as an inquiry. Finally, Jana had to tell her mother the truth when she opened a letter addressed to her mom stating that Jana would not be accepted back in school for the following semester.

IMPLICATIONS FOR YOUR MINISTRY

This area of problems at school is difficult for you to monitor unless your church is affiliated with a school. If it is, then you may have the opportunity to monitor grades, general behavior, tardiness, absenteeism, and cutting.

Much can be learned by a pastor or youth pastor by staying in touch with the school officials (including the school nurse). I know of a youth pastor who automatically hears from the attendance secretary at the Christian school associated with his church whenever a child or teen misses more than three consecutive days of school. Affiliation with any school attended by the children and teens in your church can provide access to information you might otherwise miss.

Whenever you have children whose parents are divorcing or have divorced within the last two years, you may consider talking to their teachers about the situation. Let the teachers know that you are watching and would like their assistance in monitoring these children. Request that you be notified whenever a child has been tardy to school on a consistent basis or when the child does not show up at all.

FINDING 25

Most children and teens think their emotional problems are obvious.

An interesting phenomenon occurs in children and teens after divorce: Their insecurity makes them believe their thoughts and problems are transparent. Almost half of the children I interviewed believed that anyone and everyone around them knew of their problems.

This tendency is linked closely to children's inclination to see themselves as either all good or all bad. In other words, children and some teens have what counselors call an *overactive conscience*. When they are thinking or doing something wrong, their minds produce paranoid thoughts, and they feel guilty and exposed. This is why when a child is unable to look you in the eye, it usually means you're not hearing the complete truth. Adults, on the other hand, have had years of practice at hiding or burying their feelings.

IMPLICATIONS FOR YOUR MINISTRY

A byproduct of the children's "black or white" thinking pattern was that many of them felt somebody should have come forward to offer help. Many were surprised, shocked, and disappointed that somebody didn't notice the impending crisis and come to their rescue. Remember, they felt their problems were so obvious that only a fool (or someone who didn't care) wouldn't notice.

This information is important to know when you are working with children and teens in your groups. Don't assume that things you notice are also being noticed at home. However, you can safely assume that the child thinks you have noticed too. Take the time to sit down with the child or teen and explain that you did notice and that you care. Explain that sometimes parents are the last to notice when their kids are having problems. Ask the child to meet with you and his or her parents to discuss the problems.

FINDING 26

Many children and teens feel responsible for their parents' divorce.

A good example of how kids can feel personally responsible for a divorce can be seen in the following case. Bret, a twelve-year-old boy, was receiving counseling for his depression. His depressed feelings had started about the same time his parents' relationship began to decline. Bret would come home from school, start his homework, and then listen to his parents fight and argue about money, household chores, sex, grocery shopping. You name it, they argued about it.

Bret started to get the idea that he was responsible for his parents' problems when they would either ignore him or snap at him after one of their blowups. (Remember, kids see things in very black and white terms.) As a result, when the marriage finally ended in divorce, Bret became isolated and depressed. Neither of his parents noticed, so they never bothered talking to him about the reasons for their divorce.

Bret's counselor told me that, during one session, Bret said, "I wish I were dead. My parents used to get along good until I came along. They were always yelling at me about my school work or my chores and other stuff. I guess the reason my dad left was because he was tired of having to yell at me. I guess it was my fault."

IMPLICATIONS FOR YOUR MINISTRY

I can't stress enough how important it is that you help children and teens keep their parents' divorce in perspective. One tool for doing this is simply asking the child basic questions that are designed to help him or her process through feelings.

Question 1: What do you think were the biggest problems between your mom and dad?
Wrong Answers: Me, my brothers/sisters, my school grades
- If the child answers "me," you have your work cut out for you.

Question 2: Do you really think you had that much power over your parents?
Wrong Answer: Yes

Question 3: Who do you think had the most control over whether your parents stayed together or not?
Wrong Answers: Me, my family

Question 4: Do you think Jesus wanted your parents to divorce?
Wrong Answer: Yes
- If this is the answer you receive, be prepared to talk about biblical perspectives on marriage. Talk about how God created us and how, since the fall of Adam and Eve in the garden, we all have a sin nature. As such, we are all capable of making bad decisions for ourselves and others. Explain that one fact remains true: God loves and accepts us even when we mess up and sin. Be sure that children understand that divorce is not okay with God (in most cases). But children also need to understand that God is fair and is not punishing them or their parents for some sin.

I think you get the picture. My hope is that you can help children (1) see their lack of power over their parents, and (2) understand that they could not have possibly caused their parents' divorce.

FINDING

27

Children believe the responsibility for divorce lies with their fathers.

At first it seemed unusual that so many children felt this way. Yet, some of this perception can be explained by an examination of family dynamics that can go on following a divorce. Time after time, I have seen moms who have custody of their children unconsciously (and sometimes consciously) bash the ex-husband. Children, more than teens, are apt to pick up on this negativity and believe it to be fact, even if they started out knowing the perception was not totally accurate.

Other reasons exist as to why more teens and children believed their fathers were responsible for the divorce:

- It may be true.
- Moms are telling children that fathers are responsible for the divorce.
- Most children are living with their mothers and would naturally side with them.

FINDING 28

The most common reasons given for divorce are money, physical violence, arguing, communication, and an affair.
A few years ago, I recalled seeing a survey (although I can't remember where) of the things married couples argued about most. The survey concluded that money was the most common reason couples argued, followed by the children and sexual issues.

It comes as no surprise that money is one of the highest responses among teenagers, as they have such an increased awareness of money during these years. It is also understandable that teens would be more aware of arguments about financial matters because these issues often affect them personally.

The subject of communication came up quite often in the survey. Teens in particular felt that poor communication between their parents was a major factor in the marriage failing. Children seemed to pinpoint arguing (a major element of poor communication) as playing a major role in their parents' divorce. The fact that children who were surveyed cited arguing more often than their parents did would seem to provide evidence that children are more sensitive to arguments and general disruptions at home. Although teenagers are certainly sensitive to these issues as well, many may have become desensitized to these conflicts by the time they reach their teen years.

Leon, a sixteen-year-old boy who was in an inpatient treatment program following an attempted suicide, told me about some of the arguments his parents used to have. "My dad used to come home from work at around dinner time and the first thing he would do is start yelling at my mom. He would yell at her because the house wasn't picked up or because he didn't like what she made for dinner. My mom would yell back at him and call him names. Sometimes they would hit each other and throw things, and sometimes the neighbors would call the cops. One time, my dad hit my mom and gave her a cut lip and a black eye. When the cops came out, my mom had them take him away. He came home that night, and they fought again all night. I remember just lying in my bed and crying with my pillow over my head. I was scared that my dad would hit my mom again or that he would come in and hit me. I just lay there all night and cried."

On the subject of domestic violence, more than one out of four teens and children reported some degree of violence between their parents.

In an outpatient counseling session in my office I met a seventeen-year-old girl who told me that, prior to her parents' divorce, they would fight constantly. One night, Jill's father came home drunk, and her mom had been drinking all

More than one out of four teens and children reported some degree of violence between their parents.

evening as well. They got into a violent argument, and her mother took out a pair of scissors and, right in front of the kids, stabbed him in the leg.

As a police officer, my recollection is that the most common acts of domestic violence involved slapping, hitting, and pushing. Although these incidents may seem mild in comparison with an assault with a deadly weapon, they did sometimes require medical attention. Fortunately, most states have enacted laws requiring the police to file criminal reports against husbands (and wives if necessary) who assault their spouse.

Another surprising area of the survey revealed that two out of ten teens thought an affair was at the root of their parents' divorce. Slightly more than one out of ten children felt the same.

Heather, a fourteen-year-old, was doing very well after having been admitted into a psychiatric facility following a suicide attempt. She told me about how her father's affair not only ruined the marriage but also affected her. "About six months before my parents got a divorce, I found out from my mom that my dad had a girlfriend. She told me that he had been seeing her for a long time and that he must not love me or my mom to be able to do such a terrible thing. For a long time I believed what she was saying, and it made me real hurt and angry that my dad could do this to us. I guess I didn't know what to do, so I just decided that life wasn't worth living anymore. Now that I've had a chance to look back at it, I guess my mom was so angry at my dad that she wanted me to hate him as much as she did."

IMPLICATIONS FOR YOUR MINISTRY

It is really not so important what reasons the children and teens gave for their parents' divorce; it is vitally important that they need a safe place to work through those thoughts. You may recall that children and teens don't go to their parents with their problems. You may also recall that, most of the time, someone at school noticed there was a problem. At the risk of beating this point to death, some person (or a group of people) at each church participating in a single-parent family ministry should be available to listen and assist. A combination of concerned listening and actively participating in a single-parent ministry will help provide the support these families so desperately need.

ADVICE FROM TEENS AND CHILDREN WHO HAVE BEEN THROUGH DIVORCE

Alicia. I met Alicia, a sixteen-year-old high school sophomore, while she was being treated at an inpatient hospital for a drug addiction. Alicia talked about the pain she experienced as her parents were going through a separation, which ultimately led to a divorce. "I just kept having the same questions going over and over in my mind," Alicia stated. "Weird stuff like, Where am I going to live after the divorce? Does my father even want to see me anymore; and if so, how often? What if he remarries; would his new wife try to act like my mom? Will I have to go to a new school? Will the other kids at school think I'm weird because my parents got a divorce? My mom said we don't have enough money anymore. Will I be able to get new clothes when I need them?"

Thoughts such as these affected Alicia so much that she couldn't cope with life any longer. "At first I began drinking wine and liquor from my parents' cupboard," said Alicia. "A little while after that, I met a couple new friends who gave me some marijuana and later acid. At first I thought it was really cool that I could get high and my problems didn't matter anymore. Then I figured out that I was getting high all the time just to forget about how rotten my life was."

Alicia talked about the time she tried to talk to her mother about her fears but felt shut out when her mother started to cry. "I went to my mom to talk to her right after my dad left. I know she wanted to help me understand, but she started crying and got really sad and depressed. After that, I was afraid to go to her because I didn't want to see her so unhappy."

Alicia kept everything bottled up inside after that. She didn't have anyone to act as a support system, and she didn't think to look for others to help her through her crisis.

Alicia had this advice to share with other teenagers going through similar circumstances:

- Tell your mother or father that you *need* to talk, even though it hurts. If they won't listen to you, then you have to find somebody else who will.
- Talk to a school counselor or a teacher you like.
- Talk to other kids at school whose parents are divorced to see what they went through.
- See if you have an aunt or uncle or other relative who will help you through some of your problems.
- If you go to church, talk to your pastor to see if he can help your mom cope with her problems. Maybe he can help her with some counseling.
- Don't do what I did and take drugs. Even though you think it is making you feel better, it's not. After you get sober, the problems are still there. In fact, they are worse because then you have a hangover, or you're already thinking about the next time you can get high.

Ron. I met Ron as he was finishing his sixth session with his outpatient counselor. Ron, an exceptionally bright twelve-year-old, started seeing a counselor for the problems he was experiencing adjusting to his parents' divorce six months earlier. Ron related, "Right after the divorce, I just stayed in my room. I didn't know why, but I would just lie on my bed and cry all the time."

Ron's mom added, "When he came out of his room, he would follow me around the house everywhere I went. I couldn't leave the house to go next door or to go out to water the plants without Ron at my side. Often I would get a call from the school nurse telling me that Ron was in her office and he was feeling sick. I was in jeopardy of losing my job because I had to keep going to the school to get him."

Finally, the school counselor suggested to Ron's mom that he should see a counselor to help him work through his problems brought on by the divorce. Ron

Alicia talked about the time she tried to talk to her mother about her fears but felt shut out when her mother started to cry.

related, "I learned that I didn't want to leave my mom because I was afraid that she might leave me like my father did." Ron now realizes his fear was unfounded, but he did not realize he could ask her about it.

Ron offered this advice: "If you don't talk to someone about the things you are feeling, it just gets worse and worse. I started feeling like I wasn't a good guy and that I caused my dad to leave us." Ron concluded, "You just have to talk to your mom or dad about what you are feeling. Don't keep it inside."

Kelly. I spoke with Kelly, a seventeen-year-old who was in her second year of outpatient counseling after being treated at an inpatient hospital. Kelly related, "Right after I found out that my parents were getting a divorce, I freaked out and ran away from home. I went to the city where my old boyfriend lived. He was twenty-two and had his own apartment. When I got there, he said he had a new girlfriend and told me to get lost.

"I guess it was just the pressure of my parents' divorce and my old boyfriend's refusing to help me that put me in shock. I just sort of moved around to different friends' houses, garages, and cars for about nine weeks."

Kelly was finally found by the police and was brought to the treatment center for counseling. "I didn't want to go home to my mom because she was just freaking out all the time. She was always yelling at me and taking out her anger at my dad on me. I was also pregnant at the time; and if she knew, it would have made her totally crazy. I felt like I had no choice but to leave," concluded Kelly.

Kelly offered this advice. "I learned that you can't run away from your problems. No matter what, they are still there when you stop running. They just go with you. In my case, my problems got worse because I was pregnant when I ran away. Now I realize that I was looking for a husband to replace my father, even though I was never really very close to him. That made me feel really insecure about men and boyfriends, so I thought I had to sleep with a guy for him to really like me."

Kelly is now a peer counselor and attends groups such as ALANON and ALATEEN (for teens who have drinking or drug problems) and talks to them about why they shouldn't run away from home.

Andrew. Andrew, one of the teenagers, summed up his feelings in a short (but profound) answer. He said, "Look, you guys, don't get depressed and try to hurt yourself like I did. It will get better if you just hang in there and find someone to listen to you."

THE CHURCH BODY AS COUNSELORS

Many churches are now implementing programs that train interested church members in basic counseling skills. I believe the programs are valid when they are closely supervised by a pastor or licensed therapist and where ongoing training is conducted. Most communities have training resources available, and many churches have members who are counselors or specialists in various fields and can help serve the church body in this capacity.

FIGURE 5.3
SUMMARY OF THE FINDINGS IN CHAPTER FIVE

1. The child and adolescent survey verified the Windows of Opportunity theory—a time frame between six months and one year following the divorce where crisis can be prevented with children and teens.
2. Children and teens view parental arguments differently. Children tended to view life in extremes while teenagers had a more life-like view of their parents' conflicts.
3. Domestic violence is prevalent prior to divorce.
4. Marital problems are seldom a surprise to children or teens.
5. Girls tend to feel post-divorce stress more than boys—or do they? Boys are probably in stages of greater denial of their feelings than girls.
6. Most teens and children have nobody to talk to about the divorce.
7. Over two-thirds of teens and children believed divorce led to their serious personal problems.
8. Three out of four teens shoplifted after their parents' divorce.
9. More than half of the teens and children used drugs or alcohol during or after their parents' divorce.
10. Running away from home is prevalent in single-parent families.
11. Fighting is often a sign of emotional struggles.
12. Suicidal thoughts are common among children and teens following the parents' divorce.
13. Anger toward self and others is normal in kids during and after divorce.
14. Sleeping problems were present in most cases after the parents' divorce.
15. After parents divorce, one in ten girls develops troublesome eating habits that can lead to an eating disorder.
16. One in three teens commit theft after divorce.
17. Many teens and children drank alcohol after their parents' divorce.
18. A majority of teenagers and nearly 20 percent of children got sexually involved during and after their parents' divorce.
19. Cruelty to animals often reflects past child abuse.
20. After divorce, more than half of the teens and one-third of the children feel like hurting others.
21. Following a divorce, few teens or children talk to parents about their real problems.
22. Nearly two in ten teens and one in ten kids are arrested after their parents' divorce.
23. Only 2 percent of those surveyed reported their problems were observed by church staff.
24. Most problems are discovered by teachers and school officials.
25. Most children and teens think their emotional problems are obvious.
26. Many children and teens feel responsible for their parents' divorce.
27. Children believe the responsibility for divorce lies with their fathers.
28. The most common reasons given for divorce are money, physical violence, arguing, communication, and an affair.

THE TWENTY-ONE WARNING SIGNS OF CRISIS

O LORD, do not Thine eyes look for truth?
Jeremiah 5:3 (NASB)

A major goal of the single-parent survey was to identify specific warning signs or symptoms that were commonly found among children and teens following their parents' divorce. For those of you who work with teens and children, the significance of knowing these warning signs (along with the other information in *Helping Single Parents with Troubled Kids*) is that it will help you to move from a *reactive* position to a *proactive* position.

In other words, when everyone else is wondering what is wrong with a child and what to do, you will have the insight needed to take action. You will understand that what you are observing is a typical warning sign of an approaching crisis. You will also know the Windows of Opportunity theory, which tells you that you have six months or less in which to help the child work through his or her problems before the likelihood of a major crisis.

The Twenty-One Warning Signs of Crisis were collected from observations of and interviews with the 640 parents, teens, and children who responded to the survey. Sadly, the majority of parents stated they noticed these changes in their children but didn't realize their significance until after the crisis.

I should mention that changes in behavior are normal and should be expected in children when the problems between parents increase. Problems generally intensify as the divorce draws nearer, and they will generally continue during the postdivorce period as well. I would be remiss if I did not also voice my concern about a child who does *not* exhibit symptoms related to stress after this period.

A child's natural reaction to the trauma of divorce can generate any number of emotions. Some of these are clear warning signs, and others are not. Where the line is drawn between a child's natural responses and the characteristic warning signs is far less clear, however.

Many differences also exist in the length of time a child or teen grieves about the divorce. Nobody can predict or control the time it takes for this process to conclude and for life to resume a sense of normalcy. In the cases I studied for the survey,

IN THIS CHAPTER

● *Steps to take when you notice a child's depression.*

● *How to confront a disruptive child or teen.*

● *Guidelines for helping both parent and child to set healthy boundaries .*

it would be safe to conclude that the average time for this process is generally between three and six months. Some children will process their trauma more quickly, and others will take more time.

Although there are no right or wrong answers as to how long this grieving process should take, there are some general guidelines. If a child seems undaunted by the divorce and has not shown signs of grief, loss, stress, unhappiness, or reduced levels of functioning, the child may be masking his or her feelings. In these cases, the child may be in a state of shock, which can make it nearly impossible to show emotions. These children are most easily recognized if they seem just to go right on with their lives as though nothing has happened. In other cases, children may be feeling so insecure and tentative about the family and their position in it that they are unable to express their feelings honestly.

On the other hand, teens tend to act out their stress more openly. A teenager's grieving process can go on for many months or, in some cases, years. If a teen is showing signs of distress over the divorce, then unresolved problems and emotions are likely. If this condition goes on for a period in excess of thirty days, the only safe course of action is to initiate some conversation and evaluate if counseling is warranted right away.

As a rule of thumb, anytime you observe one or more of the following warning signs—in either children or teens—you should confront the behavior by following the guidelines that accompany each warning sign.

Additionally, I would encourage you to complete a weekly Wellness Checkup (see appendix A) on each child or teen whose parents are having severe problems or are divorcing. Maintain this weekly maintenance check until you see improvement in the child or until you have documented irrefutable evidence that the child's condition warrants further counseling.

WARNING SIGN 1

My child became extremely lonely, quiet, or moody.
The terms *lonely, quiet,* and *moody* are words commonly associated with depression. As such, they should be viewed as classic pre-crisis warning signs of depression. I learned from many of the parents that these signs were more apparent following the child's visit to or phone conversation with the other parent. While a feeling of loneliness, quietness, or moodiness might be considered normal after the emotional stress of visitation, these feelings should be monitored. Prolonged symptoms (lasting weeks or months) are definitely cause for concern. Short-term symptoms (lasting one or two weeks to a month) are generally viewed as children's ways of working through their pain.

One parent described her daughter's overall mood following the divorce in this way: "Nearly every day Christina's pattern would include getting herself ready to go to school, sitting quietly while having her breakfast, and then going to school without more than a quick goodbye. After school, she would come home and go to her room, again without saying much. She would sit at the dinner table and barely look up from her plate, and then she'd go back up to her room to do her homework. When I would ask her how her day went, she would quietly answer

'Okay' and then sigh deeply. After a while, I felt like I was pulling teeth just to get her to say anything.

"Something else I noticed is that Christina was starting to act impatient and grouchy with me, her sister, and her friends. After a while, I noticed that her friends weren't coming around the house anymore."

HERE'S WHAT YOU CAN DO TO HELP

Precautionary procedures. Talk to the parent(s) about what you are observing. Let them know that a child who is suddenly acting lonely, quiet, or moody can sometimes be sending out a warning signal of depression. Let them know that time is of the essence and that an appropriate and timely response is indicated. Tell them that it is better to be safe than sorry, and bombard them with any other clichés you can think of on your own to get the point across. You may consider offering your counseling assistance, or you may wish to refer the family to another counselor.

Initiating the conversation. Sit down with troubled children and teens and let them know that you have noticed the changes in their behavior. Ask them to talk to you about those changes. Prepare yourself for children or teens to deny that anything is wrong and to resist your help. Encourage them to begin talking about their home life and personal problems as soon as they are ready. Often, a child's or teen's initial response will be to resist attempts to help, but later these same children will come around to the point of accepting help. Encouragement and persistence on your part will increase the likelihood of their cooperation.

The counseling process. If you are able to begin counseling with children or teens, I recommend that you simply provide them with a forum to begin talking about their feelings. Be prepared to discuss their sense of abandonment, fear, frustration, loneliness, anxiety, isolation, and anger.

Be mindful that the child or teen may view you as a parental or authority figure. As such, you may be the recipient of some angry feelings that the child can't express at home. This process is called *transference*. If it occurs, the best thing for you to do is calmly to accept it and help the child understand what he or she is feeling and why. It is important to validate children's feelings so they don't feel as if they are going crazy.

If the child refuses your assistance, at the very least you have sent a clear message that you are taking a special interest in him or her. Let children and teens know you are on their side and will be there if and when they need help.

Peer support. Regardless of whether children and teens begin counseling or not, consider asking one or two of their close friends to help you in providing a little extra support. Let them know that they can help by staying close and providing support and friendship as well. Encourage other kids who also come from divorced families to connect with the child until you get your support groups up and running.

Ongoing points to monitor. Closely monitor how the child is doing in these areas:

- Is the child connecting with friends, siblings, or any other children?
- Is the child continuing to isolate from his or her peer group?

- Is the child still coming to groups/church/Sunday school?
- Is the child displaying any of the other warning signs?

Regrouping. If you don't perceive the situation to be improving, you should call the parent(s) in for another consultation. Let them know that you feel the situation is potentially escalating and urge them to consider directing their child into some form of counseling. Be prepared with a referral list of counselors for the parent's consideration.

SCRIPTURAL PERSPECTIVE
Do not tremble or be dismayed, for the LORD your God is with you wherever you go. (Joshua 1:9, NASB)
Do not fear, for I am with you; do not anxiously look about you for I am your God. (Isaiah 41:10, NASB)

WARNING SIGN 2

My child just seemed depressed.
Depressed moods in children and teens are common after a divorce. Some of the typical feelings reported during this time were:

- Hopelessness
- Helplessness
- Poor concentration
- Low energy
- Little or no emotion
- Difficulty in making decisions
- Low motivation
- Low self-esteem
- Tearfulness
- Sleep problems
- Reduced affect (no laughter, crying, smiling)

Here again, after a divorce these feelings could be considered normal in small amounts or short intervals. Depressed feelings start to become warning signs of crisis when they go on for extended periods of time. A safe rule to follow is to consider anything over a few weeks as serious. I know this seems like a short time, but depression is very serious, especially in teens who are inclined to feel completely overwhelmed emotionally.

Many clinicians feel that depression left untreated for a period of six months or longer can have irreversible effects. Therefore, it is very important that you learn how to identify the symptoms of depression quickly, as depression may otherwise lead to long-term problems or even suicidal thoughts.

One senior pastor told me that one of his youth pastors had come to him with a concern about a new girl in his summer youth group. This girl was becoming very quiet and depressed near the end of each group meeting. As it neared time to go home, she would often start to cry and would excuse herself from the room.

After about a week of this, the youth pastor realized he needed to investigate the girl's situation further. After taking her aside one evening, he discovered that she was feeling abandoned by her parents, who had divorced a few months earlier. Church reminded her of the good times when her family was together. Nearing the end of the evening when it was almost time for her to go home, she would become sad at the thought of returning home to an angry mom and a broken family.

HERE'S WHAT YOU CAN DO TO HELP

Looking for patterns of depression. Any signs of depression are cause for concern. Sometimes it is easier to see signs of depression in patterns. Similar to the above example, a child or teen will often consistently display depressed symptoms. When you notice these potential signs of depression, you need to discuss your observations and concerns with the child as soon as possible.

Initiating the conversation. A good approach is not to overemphasize a child's behavior and your observations, but don't minimize them either. Let the child know that you are just a concerned friend and that you have noticed some signs of depression or seeming down lately. After your statement, look for changes in the child's facial expressions or posture that might give you a hint if you were right about your observations.

The counseling process. The goal is to get the child comfortable enough to start talking. Some effective techniques for this include:

- Humor (Don't overdo it because the child may not think you are taking him or her seriously.)
- Agreement (Try agreeing unless the child's point of view is really out of the question or dangerous.)
- Openness (Share similar difficult areas of your life so the child can see how you have coped with and overcome hardship.)
- Mutual interests (Find out what the child's likes and dislikes are—hobbies, friends, school, etc.—and talk about those interests.)
- Empathic listening (Reword what the child says, nod, and say "uh-huh" frequently.)

Be a friend. Remember, you are perhaps the only person who is interested in hearing about life from the child's perspective. Be a good friend and listen.

Let the child talk. Let the child do most of the talking if you can. A good one-hour therapeutic session should look something like this: child's conversation, 85 percent; your responses, interpretations, and advice, 15 percent. Remember, the child *needs* to talk. Most of us are already expert talkers.

Don't be a fixer. You are not going to be able to fix a child's problem in one, two, or even three sessions. It is going to take time for the healing process to begin and to run its course, so don't get discouraged if you don't see immediate improvement.

Set and keep regular appointments. The child will need to be able to look forward to seeing you at regular times, week after week. In some cases I have heard from teenagers that the weekly meetings with the pastor were the only things that kept them going through the tough times.

A good one-hour therapeutic session should look something like this: child's conversation, 85 percent; your responses, interpretations, and advice, 15 percent.

Some homework is okay. Some kids respond very well to the assignment of homework or journaling. Make the assignments easy and take a look at them at the beginning of each session so they know it isn't just busy work. Try to avoid assigning books or studying Scripture unless the child expresses an interest in this.

If you get in over your head, punt! Don't be afraid to ask for help or to admit when a case gets too difficult to handle alone. A sign of a good counselor, even the most experienced one, is to be able to admit when you may need expertise or experience you don't have.

If children talk about hurting themselves, take them seriously. Talk of serious suicidal thoughts or suicide plans need to be addressed immediately. With all the children and teens I have counseled for severe depression with suicidal thoughts, I let them know that I will take suicidal ideation earnestly. As a result, if teens tell me that they have been feeling like they may hurt themselves or someone else, they know I will act on it. This eliminates the potential for the child to feel set up.

Report suicidal thoughts or thoughts of hurting others to the parent(s) immediately. Encourage the parent(s) to take over from there, but don't make the assumption they will. If they don't seem to be taking the situation seriously, confront them again with the facts. You also may want to consult with a counselor, doctor, police officer, or social service agency in your community.

Whenever you feel children with whom you are counseling may be having suicidal thoughts, always get them to sign a contract before leaving your office. The contract could follow this format:

I _____ do hereby promise not to hurt myself in any way. I also promise not to hurt anybody else.
If I find I am having thoughts related to these things, I promise to call _____ prior to acting on any of my feelings.

Pastor _____

Counselee _____

Date _____

If the child refuses to sign the contract, you should consider this to be a statement that he or she intends to follow through on the thought. At this point I would consider notifying the police or other social service organizations that have the authority to require treatment.

SCRIPTURAL PERSPECTIVE
Why are you downcast, O my soul? Why so disturbed within me?
Put your hope in God for I will yet praise him, my Savior and my God.
(Psalm 42:5)

"What do you think? If a man owns a hundred sheep, and one of them wanders away, will he not leave the ninety-nine on the hills and go to look for the one that wandered off." (Matthew 18:12)

WARNING SIGN 3

My child's self-esteem was very low.
Self-esteem during the teen years should be considered fragile under the best of circumstances. Feelings of inadequacy seem to bleed over into nearly every aspect of a teenager's life. Feelings of insecurity over the way their body is changing, the style of clothes they wear, their hairstyle, their friends, and just about every other conceivable detail of their lives can create an atmosphere of tension and anxiety. Following divorce, self-esteem and self-image seem to take a beating. Children, as well as teens, often think to themselves, If my parents didn't love me enough to stay together, then I must not be very lovable or important.

A poor self-image can also affect the way a child or teen feels about God. Often the concern voiced by these children following a divorce is, "I must not be very important to God if he allowed this to happen to my parents and me. My life is ruined."

HERE'S WHAT YOU CAN DO TO HELP

The counseling process. Ask children or teens questions that will give you some idea of how they are feeling about themselves. Here are several examples of these questions:

- What is your best subject at school?
- What sports (activities) are you good at?
- Who are your friends?
- Why do your friends like you?
- Why does your mom/dad like you?
- Do you think you are popular?
- Do you think you are nice looking?
- Do girls (boys) like you?

Most young people with low self-esteem will answer these kinds of questions very negatively. They will tell you that they do okay in school, that they really don't have any friends, or that they don't think they are very nice looking.

Gauging self-esteem in children. In children, an effective technique for determining self-image is called *play therapy.* Consider having children draw pictures of themselves and of their mom, dad, brothers, and sisters. Ask them to draw their house and anything else they feel should be in the picture.

In a recent session with two children who were going through their parents' divorce, I had them draw pictures of their families. The older of the two girls, a five-year-old, drew her parents and her brother crying on one side of the house and drew herself on the other side of the house. When I asked her why she was alone in the drawing, she said, "Because my dad wants Shelby to live with him, and my mom wants Shelby to live with her. I guess I'm too old for them to want me."

Keeping reality clear. Let children and teenagers know that their lives haven't been ruined because of the divorce. Let them know that about 50 percent of their friends also come from divorced homes and that they have a lot of company. By letting them know that there are other kids at the church whose parents are divorced, they will see that life does go on.

It would also be helpful to introduce them to kids their age who have been through the same things. This should take place naturally after you get your children's and teens' support groups started, but you may not want to wait until then. Remember, an important goal is to help these children feel less exposed and different, even though they live with only one parent.

Some image-building techniques. Take extra time to help teens and children build their self-esteem. Usually, just spending time and showing a genuine concern will have a great effect in this process. While you are working with these children, give timely compliments to the work they are doing, but be careful not to exaggerate or be obvious. The best way to do this is to find out what they really do well, and then compliment them for it.

Asking for help. Talk to moms and/or dads about your observations of their child's low self-esteem. Let them know that your plan is to try to increase self-esteem by working with the child and connecting him or her with other kids within the church who are from divorced homes.

Let parents know that there is a connection between what children pick up at home in the form of negativity and how they feel about themselves. Encourage the mom and/or dad to monitor their conversations and conflicts. Kids pick up on this negativity, and it causes them tremendous self-doubt and anxiety. Ask the parents to spend some quality time with their child and to reinforce a positive attitude.

Possible referrals. If no improvements are seen within thirty to forty-five days, you should consult again with the child's parents about referring the child to a therapist who specializes in issues related to building self-esteem.

SCRIPTURAL PERSPECTIVE
For through the grace given to me I say to every man among you not to think more highly of himself than he ought to think; but to think so as to have sound judgment, as God has allotted to each a measure of faith. (Romans 12:3, NASB)
And have put on the new self who is being renewed to a true knowledge according to the image of the One who created him. (Colossians 3:10, NASB)

WARNING SIGN 4

My child began having difficulty sleeping.
Many of the teens and children described episodes of severe problems related to sleeping. Most of them reported an inability to get to sleep; however, fitful sleep, nightmares, interrupted sleep, and oversleeping were also common. A sleeping problem is often our subconscious mind's way of telling us something is wrong. We must pay attention! Disrupted sleeping patterns could be a sign of depres-

sion, anger, excessive pressure, or anxiety. It is also important to note that one of the critical symptoms of post-traumatic stress disorder (PTSD) is sleeping problems.

Quite often, the disrupted sleep patterns can be traced back to the absence of the other parent. Children in particular are creatures of habit, and as such, feel insecure when both parents are not sleeping in the next room. When parents separate or divorce, this change in the sleeping arrangements can cause a short-term disturbance in a child's sleeping patterns. Usually, these manifest themselves when the child is trying to go to sleep or if he/she awakens at night.

Probably the only way you will discover that one of the children or teens in your group is having difficulty sleeping is either if they tell you or if a parent comes to you for advice.

HERE'S WHAT YOU CAN DO TO HELP

The counseling process.

Dream interpretation. If the sleep disruption involves nightmares or frequently recurring dreams, ask the child about the dream. By letting the child talk about the dream, you are allowing the child to release some subconscious thoughts and feelings.

You will probably find that feelings of anger, helplessness, isolation, and anxiety are at the foundation of the nightmares. By helping the child to feel connected to you and to others, you will reduce the child's anxiety, which in turn should reduce the frequency of nightmares.

Be careful about making dream interpretations unless they are obvious. Dream interpretation is a study in itself, and many good books available at the public library will help you understand dreams.

Keeping track of nighttime thoughts and feelings. You may also request that children with sleeping disorders keep a diary next to their bed. When they have awakened from a nightmare, ask them to make notes that will help remind them of the dream when you get together next.

Many older children and teens find it comforting to read a few Bible verses when they awaken from a bad dream. You may consider walking them through some verses that point out how God loves and comforts us and that remind us we are never alone when we believe in Him.

Helping kids get to sleep. We frequently hear of children and teens who have difficulty getting to sleep. This is often due to a process called *racing.* This occurs when many thoughts (often sad) move very quickly from our subconscious to our conscious mind, leaving behind the feeling of being anxious or overwhelmed.

You can make the following suggestions to help these children and teenagers get to sleep:

- Ask them to keep a diary next to their bed. Have them make notes of what they are thinking and feeling when their thoughts race.
- Advise them that they have a "worry" period of only fifteen minutes just before going to bed. Set a timer and let them know they have to begin worrying immediately. When fifteen minutes is up, tell them it is time to go to sleep or move on to more pleasant subjects.

- Recommend to them that they set aside some time just before going to bed to read the Bible and to pray. This is a time to share the deepest secrets and most distressing thoughts of the day with God. Teach children to ask God to take control over their lives and their problems.
- Suggest to mom and/or dad that they set some time aside for just chatting each night before bedtime. This will have a calming effect, especially on younger children, and should allow them to feel more safe and connected.
- Suggest that they avoid eating sweets or drinking beverages containing caffeine for at least two hours prior to going to bed.
- In the case of younger children (ages three through nine), suggest that the mom or dad let the child sleep in the parent's room. Once asleep, the child can be put to bed in his or her own room. As a word of caution, make sure the parent conveys to the child that this is a temporary situation, or it will be difficult to get the child back to his or her own room.
- Suggest that the parent(s) consider light exercise or other play activities to help the child wind down before bedtime.
- Other miscellaneous ideas parents might consider are leaving a radio on, reading bedtime stories, drawing or coloring together, or lying down or sitting with the child for a short time.

There are no right or wrong answers to solving a sleep disturbance dilemma with teens and children. Take whatever appropriate measures are necessary.

SCRIPTURAL PERSPECTIVE
I will lie down and sleep in peace, for you alone, O LORD, make me dwell in safety. (Psalm 4:8)
"Come to me, all you who are weary and burdened, and I will give you rest. Take my yoke upon you and learn from me, for I am gentle and humble in heart, and you will find rest for your souls. For my yoke is easy and my burden is light." (Matthew 11:28)

WARNING SIGN 5

My child seemed so negative about everything.
Negativity is a feeling that is interwoven into many emotional problems. Perhaps the most serious emotional problem in which negativity is frequently apparent is depression. Negativity, however, is also commonly associated with anxiety, stress, and eating disorders.
Let me give you an example of how negativity often manifests itself in teenagers. I began working with a seventeen-year-old girl named Laura after her mother brought her in because she had become so negative. Whenever I work with teens and children who exhibit negativity or depression, I first look at their relationships with their mom and dad, brothers and sisters, friends, family, and school classmates.

Laura's response to nearly every question or piece of advice I gave her was negative. For instance, in one of our sessions, I suggested she talk to a boy in her church youth group about the things he said that made her feel put down. Laura's response was, "That won't do any good. I've tried all those things. None of them work."

Laura continually exhibited what I would term contrary thoughts and feelings about nearly every aspect of her life as well as about her own therapy. These contrary feelings are often found in oppositional behavior disorders (see chapter 4) in children and teens and should be signaling you to look for the underlying anger. Sometimes this anger can be quite old and may require considerable probing, or it can be recent and easily recognized.

| **HERE'S WHAT YOU CAN DO TO HELP** | ***Take a brief history.*** Talk to the child's mom and/or dad to determine when these negative or contrary feelings were first |

noticed. Many times you can track the onset of the feelings back to a major emotional event, such as a divorce or a death in the family. Remember you're looking for a major event that could produce feelings of anger.

Sometimes you will find out that the negativity was not so much caused by a major event alone, but was instead learned from a parent. Children as well as teens will pick up negativity and will begin emulating how they see a parent coping following the divorce.

The counseling process. Following are several issues to consider.

Labeling and owning the negativity. Often a good approach is to point out gently the times that you notice negativity. If you have been successful in determining the event that started the negativity, then bring it up. If you find the negativity is being learned from the parent(s), then call the child's attention to this as well.

If these feelings are being passed from parent to child, you will want to include the parent in some of your counseling sessions. During these sessions, feel free to call parents' attention to their negativity and discuss how common it is for parents and children to share these feelings without even knowing it.

It is very common for negativity to filter into our lives. We don't see it coming as a major event; and before we know it, we just seem down on everything. Don't be surprised by children or teens insisting that they are not negative. (No! Absolutely not! No way, uh uh!)

Steps to regaining control. Ask older children and teens to begin listening to themselves throughout the day and during your meetings with them. Ask them to keep a mental scorecard of conversations throughout the day. The goal is (1) to help them identify the times they are acting contrary, and (2) to get them to experience the feelings that are causing the negativity.

When you get together after that, ask them to relay some of the incidents in which they caught themselves responding negatively. After you have heard a few of these situations, consider any common links between them. Often you will find the negativity was targeted at an authority figure. You should point out all similarities you find and encourage discussion about them.

The cyclic pattern of negativity and isolation. Children and teens who express themselves negatively often don't have many friends. Point out during a counseling session that a negative attitude makes it hard for others to want to be around a person. You will often hear a response such as, "I don't care about friends. I am the way I am." Let children know that you are not asking them to change their personality but to consider just one small element of their personality.

Consider enlisting the aid of other children within your youth group. Ask them to take some extra time to be with the person you are counseling, and let them know why. Their good attitudes and positive natures will rub off on the child, just as the bad attitudes did.

Looking beyond the surface. Even if you are successful in showing a child how to respond more positively, don't assume the underlying anger is gone. This situation resembles the story of the wolf and the mouse. Even though the mouse saved the wolf's life by freeing him from the trap, the wolf ultimately ate the mouse. The wolf was able to act okay for a while; but eventually his old familiar ways returned, and he was unable to resist his basic nature.

Keep children focused on trying to form good relationships and on resolving the underlying angry feelings. If Mom or Dad is perpetuating these negative feelings at home, try to get their cooperation as well.

A paradoxical approach. A paradoxical technique in therapy is sometimes helpful with older children and teens. To do this, very subtly begin responding to them negatively, but don't make it obvious that you are doing so. Quite often, after you have responded this way for a session or two, the child will exhibit some frustration with you but not know why. Pay attention to when this happens, and then relate to the child why he or she is frustrated with you. In this way you can demonstrate how negativity affects those close to us.

Working toward long-term change. With older teens like Laura, negativity is an ingrained pattern. She has been acting negatively for such a long time that helping her change her behavior will be slow and difficult.

Negativity is a bad habit that is tough to break. You may want to schedule regular meetings with the child and semi-regular meetings with the mom or dad

---

FIGURE 6.1

HELPING PARENTS SET BOUNDARIES

Learning to establish—and live within—healthy structure and boundaries is always helpful for the development of children and teens. But it can be especially helpful following a divorce, providing additional stability during a high-stress time in life. One way to accomplish this is by meeting with the parent(s) to enlist assistance and to volunteer your support. Suggest that they take a hard look at the limits and boundaries they have placed on the child. Help them examine the following questions related to boundaries:

1. Are there any boundaries at all?
2. Are they clear?
3. Are they fair?
4. Have they been communicated to the child?
5. Are there consequences for crossing the boundary?
6. Are the consequences fair?
7. Are consequences forgotten when it's time to enforce them?
8. Are the consequences consistent from event to event?

(or both). If you (or someone on staff) don't have this kind of time, consider referring the child to a counselor who will be able to promote positive thinking patterns.

SCRIPTURAL PERSPECTIVE
Each heart knows its own bitterness, and no one else can share its joy. (Proverbs 14:10)
Get rid of all bitterness, rage and anger, brawling and slander, along with every form of malice. Be kind and compassionate to one another, forgiving each other, just as in Christ God forgave you. (Ephesians 4:31-32)

WARNING SIGN 6

My child began to isolate himself or herself.
The single-parent survey revealed that isolation (in varying degrees) was present in eight out of ten cases. Isolation, which is usually accompanied by low self-esteem, is considered to be a universal warning sign of many emotional problems. The more common disorders where isolation is present are:

- Depression
- Stress
- Eating disorders
- Anxiety disorders
- Learning disabilities
- Attention-deficit disorders

Children and teens often isolate because it helps them to feel more secure and less vulnerable. They may feel that if they isolate from others, then they cannot be hurt again by failed relationships, such as happened with their parents' divorce.

Within your church, you will have relatively few opportunities to notice a child or teen who is in the early stages of isolating. This is because these kids tend to blend into the crowd. They don't draw attention to themselves like the kids who are displaying their problems by acting out. Before you know it, they have faded out of church activities altogether as their feelings of isolation and depression increase.

Identifying the children and teens who isolate. There are some specific things you can look for in children who are beginning to isolate. Some of the indicators may signal trouble:

- Attendance may become infrequent.
- There is a drop-off in interest in group activities.
- The child may begin to alienate from individuals or the group by saying or doing mean things. Sarcasm is a key element to look for.
- The child may act disinterested or negative about church activities and never volunteer for anything.
- The child may avoid responsibilities to the group or others. This is done to avoid connections and to make isolating easier.
- At group functions, the child may isolate from the crowd. (In a large gathering, look *away from* the activity to find these children.)

Isolation, which is usually accompanied by low self-esteem, is considered to be a universal warning sign of many emotional problems.

HERE'S WHAT YOU CAN DO TO HELP

The counseling process. In cases where children seem to be isolating themselves from others, look for the underlying cause. Try to determine which of these feelings best describes the children you are trying to help:

- Feeling they do not belong
- Feeling unworthy of love or shameful
- Feeling resentment toward others
- Feeling as if they are *all* bad
- Feeling angry or hurt and feeling they have no place to go with these feelings
- Feeling low self-esteem

In your initial approach, be a safe person for children by letting them know you care. Returning from isolation is a risky step for children and teens. In order for them to begin integrating back into relationships, they first must develop trust in you and feel they have a safe place to take this first step.

Sometimes the best way to do this is simply by showing them some additional attention. Begin with acknowledgment. Make it a point to say hello and to make other small talk. You may find that even a small amount of effort on your part can make a great difference in a child's or teen's mind.

If you get the chance, look for something that you can praise children for. But be appropriate or they will see through your efforts. You may want to consider asking them to help you out with some projects you are managing. Be careful not to make the project too large, or they may feel overwhelmed and destined for failure. After they complete the project, send a note of thanks to them at home. This is an important step because it will allow the children to show the note to their mom or dad. This will boost their self-esteem and increase their desire to connect with others at church groups.

Call parents to let them know that you are concerned about their children's lack of connection to the group. Ask if this is something they are noticing at home or in other settings. You may suggest to parents that they not discuss your phone call with the child at this time, as it could undermine your efforts.

A therapeutic technique. As an authority figure in the lives of children at your church, you have the ability to reaffirm that they are good people. You can use these three techniques to ease a child or teen away from isolation:

1. Encourage them to form attachments with others.
2. Encourage them to talk about their insecurities about their future.
3. Encourage them to be friends to others. It is hard to isolate when you have an assignment of making a friend.

The buddy system. Ask peers (not one of their current friends) to take a special interest in the children you work with. Try to select a peer who is considered popular and outgoing—someone you consider as having the gift of helps. Ask him or her to help you bring this child back into a relationship. The buddy system is quite effective in drawing the child out of isolation.

Tactics after little or no progress. If children continue to isolate, contact their parent(s) and suggest a conference. At this meeting discuss the techniques you have used and ask for their input. You may also suggest that they consult with an outside counselor to get a second opinion.

As a general rule, when you first see signs of isolation in a child following a divorce, try to take action right away. The underlying feelings that can cause isolation, if left untreated, seldom resolve themselves.

SCRIPTURAL PERSPECTIVE
"It is not good for the man to be alone." (Genesis 2:18)
Jesus said, "I have called you friends." (John 15:15)

WARNING SIGN 7

My child was often very angry and abusive.
Studying the responses from the children and teenagers regarding their feelings of hurt, frustration, and anger during the post-divorce period provided some interesting facts. More than seven out of ten teens and over six out of ten children said they were very angry and felt as if they hated everybody and everything during the divorce. Over half of the teens said their anger made them want to hurt somebody, and four out of ten children felt the same way.

Many of the older children and teens were characterized as being verbally abusive or lashing out at friends or family members. These symptoms were commonly referred to as just blowing off steam until the seriousness of their emotions was understood. Unfortunately, the discovery sometimes involved a serious event or crisis.

The mind's safety valve. The process in which children and teens reach the point at which they have to vent or release their anger usually occurs when they are unable to identify their feelings of anger, hurt, and frustration. As a result, this anger escalates until it is unintentionally released through the mind's safety valve system.

This anger is often misdirected at others who may have done nothing to provoke the anger. Most younger children and many teens lack the insight to know why they are feeling the way they do and where their anger is based. These feelings often drag on or worsen when there is nobody close to children to help them interpret their feelings of anger, hurt, and frustration. Children need someone who can point out why they feel the way they do and who is willing to help them work through those feelings.

The process in which children and teens reach the point at which they have to vent or release their anger usually occurs when they are unable to identify their feelings of anger, hurt, and frustration.

HERE'S WHAT YOU CAN DO TO HELP

Initiating the conversation. Always start by talking with the child's parent(s) about what you have been observing. There are several good reasons for this, but the two most important are (1) risk reduction (parents need to assume a role of accountability), and (2) ongoing support at home for the work you are doing.

Be very clear to both parents that anger and/or abusive actions are warning signs of impending problems. Dealing with these issues at the outset is much easier than trying to deal with them during the midst of a crisis.

The counseling process. Your initial meeting with the child or teen should be focused on establishing good communication. You may want to state that the child has seemed angry lately, but it is best to avoid the subject of anger as much as possible during the initial meeting.

This meeting is intended to establish a foundation of communication and trust. Talk about the child's interests and how things have been going in general. Keep the conversation light. And above all, let the child know you are on his or her side.

It is also important to let children know that what they tell you is confidential. The only exception to absolute confidentiality is when a clear and present danger exists.

Ongoing sessions. Set up regular weekly appointments with the child or teen. During these sessions, talk openly about anger and how the child has dealt with it during the week.

A good technique for monitoring progress is to have children keep a diary throughout the week of any angry feelings. Specifically, they should note such things as:

- Time of day when the anger is most obvious
- What events, conversations, circumstances brought on the anger
- What the child did to work through the anger
- When the child started feeling better and less angry
- How the anger seemed to control the child

A note about Scripture. With some children and teens, reading and studying Scripture together in a session is helpful. You may want to introduce it gradually into your sessions, as it tends to cause resistance in some children whose parents were very rigid in their biblical interpretations.

Bringing parents into the process. Meet with children's parents and let them know what you are observing at church. Ask if they have observed similar anger at home and what, if anything, has been done to address the issue.

You should try to keep the parents informed of their children's progress on a weekly basis. I would also encourage you to see the parents along with the child at least once a month. This will give you a more rounded perspective of what is going on at home and will also involve the parents in supporting your ongoing work.

How the mind processes anger. The first step in helping a child resolve angry feelings is to identify the most common ways in which the mind processes anger.

1. Anger is often kept inside, which is a painful, self-destructive process. Children who suppress their anger are sometimes referred to as volcanoes waiting to erupt. Kids who keep anger in often develop other

problems, such as hypertension, ulcers, headaches, or other physical symptoms.

2. Anger is sometimes vented in the form of temper outbursts or violent acts. This form of anger is often misdirected at some innocent person who is convenient or who will accept the anger.

3. Anger can be worked through by the sharing of feelings with others such as a pastor, youth leader, therapist, family member, or friend.

As you are working with children and teens after a divorce, try to identify which of these processes they use most often. After you have identified one or more of these areas, you should call it to the attention of the child. Once the child has had an opportunity to identify and talk about the behavior, it will be easier to work through it.

Learning about anger. An angry child or teen will need special attention from you to understand where the anger is coming from. For instance, following a divorce, angry feelings often stem from the child's feelings of powerlessness over the breakup. Help children to see how their feelings of vulnerability and power-lessness can make them angry. Only after this is understood can children begin to resolve their angry feelings.

Learning to process anger is like trying to improve your golf game. If every time you tee off you hit the ball into the lake, eventually you will get frustrated. At some point you will realize that you have three options: (1) keep hitting the ball into the lake and learn to live with it; (2) quit playing altogether; or (3) find someone who will help you learn how to stop hitting the ball in the lake.

When to refer an angry child or teen elsewhere. Children and teens who continue to demonstrate anger in spite of your attempts to intervene should be referred to an outside counselor. The reason for this is that some of these kids will require a greater amount of time than many of you can afford. In these situations, stay connected with the counselor and communicate information back and forth regarding your observations. You should also consider referring angry children and teens to a professional counselor whenever you feel their safety could be in jeopardy.

Children and teens who continue to demonstrate anger in spite of your attempts to intervene should be referred to an outside counselor.

SCRIPTURAL PERSPECTIVE

A gentle answer turns away wrath, but a harsh word stirs up anger. (Proverbs 15:1)

If you are angry, don't sin by nursing your grudge. Don't let the sun go down with you still angry—get over it quickly; for when you are angry you give a mighty foothold to the devil. (Ephesians 4:26-27, TLB)

Let all bitterness and wrath and anger and clamor and slander be put away from you, along with all malice. (Ephesians 4:31, NASB)

Dear brothers, don't ever forget that it is best to listen much, speak little, and not become angry; for anger doesn't make us good, as God demands that we must be. (James 1:19-20, TLB)

WARNING SIGN 8

My child's eating habits changed.

The survey revealed that more than one in ten teenage girls developed some type of troublesome eating-related problem following their parents' divorce. Many of these problems were confronted during the early stages, when they were simply undereating or overeating issues; however, many cases went undetected until they developed into serious eating disorders.

How crisis affects eating habits. As a general statement, crisis brings about a change in appetite and/or eating habits. For instance, when children or teenagers become depressed, their appetites tend to fall into the following four categories:

1. There is no apparent change.
2. Their appetite decreases and they begin losing weight.
3. Their appetite increases, and they overeat and gain weight.
4. They feel out of control and food becomes a major focus. They may binge or purge at this stage.

You may recall that we discussed eating disorders in previous chapters. Children and teens who develop eating disorders after their parents' divorce often are sending out signals that they may be feeling out of control. Their ability to control what they eat (or don't eat) sometimes provides their only sense of self-control.

HERE'S WHAT YOU CAN DO TO HELP

Looking for changes in weight or eating habits. Although it can be a difficult task even under the best of conditions, look for significant increases or decreases in a child's weight.

Being a detective. Watch the at-risk child or teen during activities, such as when the group eats together. Check to see if she is eating, and watch her after the meal. If she excuses herself to the ladies' room (usually immediately or within ten minutes of the meal) ask a staff member to check on her. If you find that she is vomiting her food, you don't necessarily have to confront her at this point in time, but further action is required.

Because eating disorders generally carry with them a great deal of guilt, shame, and denial, it is likely that, upon her behavior being confronted, the teen or child will tell you that she has the flu. A more effective way of dealing with this problem would be to try to observe her a second time. This introduces a second level of evidence that decreases her ability to deny she is having a problem.

After observing the eating disorder a second time, someone needs gently but firmly to confront the behavior. It is generally best for the person who is intervening to be:

- The child's mother (and father if possible). Others may be present.
- A same sex counselor, pastor, or staff person at church who has a good relationship with the child. There is less embarrassment for girls when a female addresses the behavior.

- Someone who has witnessed the eating disorder so that the denial factor is reduced or eliminated.
- Someone who has knowledge of eating disorders so that the ramifications of the disorder can be discussed. This person can be a counselor or someone who has studied eating disorders.

Whoever talks to the person about the eating disorder should avoid any confrontation that could cause her to retreat in shame. Instead, let her know that you are a friend and that you are genuinely concerned for her health and well-being.

Informing parents. As soon as you are relatively sure of what you are dealing with, talk to the child's parent(s) and let them know. It would also be a good idea to let the parent(s) know what you have learned about eating disorders and that early detection and counseling are important to overcoming the disorder before serious side effects occur.

Let them know that an eating disorder is often a symptom of a deeper problem. Their assistance is crucial in helping you look for the underlying problems that have led to the eating disorder. Eating disorders are usually based in feelings of:

- Being out of control
- Anger
- Depression
- Anxiety/stress
- Low self-esteem
- Insecurity
- Victimization

Specialized training. I would estimate that most marriage, family, and child counselors, as well as many psychologists, do not feel qualified or comfortable in treating problematic eating disorders. This is a highly technical and sensitive area of patient care that should be left to the specialists.

A good course of action for people in the ministry to take is to help the parents select a therapist who specializes in eating disorders. The best place to begin looking is the Christian counseling centers in your area. I would also encourage you to continue your pastoral counseling along with the clinical counseling. It is important for the child or teen to stay connected to you, her church, and God's Word during her treatment.

SCRIPTURAL PERSPECTIVE
I am holding you by your right hand—I, the Lord your God—and I say to you, don't be afraid; I am here to help you. (Isaiah 41:13, TLB)
For since He Himself has now been through suffering and temptation, He knows what it is like when we suffer and are tempted, and He is wonderfully able to help us. (Hebrews 2:18, TLB)

Whoever talks to the person about the eating disorder should avoid any confrontation that could cause her to retreat in shame.

WARNING SIGN 9

My child became argumentative and lied to me.

When we looked at oppositional defiant disorders (see chapter 4), you may recall that some of the common symptoms in teens and children were arguing and lying. Many parents responding to the survey also reported that their children were talking back, swearing, or resisting rules, requests, or limits. Oppositional behavior that occurs outside of the home is fairly easy to recognize. For instance, a mom participating in the survey told me that she had no idea her teenage son was having emotional problems until she received a call from his youth pastor at church. The youth pastor told her that her son was on the verge of being asked to leave the youth group. According to him, her son constantly refused to follow instructions. He argued with the pastor and youth leaders, picked fights with the other boys, and basically terrorized the entire group.

A meeting between the senior pastor, the youth pastor, the mom, and her son led to some therapy sessions with an outside counselor. These sessions revealed that the boy was angry at men, especially those in authority positions within the church. The underlying reason seemed to be that the boy's father had been active in the church prior to the divorce. In the boy's mind, he associated the divorce with anything having to do with church, including the pastors.

HERE'S WHAT YOU CAN DO TO HELP

The counseling process.

Confronting in a loving manner. Confront the activity. Most of the time when children and teens are acting out of control or are lying, they are looking for more control or structure in their lives. By gently but firmly confronting the behavior, you are telling the child that boundaries need to be observed. In essence, you are letting the child know (1) that you understand he or she is feeling lost and confused, and (2) that you will provide love, direction, and support.

The most important part of the confrontation is that it establishes boundaries on behavior. Be very clear about what is acceptable behavior and what is not. Also be clear about any consequences for violating the established boundaries. As a word of caution, be sure the punishment fits the crime.

Staying calm, cool, and collected. Don't lose control. This is often easier said than done, especially with kids who are testing your patience and forgiveness. You should keep in mind that children may test you to see if you will abandon them. Recalling past events, these children may be feeling unlovable and unworthy of relationships with grown-ups. By acting out, they are more or less daring you to place limits on them. If you let them know you aren't going to leave them and they are welcome to stay in the group as long as their behavior is appropriate, you've won a friend. Be prepared for them to test your limits a few times; but above all, don't give in by compromising your boundaries.

Keeping parent(s) informed. Let Mom (and/or Dad if appropriate) know what is going on at church. Children and teens with this particular problem typically are manipulative and will go home and tell Mom you've kicked them out of church for no reason. If parents are kept aware of recent behaviors, then you should have no problems if you have to take definitive action.

Taking the time to work through severe acting out and lying. Defiant behaviors and lying are not solved by a few sessions of sitting around the campfire, holding hands, and singing "Feelings." Children and teens who are behaving in this manner are showing you some potentially severe signs that can take months or even years to work out. If the acting out and lying behaviors continue after you have confronted the child, don't feel you have failed by referring the child to a therapist.

SCRIPTURAL PERSPECTIVE
Surely you desire truth in the inner parts. (Psalm 51:6)
In everything you do, stay away from complaining and arguing, so that no one can speak a word of blame against you. You are to live clean, innocent lives as children of God in a dark world full of people who are crooked and stubborn. (Philippians 2:14-15, TLB)

WARNING SIGN 10

My child began fighting at school and at home.
Fighting, a more extreme form of acting out, can be a symptom of oppositional behavior disorder discussed both above and in chapter 4. The vast majority of the teens and children I interviewed said they fought basically because they were angry. Their anger often stemmed from feelings of frustration, helplessness, abandonment, and low self-image. This behavior pattern was verified by the children and teens who said they fought as a way of releasing their anger and hostility toward their mom and dad for the divorce.

The common reasons for fighting. Frequently, fighting is also a type of defense mechanism. When children fight, they are trying to accomplish the following:

- The child is trying to keep someone from getting too close, and thus to avoid pain.
- The child is reacting to someone who has already penetrated his or her armor and has already caused pain.
- The child is venting anger, resentment, or jealousy.

Diagnosing the reasons for fighting. When you have a child or teen in your group who is fighting, remember to look past the behavior for the underlying reason. Some motives are listed above, but others involve more severe oppositional behavior. These behavior disorders are relatively rare and involve children who may need some more intensive counseling. You can usually identify these kids, as they show little or no remorse or conscience when they do bad things. Once you have determined the reasons you believe the child is fighting, you can then make a decision about whether or not to begin counseling the child.

HERE'S WHAT YOU CAN DO TO HELP

Talking with the parent(s). As we have discussed, in any situation that involves a child's conduct or misbehavior, you should immediately inform the parent(s). Learn from them what similar types of behavior may be going on at home and if they have any insight as to why.

The counseling process. The first step in working with children and teens (mostly boys) who are fighting is to determine if they know why they are fighting. Not surprisingly, you will find that about one out of a hundred children will know why. Most children and teens will give you a myriad of reasons for their actions, but few will accept ownership for their actions and try to understand the real reason for their behavior.

After children have determined the reasons why they believe they get into fights, then you can proceed. The next step is to sit down with the child and dedicate an entire one-hour session to some other possibilities as to why the fights occur.

Refer to the three main reasons listed above, and talk about each one of these areas. Allow the child to think through each possibility to determine which most closely reflects his or her feelings. To facilitate this, you may ask what events, thoughts, feelings, and emotions precipitated each of the child's most recent fights.

Eric was a seventeen-year-old boy who found himself in the principal's office for frequent fighting. When Eric and I were discussing his last episode, he told me that the boy he was fighting lived down the street from him. He really didn't know why he disliked this kid, he just did. What Eric learned about himself in subsequent sessions was that he was jealous of the boy because he often saw him going places with his dad. On weekends, the boy would be outside playing catch with his dad or helping him wash the car. Eric didn't understand his anger toward this boy because it was well hidden in his subconscious. Once we took a look at what Eric knew about this boy, it became obvious that his motivation to fight was based in envy, which triggered his insecurity and showed up in the form of anger.

Setting boundaries. Once you have helped children or teens understand that their desire to fight is connected to some very powerful subconscious feelings, the rest is downhill. The next step, as with any child who is acting out, is to develop firm, fair boundaries regarding their behavior.

In Eric's case, I asked him to set his own boundaries. Eric responded by saying, "If I feel like I'm going to get into a fight, I'm going to stop and think about what I'm doing. If I still get into a fight, then I know there will be some consequences like losing my allowance or being on restriction or suspension from school." I then put Eric's plan on paper in the form of a contract and we both signed it.

Part of the reason Eric didn't have any further problems with fights was because he finally understood why he wanted to fight. Additionally, he felt he had something invested in the consequences, which made backsliding more difficult.

Some ongoing counseling tips. With kids like Eric, you might consider weekly counseling sessions. In these sessions, you should encourage them to talk about their unresolved feelings about the divorce and how it affects them. Help them to understand how we must all take responsibility for our behavior and that fighting will never result in anything positive.

Knowing when to make referrals. If the acting out and fighting continues even after you have progressed through some of the above steps, I would consider referring the child to a therapist. This pattern is generally a sign that deeper issues are at hand and that more time will be required to work them through.

SCRIPTURAL PERSPECTIVE

"I am leaving you with a gift—peace of mind and heart! And the peace I give isn't fragile like the peace the world gives. So don't be troubled or afraid." (John 14:27, TLB)

Don't worry about anything; instead pray about everything; tell God your needs and don't forget to thank him for his answers. If you do this you will experience God's peace, which is far more wonderful than the human mind can understand. His peace will keep your thoughts and hearts quiet and at rest as you trust in Christ Jesus. (Philippians 4:6-7, TLB)

WARNING SIGN 11

My child's school grades began to fall.
School problems of some type or another were identified in nearly all of the children and teens involved in the survey. You may recall that nearly eight out of ten teenagers stated they have cut school, and almost half stated they were failing at least one class. As a pastor or someone in the ministry, you will probably hear about poor school grades in three ways:

- If you have a school affiliated with your church
- If the child or parent tells you
- If you hear it through the grapevine

In support of the findings from the single-parent survey, another survey conducted by the National Center for Health Statistics in 1988 reported that children ages five through seventeen who live with both biological parents had to repeat a grade in 12 percent of the cases. Conversely, 22 percent of children living with a divorced mom needed to repeat a grade.

Common reasons why grades drop after divorce. Some reasons for a decline in grades or for poor school conduct can be attributed to some or all of these three areas:

1. The distraction of the divorce. This included such areas as levels of concentration, depression, lower motivation, changing environments, or relocation to other schools.
2. Teenagers will test limits whenever possible. With just one parent left at home to watch over school work, a child has a natural interest in wanting to see just how much he or she can get away with.
3. School teachers and administrators represent authority figures and, as such, are identified in the child's or teen's mind with the parents and the divorce.

> *School problems of some type or another were identified in nearly all of the children and teens involved in the survey.*

HERE'S WHAT YOU CAN DO TO HELP

Ruling out physiological problems. As a general rule with the children and teens I work with, I follow a course of action that is termed a rule-out. This process involves checking to make sure the child is medically okay prior to assuming that his or her school problems are psychological. If the child has not had a routine physical during the past year, recommend a visit to the family doctor. Once you have established that the child is physically sound (i.e., hearing, vision, blood work, etc.), then you can proceed with other areas of consideration.

Collecting a brief school history. Ask the parents for a profile of how the child has done in school over the past three years. Pay particular attention to English grades (especially reading, writing, and spelling) and citizenship. English grades are important because they will generally be the first areas in which a learning disability or attention-deficit/hyperactivity disorder will be detected.

Citizenship, or conduct while in class and around other kids, is important to look at as well. If a child is hyperactive or disruptive in class and has poor or failing grades, then further specialized testing is in order. The child's school should be able to help you find a counselor who specializes in testing for learning disabilities or attention-deficit/hyperactivity disorders.

If the child's grades have fallen over this three-year period of time *prior to* the disruption in the family, then one of the above disorders may be a factor in the child's learning patterns. Falling grades that coincide with the onset of the parents' marital problems and subsequent divorce are likely to be more stress-related.

Countering the disruption. Talk to the parent(s) about the child's level of distraction after the divorce. Suggest that they refocus some of their attention toward getting back into the child's schoolwork/homework routine. Suggest to them that they try to create an atmosphere similar to when the family was together. Often a disruption in routine is enough to distract the child and cause grades to fall, due to poor study habits and lack of concentration.

A second area of countering the disruption is to find out if the child is anticipating changing schools. One of the excuses I often heard from teens whose parents had recently been divorced is that they anticipated changing high schools. As a result, their logic told them they didn't have to try so hard at their present school.

The counseling process. Consider the three following issues.

Anger and schoolwork. Determine if anger is playing a part in the child's failing grades. Poor grades with no obvious acting out behavior are often caused by the child's feelings of frustration, confusion, and unhappiness over the family situation. When poor grades are accompanied by acting out, the situation tends to be based more in emotional problems such as anger, depression, stress, or feelings of abandonment.

A high school teacher called my attention to the class work of a teenager whose grades were falling steadily. The teacher stated, "I could tell that the boy was quite angry just by looking at his handwriting and the neatness of his papers." The teacher went on to tell me that the child's penmanship became very sloppy and his work was often incomplete. In addition, he told me that the child was not reading the instructions before completing assignments. All this, he said, indicated the child was angry, which was causing a distraction in his work.

Talking through the problems. Sit down with children and teens and let them know that many people in their lives are concerned about them. Ask them if they know why their grades are falling and if that seems important to them. Allow them some time to think about the connection between their parents' marital problems

> *One of the excuses I often heard from teens whose parents had recently been divorced is that they anticipated changing high schools. As a result, their logic told them they didn't have to try so hard at their present school.*

and their own trouble in school. You'll be surprised how many kids don't see the connection until you point it out.

Monitoring progress. In most cases, the child's report card will not show improvement until at least the quarter following the time when counseling begins. It is easier to note ongoing progress by suggesting the parents have regular conferences with the child's teacher(s).

WARNING SIGN 12

My child began violating curfew times.

Many parents who took part in our survey reported that their teens stayed out late at night, even though they knew it was in violation of their curfew. Also commonly reported were teens, as well as children, who failed to come home after school, even though they knew this would upset their parent(s).

Although you as someone in the ministry may not know when children are breaking rules at home, you are likely to see some similar behaviors from them as they interact within your youth group. If children are angry and defiant at home, they will be angry and defiant away from home.

Often, children and teens who violate limits (such as curfews) are feeling angry, hurt, abandoned, and insecure. These feelings often create a greater sense of being out of control and in need of even more direction and structure. Instead of being able to recognize these feelings and ask for more structure, they resort to acting out, hoping subconsciously that more limits and structure will be imposed.

The teens and children who fall into this pattern of passive resistance are usually fairly easy to work with. Since their lack of structure and attention was a primary reason they got into trouble, the addition of attention and structure will usually help them alter their behavior.

On the other hand, some teens and children defiantly disregard rules and authority. Their defiance also stems from feelings of abandonment, hurt, anger, and insecurity; however, they show these feelings aggressively rather than passively. These are the kids whose motives are based more on punishing others for their parents' divorce. Working with these children and teens will present more of a challenge due to their open anger with life in general and with authority figures.

HERE'S WHAT YOU CAN DO TO HELP

A controlling environment versus a structured environment.

Talk with the parent(s) about creating a more structured environment for the child. Help them to understand the difference between a controlling environment and a structured environment. The differences in these two approaches can be seen in the following two parenting styles.

Parent A (controlling environment). "You have been coming home late from school, and you haven't been home by your 10:00 p.m. curfew on weekends. Starting now, I want you to come home right after school, no later than 3:30. As for weekends, you are on a four-month restriction until I see a marked change in your grades and until you show me you can be more responsible."

Parent B (structured environment). "I'm concerned with what has been going on lately. I have noticed that you aren't getting home from school on time. When you go out on weekends, you don't seem nearly as concerned about what time you come in as I think you should be.

"I think it's important that we talk about a new system to help you get your homework and your chores done as well as to follow the rules. I'd like your input on the best ways we could go about accomplishing this. Let's both think about how we can best accomplish these goals and agree to talk about some solutions tomorrow."

The counseling process. Consider the four issues discussed here.

Lending an ear. Make some time to talk to children in private about how they are dealing with life after divorce. Again, many of the kids who are defying rules at home are doing so subconsciously. Their angry feelings haven't surfaced to the point where it has occurred to them what they are doing. Just the fact that you are on their side, taking the time to talk with them, will help immeasurably.

Passive-aggressive behavior. Take a look at the following example of this type of behavior and consider how you might handle it in your teen group:

> Denise, age fifteen, has been coming to your teen group for almost two years. About three months ago, her parents started divorce proceedings. At first, Denise seemed to be taking the divorce in stride; however, for the last four weeks or so, Denise's behavior has been changing.
>
> At first, she was somewhat disruptive in group activities. She talked during Bible study, drew pictures, doodled in her notebook, or passed notes to other girls. Then she began coming late to groups and tried to draw attention to herself by being loud. On one occasion, when she was asked to help in planning an activity, she commented, "I'd love to help out; these events are so much fun." But when the time came, she made excuses why she couldn't help. You later heard from one of her friends that she hated working on these types of projects because they bore her.
>
> Finally, you heard from someone in the group that Denise had been talking about how youth group isn't fun anymore. She told someone that if the youth group had a good leader things would be better—like they are at youth groups in other churches.

Denise provided us with a classic example of passive-aggressive behavior. In this case she was misdirecting the anger she felt toward her parents and, instead, directing it toward the group and its leaders. The most effective way of dealing with children and teens like Denise is lovingly to confront their behavior. Let them know that they are okay, but what they are doing is not okay. In other words, confront only the behavior, not the person.

Helping parents set boundaries. When children are acting in a passive-aggressive manner, there is often a need for more structure and boundaries in their lives. The best way to accomplish this is by meeting with the parent(s) to enlist assistance and to volunteer your support. Suggest that they take a hard look at the limits and boundaries they have placed on the child. I suggest you help them examine the following questions related to boundaries:

When children are acting in a passive-aggressive manner, there is often a need for more structure and boundaries in their lives. The best way to accomplish this is by meeting with the parent(s) to enlist assistance and to volunteer your support.

1. Are there any boundaries at all?
2. Are they clear?
3. Are they fair?
4. Have they been communicated to the child?
5. Are there consequences for crossing the boundary?
6. Are the consequences fair?
7. Are consequences forgotten when it's time to enforce them?
8. Are the consequences consistent from event to event?

A good idea for kids (especially teens) who are not observing boundaries, rules, and responsibilities is to help the parent(s) place them on a behavioral contract. This contract calls for the writing down of certain specific tasks, responsibilities, and expectations along with the consequences for each, both positive and negative. Here is an excerpt of a contract between a parent and child.

---

1. You will be home by 4:00 p.m. each day after school. For the first hour after you get home, you are expected to do your homework. I will check your homework each evening after you finish. If it is not done correctly, you will be expected to correct it right away. If you argue or cause a scene, you will not watch television that night.
2. If you come home late from school, I will ask you the reasons why. If you have a good reason, I may forgive the situation. If not, then you will not be able to watch television or listen to your stereo that night, and you will be grounded for one night of the next weekend.

_____   _____
Parent's signature   Teenager's signature

Knowing when to punt. As a general rule, a child or teenager who needs more structure should start showing signs of improvement very quickly. If the combined efforts between you and the child's parent(s) have not produced the expected results, you may want to examine and redefine the contract. You may also think about suggesting to the parents that they consider referring the child to a counselor. It is best to control this behavior of exceeding boundaries while it is still in the stage of being a nuisance and before it becomes a serious conduct disorder.

SCRIPTURAL PERSPECTIVE
A gossip betrays a confidence, but a trustworthy man keeps a secret. For lack of guidance a nation falls, but many advisers make victory sure. (Proverbs 11:13-14)
A perverse man stirs up dissension, and a gossip separates close friends. (Proverbs 16:28)

WARNING SIGN 13

My child was arrested for shoplifting.

When you stop to consider that three out of four teenagers had shoplifted subsequent to their parents' divorce, you have to conclude that this is an area that merits further attention.

Frequently during the survey's follow-up interviews, teens and children who had shoplifted told me they knew they would be caught but didn't seem to care. Many felt they had nothing to lose, since their lives were already in chaos. This indifference to being caught might also explain why most children and teens who shoplift have enough money with them to pay for the item.

I recall working with a small boy who had become the Al Capone of shoplifters. At the ripe old age of eight, Timmy had a shoplifting routine that featured a specially altered lunch box and a school back pack. Timmy's secret was finally discovered when his mother just happened to be shopping in the same department store and she saw him stuffing a Ninja Turtle toy into his lunch box. His mom watched him as he made his way around the aisles of toys and looked for specific items to fill his shoplifting list.

After she discovered Timmy, his mother learned that he had been shoplifting for a period of about one year. He estimated that, during that time, he had taken more than 600 toys. Yet not one was for him.

Mom discovered that since her divorce from the boy's father almost a year earlier (what a coincidence, huh?), Timmy had been feeling quite abandoned and hurt. His self-esteem had dropped so low that the only way he could feel important was to give presents to his friends. In the boy's mind, he had to maintain his toy shoplifting in order to be worthy of relationships and to feel better about himself.

A meaning behind shoplifting. Many therapists interpret stealing in general and shoplifting in particular as a subconscious request for attention and limits. Like in Timmy's case, shoplifting provided him with the attention he needed to feel important.

In other cases, however, shoplifting is connected to out-of-control feelings. These kids often feel that their lives are falling apart. The structure that was once there is suddenly pulled away, often leaving them feeling very confused. Since their confused lifestyle doesn't feel comfortable, they begin subconsciously to look for ways of getting control back in their lives. Because most children and teens lack the insight to ask for more limits and attention, they resort to acting-out behaviors. These kids will do anything they can to cause the authority figures in their lives to increase the attention and limits.

If these signs are missed, the significance of the act usually increases, such as is the case with shoplifting. In the subconscious mind of children who shoplift, the worst thing that can happen is that they will get into a little trouble but will receive the attention and increased limits they need.

HERE'S WHAT YOU CAN DO TO HELP

The counseling process.
Confronting the behavior. If you hear that one of the teens or children in your group

is shoplifting, try to talk with him or her about it. Be careful not to approach a child from a judgmental position.

If you are working with younger teens or children, let them know that it is not uncommon to have one shoplifting experience in a lifetime—but that's usually it. Let them know that you are more interested in helping them understand why they shoplift than in talking about the shoplifting itself. A good way of doing this is to ask:

1. If they know why they shoplifted.
2. What type of things they shoplifted.
3. How they felt when they shoplifted.
4. What they do with whatever they shoplifted.
5. If they understand that there are legal consequences for shoplifting.

Pay particular attention to children and teens who do not show any signs of remorse or guilt. Many kids report a feeling an exhilaration while shoplifting, which can signal that the problem may escalate.

Explaining the ramifications. When you are counseling with kids who don't seem to be understanding the seriousness of shoplifting, you may consider ways of increasing their awareness. One such way is to have someone from your church who is an attorney or police officer talk to the child. I would suggest you get the approval of the child's parent(s) first. You may also want to let the child know of the legal ramifications of shoplifting, which can include fines, probation, or juvenile hall. Repeated offenses generally involve heavier fines and/or longer time in a juvenile hall.

Involving the parent(s). Consider a meeting with both the child and the parent(s) to discuss the shoplifting. If you get an indication that the shoplifting is a chronic problem, you may want to refer the family to a therapist.

SCRIPTURAL PERSPECTIVE
"You must not steal." (Exodus 20:15, TLB)
"Don't kill, don't commit adultery, don't steal, don't lie." (Matthew 19:18, TLB)
So overflowing is his kindness towards us that he took away all our sins through the blood of his Son, by whom we are saved. (Ephesians 1:7, TLB)

WARNING SIGN 14

My child dropped out of once-loved activities.
Parents, teens, and children who participated in our survey reported the following activities as those most frequently given up:

- Scouts
- Church groups
- Music lessons
- Afterschool sports
- Other social organizations

A classic interpretation for why children and teens quit these types of activities following their parents' divorce is that they are angry and confused. In their minds, they may subconsciously feel that quitting activities their parents had encouraged is a form of retaliation or punishment.

In another way, children look at these activities as commitments. Subsequently, when children see parents break something as important as the marriage commitment, the children may subconsciously see it as okay to break their lesser commitments.

Another group of children and teens quit activities as a response to the divorce trauma and thus exhibit a possible sign of depression. Depression is often accompanied by a decrease in activity, motivation, energy, and by an increased desire to isolate. Quitting activities, in these cases, is the mind's way of acknowledging its depression and of minimizing the chances of discomfort.

HERE'S WHAT YOU CAN DO TO HELP

The counseling process.
Initiating a conversation. Since one of the areas you are likely to recognize first is a drop off of interest in church groups, here is the approach I would recommend for pastors and other ministry leaders.

1. Meet with children and teens who are thinking about quitting the youth group and let them know you are concerned. Even if they have already quit, make it easier for them to come back by stating, "I heard you are thinking about quitting. Want to talk about it?"
2. Tell them you understand that after parents divorce, kids often feel like quitting groups and activities. Try to learn if they are quitting out of subconscious anger at their parents or if they are possibly suffering from depression.
3. Let them know that they are valuable to the group and that they would be missed if they chose not to attend.
4. If you are not able to change their mind, try to talk them into a temporary break from the activity or group. Set a specific time frame in which you expect they will return, and then stay connected with them during their absence.

Encouraging peer support. While children and teens are still considering whether to leave the group or not, connect them with other boys or girls who are close in age and who have been through similar circumstances. There is a very powerful and positive dynamic that occurs between two kids who share similar backgrounds. You may find that this is all it takes to keep the child active in church.

Involving the parents. Meet with the child's parent(s) and let them know of your concern for their child. Inform them of what you know about why children quit activities and groups after divorce. Enlist their assistance in keeping their child connected during this difficult transition.

WARNING SIGN 15   I caught my child drinking or taking drugs.

It was often reported, especially by mothers of teenagers, that they found alcohol or drugs while cleaning their child's room. I always tell parents there are no points off for good detective work. Alcohol is often the first level of escape for teens and children, just as it is for adults who would prefer to avoid reality.

A secondary problem with alcohol, as with many drugs, is that it is a depressant. When taken by kids who are already feeling depressed following a divorce, it can compound and intensify their depression. Many scenarios involving teen suicide include the use of alcohol and drugs on top of layers of depression.

When and why teens drink. The cycle of alcoholism and drug abuse commonly begins when the teen drinks to numb his or her painful feelings. When the effects of the alcohol or drug wear off, the old depression returns along with the new depression caused by the sobering process. Since this is an even more painful place to be in than before, the adolescent drinks again to escape that pain, which completes the alcohol-depression-alcohol cycle.

The single-parent family survey discovered that an alarming 82 percent of the teenagers and 48 percent of the children drank during the time of the divorce and the period following it. This behavior, they stated, went on until they were caught or received treatment.

As a point of reference, in September 1991, the Associated Press reported that 51 percent of the nation's 20.7 million junior and senior high school students had had at least one drink in the previous year, and eight million students drank weekly. The study added that 454,000 students said they binge on alcohol weekly.

You need to understand that kids who drink or use drugs are champion manipulators, and you are the next target.

HERE'S WHAT YOU CAN DO TO HELP

The counseling process. Frequently, the first reaction of some youth leaders when they find out a child or teen has been drinking is to try to be a friend, keep it a secret, and fix the problem. This is usually not meant to be a cover-up, but rather a way of trying to build confidence and a relationship. At all costs, avoid the temptation to try to help the teen by yourself. This is an area that requires a great deal of attention, expertise, and teamwork.

Notifying parents. For liability as well as for clinical reasons, talk to the parent(s) immediately. Also, it is generally best to let the teen know you will be talking with the parent(s) about the situation. The only exception to this rule is if you feel the teen may run away or hurt himself or herself if you call a family meeting.

Often children or teens will tell you that their parent(s) will kill them if you tell. They may tell you that they will be severely beaten and plead that, if you just let them slide just this once, they promise to stop drinking. You need to understand that kids who drink or use drugs are champion manipulators, and you are the next target. Let them know that you are talking to their parent(s) because you care about them and want to help them see this through.

Intervening. Although it may be uncomfortable, call a meeting between the teen and the parent(s) to talk about the alcohol problem. Start by presenting some ground rules for the session. The rules are as follows:

1. Tempers stay under control.
2. No violence is allowed.
3. This is a problem-solving session.
4. No blaming, finger-pointing, or I told you so's are allowed.

During the session, stay out of the cross-fire as much as possible. Your position should be that of moderator, and as such, you should remain as neutral as possible. Keep the meeting on target by staying with the facts and seeing to it that all parties obey the rules listed previously.

Assessing the problem. At some point you should try to help determine how serious the drinking problem is. I will, however, go on record as saying all drinking problems are serious and potentially life-endangering. The importance of learning the severity of the problem is so that you can make an informed recommendation.

To determine the severity of the drinking problem, you should ask these ten clarifying questions:

1. "How often do you drink, and how long have you been drinking?"
2. "What do you drink?" (Note: Beer and wine are no less serious than hard liquor.)
3. "When do you find yourself wanting to drink?" (Does the child drink when under stress, when he or she wants to escape, because he or she likes it, when he or she wants to be able to socialize? If the drinking is tied to making life easier or more bearable, then you are most likely dealing with a problem drinker.)
4. "How does the alcohol make you feel?" (Does the adolescent or child feel better, calmer, more social?)
5. "Who knows you drink?" (Do family and friends know, or is the drinking a secret?)
6. "What problems has your drinking or drug use caused?" (Are there problems with school work, relationships, an after-school job?)
7. "Do you think you could give up the alcohol?"
8. "Is there any history of alcohol or drug problems in your family?"
9. "Where do you get your alcohol?"
10. "Do you get drunk when you drink?"

These questions should clarify how severe the drinking problem is. You want to key in on when and why the teens drink, what problems they have experienced as a result of their drinking, and how long they have been having these problems.

Making referrals and the process of denial. Most teens and children (I estimate 99.999%) rarely believe they have a serious alcohol or drug problem. If you suspect a serious drinking or drug problem, at the very minimum recommend they receive specialized counseling and begin attending Alcoholics Anonymous (AA)

FIGURE 6.2

DETERMINING THE SEVERITY OF A DRINKING PROBLEM

Frequency x Reason x Dysfunction = Extent of Drinking Problem
    Frequency = How often they drink
    Reason = Why they drink
    Dysfunction = Problems the alcohol or drug has caused

meetings. You can find this resource by calling your local council on alcoholism or by calling information for the nearest AA group in your area.

For drinking or drug problems that appear more serious, remember *Frequency x Reason x Dysfunction = Extent of Drinking Problem*. (Refer to figure 6.2.) Children and teens with extensive drinking and drug problems should be directed to a qualified substance abuse counselor or inpatient hospital program.

SCRIPTURAL PERSPECTIVE
Wine is a mocker, strong drink a brawler, and whoever is intoxicated by it is not wise. (Proverbs 20:1, NASB)
Envyings, drunkenness, carousings, and things like these, of which I fore warn you just as I have forewarned you that those who practice such things shall not inherit the kingdom of God. (Galatians 5:21, NASB)

WARNING SIGN 16

My child refused to go to church anymore.
Aside from the child's quitting church groups or other activities, there are three basic reasons why children and teens refuse to go to church.

1. Children and teens sometimes subconsciously show anger at God for allowing their parents to divorce.
2. Some children believe God is punishing them for not being good enough, and they may actually be seeking to avoid God by avoiding church.
3. Some children avoid going to church in an attempt to avoid the kids at church who may be perceived as normal, meaning they have both parents.
4. Children sometimes subconsciously avoid going to church to punish their parent(s) for getting a divorce. These children think that because their parents are Christians, they should have known that divorce wasn't okay.

Some children believe God is punishing them for not being good enough, and they may actually be seeking to avoid God by avoiding church.

HERE'S WHAT YOU CAN DO TO HELP

Assessing the situation. Try to determine which of the above four descriptions the child most likely fits. After identifying the source of the child's resistance to going to church, concentrate your efforts on helping the child to work through those feelings. This is best done by listening to the child and providing positive and appropriate feedback. See if the child's perception of God is accurate.

A particular case I recall introduced me to thirteen-year-old Michael. Since he was three, Michael had been going to church regularly with his mom and dad. After the divorce, he refused to attend church or any of the youth groups he had been active in. The youth pastor called a counselor to consult with him about the case. The counselor correctly diagnosed the problem to be the child's anger at God and suggested the youth pastor provide counseling in that area.

The youth pastor counseled with the youngster and helped him to understand that we live by God's will and timing. We often don't understand why bad

---

A MESSAGE FOR YOU TO GIVE PARENTS
WHEN THEIR CHILD DOES NOT WANT TO ATTEND CHURCH

Encourage parents of teenagers not to allow them just to refuse to go to church, but don't advocate high pressure tactics either. Teenagers should be able to talk about their feelings and help you identify why they are not willing to attend church. If they tell you they don't understand their resistance to going to church, I suggest they attend until they are able to get in touch with their feelings.

On the other hand, if teens tell you they are very angry and feel anxiety about going to church, listen to them. They are probably telling it to you straight. It usually serves no purpose to force a teenager, with feelings this strong, to go to church. As a pastor or someone who works with the youth, you should stay in touch during the time children are working through their feelings. This will make their eventual return to church easier.

But if at all possible, children should be persuaded to continue attending church during these confusing times. My philosophy is that during and after divorce, the church should be providing a continuity of caring relationships for these kids.

---

things happen, such as divorce or death. The youth pastor reminded Mike that God has a plan for all of us, like we read in Jeremiah 29:11-13: "'For I know the plans I have for you,' declares the LORD, 'plans to prosper you and not to harm you, plans to give you hope and a future. Then you will call upon me . . . and I will listen to you. You will seek me and find me when you seek me with all your heart.'"

SCRIPTURAL PERSPECTIVE
We know that God causes all things to work together for good to those who love God, to those who are called according to His purpose. (Romans 8:28, NASB)

WARNING SIGN 17 **My child became lazy and procrastinated regularly.**
Parents often described their teen or child as putting off homework assignments, chores, and responsibilities until it was too late or no longer necessary for them to be completed. They also often referred to these children as having an "I don't care" attitude. Kids with this type of attitude following a divorce also fall into the category we discussed earlier as passive-aggressive. Again, this usually means that they are showing their anger or protest in a more passive manner than other kids who act out their anger. Don't assume, however, that they are not as emotionally disrupted as the kids who drink, take drugs, or shoplift after divorce.

A significant difference in these kids is that they don't feel powerful enough (emotionally speaking) to disobey openly. For these children, procrastination and laziness are much more typical. Blatant rebellion could prove too risky and could

increase fears that the parent might also withhold love from the child, as they did from the spouse.

Ruling out physical problems. The most common reason kids become lazy or procrastinate is that they are reacting emotionally to the divorce trauma. However, in certain instances this behavior could be due to physiological problems.

Before you set out to help a child or teen who is acting in this manner, talk to the parents to see if any recent physical changes have been observed. You'll want to look for recent illness, headaches, eye or hearing problems, blood pressure problems, anemia, physical traumas (e.g., car accidents, head injuries), and other similar physiological problems. It may also be a good idea for the child to have a physical, just to make sure everything is okay.

> *The most common reason kids become lazy or procrastinate is that they are reacting emotionally to the divorce trauma.*

> ### HERE'S WHAT YOU CAN DO TO HELP

The counseling process.
Making sense of feelings. Try to illustrate for children or teens the connection between their feelings of hurt and anger and their laziness and procrastination. Explain that they may be acting out of rebellious feelings toward their parents.

These children should also understand that their passive responses and avoidance of feelings and responsibilities are unhealthy and will cause them future problems with friends, family, teachers, and employers.

Setting boundaries: an antidote for laziness and procrastination. At the risk of beating a dead horse, this is another area where parents need to implement boundaries and limits. Kids who are avoiding responsibility, procrastinating, or acting lazy are indirectly telling parents, "I don't think you are in control here; in fact, I am." There are many reasons kids may feel their parent(s) is (are) not in control. It is important to try to learn where the child first perceived that laziness and procrastination were acceptable. You may have to do a great deal of backtracking to see if this tendency was a common trait of either parent.

Getting the parent(s) to set boundaries is easier said than done. As we discussed before, it will be important for the parent(s) to address the laziness and procrastination issues with a behavior contract. All areas where the child or teen displays these tendencies should be addressed in a contract, along with specific consequences for failing to improve. Only through this system of establishing and maintaining clear boundaries and expectations can a child feel that the parent(s) is (are) back in control.

SCRIPTURAL PERSPECTIVE
Lazy hands make a man poor, but diligent hands bring wealth.
(Proverbs 10:4)

WARNING SIGN 18

My child dated/befriended kids against my wishes.
Two basic things are happening when teenagers begin dating or running around with kids they would not have been attracted to prior to the divorce. First, they may be indirectly taking out their anger toward their parents for the divorce. Again, like procrastinating, these are passive-aggressive and attention-seeking behaviors. The second reason concerns issues related to self-esteem. These kids

reported wanting to be around other kids with whom they felt safe and less likely to be criticized for their broken home. The survey revealed that these kids often were attracted to other kids from broken homes. This was likely due to their insecurity of being around kids from two-parent families.

While you are working with these kids, you'll want to keep in mind that they are telling you one of two things: either their self-esteem has declined after the divorce, or they are angry and are trying to punish their parents for the divorce. You should attempt to determine which category the child in your group most closely fits.

You can do this by getting an idea of how children and teens feel about their parents and how the divorce has changed their lives. If through your conversations you discover underlying angry feelings, then you probably know which category best describes them. If, on the other hand, children seem embarrassed or withdrawn about their parents' divorce, then you can safely guess that they are seeking out other divorced kids because they feel more secure with them.

Peer group support. If you find out (or if parents tell you) that their child's recent choice in friends is a problem, you can take action. Identify one or two of the child's peers and ask them to spend some time with the child. You will be surprised how this will increase the child's self-esteem and help him or her get back on track. Be sure to follow up and keep tabs on the relationship.

| HERE'S WHAT YOU |
| CAN DO TO HELP |

The counseling process.

Elevating awareness. If you find that children are making poor choices in friends because they are trying to punish their parents or because they feel insecure, feel free to call these motives to their attention. Using these two perspectives, try to describe for children how they may be choosing inappropriate friends, and explain that neither option is healthy.

SCRIPTURAL PERSPECTIVE
A friend loves at all times, and a brother is born for adversity. (Proverbs 17:17, NASB)
I wrote you in my letter not to associate with immoral people. (1 Corinthians 5:9, NASB)

WARNING SIGN 19

My child became sexually active.
First let's discuss teenage pregnancy, perhaps "the ultimate warning sign" in teenage girls. Over the last twenty years for women nineteen years of age or younger the percentage of illegitimate births has increased from 15 percent to 51 percent.[1]

A common theory of why sexual activity and teen pregnancy are more prevalent in single-parent families is that teenage girls are desperately trying to replace the male (father) relationships missing in their lives. This is especially true when the father leaves the family while the child is between the ages of three to five, eight to ten, or ten to twelve. These are critical stages of development for girls in which they depend a great deal on their fathers.

Figure 6.3 combines information from the teenage girls I interviewed during the survey and from those I have worked with as a therapist. The chart clearly shows a direct relationship between the child's age at the time when Dad leaves and a later incidence of teen pregnancy.

Sexual activity in both boys and girls is implied due to the high incidence of teen pregnancy. Some reasons (other than the obvious hormonal changes) that teenage boys were found to be more sexually active following their parents' divorce were:

- They may be searching for love, acceptance, relationship, and attachment.
- They may be angry and view a sexual relationship as a means of expressing their anger toward their parents (defiant behavior).
- Single-parent family boys often attract single-parent family girls. As a result, they share similar mind-sets and insecurities.

HERE'S WHAT YOU CAN DO TO HELP

The counseling process. A pregnant teenager is likely to be going through perhaps the second most traumatic event in her life, the first being her parents' divorce. Accordingly, she will need a considerable amount of love and acceptance from you and her peer group at church.

Bear in mind that many emotions run through her mind at this time such as embarrassment, shame, fear, anxiety, loneliness, low self-esteem, and perhaps depression. It is important that you are there to help her work through her emotions. It is also appropriate to refer back to the warning signs of depression when you are monitoring pregnant teens.

You should also suggest to the family that they look for support groups to help all of them through the pregnancy. Teenage pregnancy support groups are available in most large cities. Check with your local department of social services for the nearest location.

FIGURE 6.3

AGES OF DAUGHTERS WHEN FATHERS LEFT HOME AND THE RELATIONSHIP TO TEEN PREGNANCIES

AGES OF DAUGHTERS WHEN FATHERS LEFT HOME	PERCENT WHO LATER BECAME PREGNANT DURING THEIR TEEN YEARS
0-2 years	8 %
3-5 years	23 %
6-8 years	19 %
8-10 years	23 %
10-12 years	27 %

Supporting parents. You will also want to provide some pastoral counseling for the parent(s) of the pregnant teen. Like the teen, the parent(s) will be feeling anger, embarrassment, and anxiety. Take special care to make sure they don't feel like outcasts within the church.

A second area of concern regarding parents is that they don't let their feelings of embarrassment and disappointment dominate their reasoning. Help them to work past these feelings in order to provide the kind of support their daughter will need.

Helping everyone understand the options. Provide a forum for discussing the outcome of the pregnancy. Be prepared to discuss these options:

- Marriage
- Adoption
- Raising the child with the parents' help
- Support from the baby's father and his family
- Abortion (You need to be prepared to discuss this option as well, since many people consider it an alternative.)

Discussing sex with teens. When discussing issues of teenage sexual activity, try to let teens know that their sexual desires are a normal part of the maturing process. Along with these increased sexual feelings come increased responsibilities, such as abstinence. (Good reference materials for issues concerning teenage sexual relationships are: *Handling Your Hormones*, J. Burns (Harvest House Publishers, 1986); *The Teenage Q & A Book*, J. McDowell and D. Day (Here's Life Publishers, 1987).

SCRIPTURAL PERSPECTIVE
Flee the evil desires of youth, and pursue righteousness, faith, love and peace, along with those who call on the Lord out of a pure heart. (2 Timothy 2:22) Marriage should be honored by all, and the marriage bed kept pure, for God will judge the adulterer and all the sexually immoral. (Hebrews 13:4)

WARNING SIGN 20

My child's appearance really changed.
Well over half of the parents commented that prior to their child's serious problems, they noticed two changes: (1) personal hygiene, and (2) mode of dress.

Personal hygiene. After divorce, many parents noticed that hygiene was not as important to their children as it was before. For instance, several parents commented on how difficult it became to get their children or teens to comb their hair, brush their teeth, or bathe regularly.

The most likely reason for these changes is the trauma of the divorce. Since we have already established that divorce can cause stress, anxiety, low self-esteem, and depression, this trauma can also affect the way people care for themselves. A common statement to hear from someone who is depressed is, "Why should I take care of myself? It doesn't matter anymore."

Lack of interest in hygiene can also have a psychoanalytical interpretation generated from the teenager's subconscious. (I apologize, but I've been looking for a place to say that throughout the book.) Children's minds may tell them to protect themselves from further painful relationships by keeping people at a distance through altering their appearance.

Mode of dress. The second change noticed most frequently was in mode of dress. Younger children (ages five through ten) are often attracted to a particular set or type of clothing.

Nine-year-old Kristin is one of the children who displayed this warning sign. After her parents' divorce, Kristin wore the same outfit day after day. She wore it to school, came home, washed it, and wore it again the next day. Her mom, who worked two jobs to make ends meet, unfortunately was not home enough. When she was home, she was too preoccupied to notice.

In essence, the child was trying to hold on to her past by continually wearing the same outfit. As it happened, her father used to comment on how nice she looked wearing that particular outfit. After the divorce, Kristin felt such a loss that she was grasping at objects (in this case, the outfit) that could bring her comfort.

Changes in dress for teenage boys and girls tend to take on a more defiant aspect. If you were to venture to your local mall and take a look at the groups of teens there, you would see two primary groups. One group is dressed normally (a relative term) and is using the mall as a nineties version of the corner malt shop of the fifties. For them, the mall is a place to socialize. But there is also a second group of teens who congregate at the malls. These kids are usually dressed in dark clothing and wear unusual-looking hairstyles. The boys are usually unshaven, and both the boys and the girls have dangling earrings and are often smoking.

If you were to take an informal poll of how many of these kids in this second group are from divorced families, you would be shocked. It amazes me how often kids from divorced families congregate together. They all seem to be looking for support and for relationships with others whom they perceive as being safe. In this way, their own inferior feelings are less likely to enter into the relationship.

Change in mode of dress following divorce probably falls under one of these three reasons:

1. Teens and children are passively seeking attention. ("Don't forget about me; you need to pay more attention.")
2. Teens and children may be trying to punish the parent(s) or themselves out of anger. ("I wouldn't look this way if you had stayed together.")
3. Teens and children feel a sense of confusion and a loss of self-esteem and self-identity. ("I don't fit in with my old friends anymore. Nobody will accept me now.")

Who's wearing what? Since you have so much time on your hands, now I'm asking you to notice the children who are dressing differently or have stopped washing their hair. The truth is, if you narrow your field of observation to just those kids who fall within the Windows of Opportunity time frame, you should be able to keep up with those who are using hygiene and dress to signal trouble. If you do

It amazes me how often kids from divorced families congregate together. They all seem to be looking for support and for relationships with others whom they perceive as being safe.

notice changes in appearance, you should immediately begin looking for additional warning signs.

For further insight, use the checklist of Twenty-One Warning Signs of Crisis, which is found at the end of chapter 4.

> ### HERE'S WHAT YOU CAN DO TO HELP

The counseling process. You may want to talk to children or teens about your observations and ask them how things are going. Try your best to get them to open up and begin talking about the divorce and its impact on their lives. One of the most appropriate things you can do at this point is to be a friend and listen. I find that kids, especially teenagers, will openly talk about the changes in their clothing if you just take the time to ask them.

I particularly remember sixteen-year-old Curt, who went from wearing typical teenage clothing to wearing an all-black outfit with sequins and metal studs. When I asked him what he liked about his new look, he said, "I just sort of like it. It makes me feel tough, you know. Like nobody better bother me."

That conversation opened the door for us further to discuss what Curt meant by "nobody better bother [him]." The result was a lengthy discussion about his insecurity, and we concluded that his changes in clothing were a defense mechanism. He believed that if people looked at him and felt intimidated, then they wouldn't talk to him and wouldn't see his insecurity because he was from a broken home.

SCRIPTURAL PERSPECTIVE
Man looks at the outward appearance, but the Lord looks at the heart.
(1 Samuel 16:7)

 **WARNING SIGN 21**

My child stopped making eye contact.
This is perhaps the most subtle of all the warning signs; however, nearly every parent identified this symptom as being present at some point prior to the crisis. Lack of eye contact, in psychological terms, is often considered a shame-based response, meaning simply that the child does not feel comfortable looking you in the eye. Lack of eye contact generally means one or more of the following:

- It could reflect that the child is not being totally truthful and is afraid that looking you in the eye could reveal that fact.
- It could reflect that the child is feeling guilty about something.
- It could mean that the child is subconsciously angry at the parent.
- It could mean that the child may be feeling insecure about himself or herself or his or her position in the family.
- It could mean that the child's self-esteem is dangerously low.

Identifying the root of the problem. Try to identify which one of the above areas the lack of eye contact is resulting from. If, for instance, you identify that the reason for the lack of eye contact is that the child is not telling you the truth, then you really have two warning signs: (1) the lack of honesty, and (2) the inability to make eye contact. This inability indicates an underlying guilt that can lead to lowered self-esteem, anxiety, or depression.

```
┌────────────────────────┐
│   HERE'S WHAT YOU       │
│   CAN DO TO HELP        │
└────────────────────────┘
```

The counseling process. Confront the behavior, not the person. This warning sign is one that you don't want to ignore and hope it will go away. I've never known troubled children or teens to wake up one day with improved self-esteem and a commitment to quit lying. Working toward a change usually requires confrontation, boundaries, consequences, and a great deal of love.

When confronting lying, depersonalize the act as much as possible. In other words, you don't want to cause further damage to the child's self-esteem during the correcting process. Try to let children know *they* are okay but what they are doing is wrong.

Being specific. Children and teens who lie will seldom admit they are lying unless you are specific when confronting them. Gather evidence about their lie; collect witnesses if you have to. When it comes time to confront the child about the lie(s), keep the confrontation as objective as possible.

For example, you might say something like the following: "You know, Billy, I've known you for quite some time now. I've always respected you and trusted you as a friend. That's why I know that, for you to feel that you need to lie to me about this incident, something must really be troubling you. Would you like to talk about it?"

SCRIPTURAL PERSPECTIVE
Then the LORD God called to the man, and said to him, "Where are you?" And he said, "I heard the sound of Thee in the garden, and I was afraid because I was naked; so I hid myself." (Genesis 3:9-10, NASB)
O LORD, do Thine eyes look for truth? (Jeremiah 5:3, NASB)

⫷ **7** ⫸

HELPING CHANGE LIVES THROUGH A PARAPARENTING MINISTRY

Carrie and Kevin came to me several months ago after deciding to seek premarital counseling. Carrie, an airline stewardess, and Kevin, a radio show disc jockey, both came from single-parent families. Carrie's mom and dad divorced when she was twelve, while Kevin's parents divorced when he was only four.

During our subsequent sessions, Carrie and Kevin learned that neither of them really knew what a good marriage looked like. Indeed, how could they have expected to know, since it had not been modeled for them during their formative years? So, an important question arises: How can children of single-parent families learn to be committed wives and husbands? Who can teach them to keep their own marriages alive and happy?

This concept of needing to introduce two-parent role models to children of divorced families took shape one day as I was beginning a counseling session with Richie, a seven-year-old boy who had been having a tough time adjusting to his parents' divorce a year earlier. During the session, Richie mentioned that he was very excited about going to a baseball game later that day with Mike and Jeannine. When I asked him about Mike and Jeannine, Richie said they used to be friends of his parents before the divorce and lately they had begun inviting him over to the house. He added that a few weeks ago they took him to a movie and ice skating along with their own children.

Further inquiries about Mike and Jeannine revealed that they were a couple from Richie's church. They had two children of their own, and prior to the divorce of Richie's parents, both families used to get together regularly. During the month or two before I started seeing Richie, Mike and Jeannine had occasionally been including Richie in their family activities. In short, they had taken a special interest in him, and he really seemed to enjoy being with them as well.

Richie was experiencing the exact concept that had first occurred to me almost eight years earlier—a concept that would enable a child of a single-parent family to spend time with a two-parent family; a concept that would allow a child like Richie to observe, firsthand, how two parents relate to one another and how they handle parenting.

IN THIS CHAPTER

• *How to provide role models for children in single-parent families.*

• *Guidelines to help you generate interest in your single-parent family ministry.*

Richie's case pointed out just how effectively this concept could work. Mike and Jeannine cared enough about Richie to take on the added responsibility of helping him through a difficult time. Thus, they served as a model for the concept of married couples sharing their time and their lives with single-parent family children. Mike and Jeannine became the first prototype for ParaParents.

PARAPARENTS: THE FINAL PIECE OF THE PUZZLE

When it came time to come up with a catchy, nineties-type name for the people who would serve as helpers to single parents and their children, I was in a quandary. I thought about names like "parent helper," but that sounded too much like something you add to hamburger. I tried several different combinations of names until I arrived at the title *ParaParent*. This seemed like a natural fit, considering my exposure to the terms paramedic and paralegal.

Webster's Dictionary defines the word *para* as "a prefix meaning: 1. Beside, beyond. 2. Helping in a secondary way, accessory."[1] What better word to describe a person who stands beside a single parent, helping out through the critical task of parenting!

Fortunately, defining the qualifications and responsibilities for ParaParents was a much easier process than coming up with the name. Here are the basic qualifications for ParaParents:

1. ParaParents should be known in the church as being of sound moral character with proper biblical values on issues such as homosexuality and premarital sex.
2. ParaParents should be at least twenty-one years of age. (Senior citizens make great ParaParents.)
3. ParaParents need not ever have been parents. (Many couples without children are great role models.)
4. ParaParents must have the desire to help.
5. ParaParents should have about five hours a month to spend with the single-parent family and/or child.

FIGURE 7.1
THE SINGLE-PARENT CHILD POP QUIZ

Instructions: To the best of your ability, answer the five questions below.

1. As the child of a single parent, where do you find positive role models, particularly if you seldom see your other parent?
2. What does a healthy marriage look like?
3. How do two good parents act when they are together?
4. How do healthy two-parent families interact with their kids?
5. How do moms and dads show affection to each other?

Note: If you answered "I don't know" to any of these questions, you may need assistance in preparing to set up your own marriage and family.

---

6. ParaParents can be relatives of the family (grandparents, brothers, sisters, aunts, uncles, etc.).

The Role of ParaParents

Just as we saw with Richie's adopted family, the role of the ParaParents is not all that complex. The most important element between ParaParents and the single-parent family is *contact*. There is no set agenda and no regimen that must be followed for the relationship to be successful. In fact, the more natural and less structured the relationship is, the better. The ParaParent should simply keep in mind that the goal is to provide a positive example of married couples or a strong role model.

Let's start by taking a look at some ways ParaParents may interact with the single-parent family.

- They attend church together.
- They are involved in a mentoring relationship with some member of a single-parent family.
- They participate in home Bible studies together.
- They are available to answer questions or just to talk.
- They provide the opportunity for single parents to take a much-deserved break.
- They help the single-parent family member to develop appreciation for the arts.
- They go to a movie with a member of the single-parent family.
- They get together for lunch or dinner with the single-parent family member.
- They can baby-sit occasionally.
- They provide friendship, companionship, and support for single moms and dads.
- They go together as part of a blended family to sporting events, picnics, outings, or other activities.

As you can see from the wide variety of possible activities, one of the main purposes of ParaParenting is to give the child of the single-parent family an opportunity to see married couples interacting. A second purpose is to provide children with a positive role model of the same sex for them to identify with. Through this contact, they can gain a perspective of life that otherwise might not have been available to them.

Finding and Matching ParaParents with Single Parents

It really is quite easy to initiate the ParaParents ministry to single-parent families. For each family in your church who volunteers to become ParaParents as well as for those single parents who would like to connect with ParaParents, you can use the materials found in appendix D.

There are two very effective ways of matching the single parents with the ParaParents. The first process—which is usually handled by a pastor, staff member, or volunteer—entails the relatively simple process of sitting down with the two

The most important element between ParaParents and the single-parent family is contact. There is no set agenda and no regimen that must be followed for the relationship to be successful.

stacks of application/information forms and matching up similarities. A phone call from the staff member to both the single-parent family and the ParaParents will serve as the introduction. I suggest that it then becomes the responsibility of the single parent to call and arrange to get together with the ParaParents.

A second way of getting the two families together is to make the ParaParents cards available to the single parents. Place the cards in the church office, and then let the single parents file through the cards until they find ParaParents they know or who appear to be a good match for their family.

GENERATING INTEREST IN YOUR SINGLE-PARENT MINISTRIES

A kick-off message from a pastor is vitally important to the success of the ParaParenting ministry for single-parent families.

A kick-off message from a pastor is vitally important to the success of the ParaParenting ministry for single-parent families. This message should clearly illustrate the need for the church's two-parent families to rally in support of single-parent families. Following the message, you should find that many families will come forward to volunteer their support and that many single parents will also want to become involved.

Here are some other effective ways of getting the word out and increasing participation:

- Include an announcement in your church bulletin (see the sample in appendix D)
- Send an announcement out in your newsletter
- Make announcements in your various support groups
- Make announcements in your men's and women's Bible studies
- Make your ministry known and accessible to single parents in other churches
- Make announcements on Christian radio stations
- Do interviews on Christian radio shows
- Provide human interest stories for your local newspapers and provide information for their calendar of events
- Send an announcement home with *all* of the children in your church or school (Try not to make single parents feel they are being targeted. If you send it to all parents, they will know about the program and will share this information with single parents.)

All of these methods are very effective in generating interest in your new or existing single-parent ministries.

Keeping Track of Your Single-Parent Families with CareCards

CareCards (see appendix D) are necessary because it is difficult to remember who the single-parent families are within your church. These CareCards will allow the pastor, singles' minister, youth pastor, or any other staff person to keep an active file of your church's single-parent families. These current records will assist you in ministering to their special needs.

The single-parent family CareCard files should be kept active for a two-year period, as this corresponds with the Windows of Opportunity theory. The CareCard sample in appendix D can be duplicated for your use, or you may prefer to come up with your own variation. These cards should be kept in an alphabetical file in the church office for easy reference.

GROUP REINFORCEMENT

It is also a positive idea to get all the single-parent families along with all the ParaParents together about once each quarter. These meetings should be primarily designed as social functions but should also include a time for learning from each other and sharing experiences.

⚞ 8 ⚟
INTRODUCING
THE SINGLE-PARENT FAMILY MINISTRY
TO YOUR CONGREGATION

One of the important elements in generating interest in your single-parent ministry will be for the senior pastor or his or her designate to make an announcement from the pulpit. The following information represents some major points to help the congregation understand the necessity for such a ministry. These points are also designed to increase awareness and to foster participation.

I encourage you to personalize these major points for your message wherever possible by adding your own stories, specific information, and biblical references.

1. Single Parents Are Valuable to God and Are an Important Part of the Body of Christ

a. Make sure the single parents in your congregation know that they are a valuable part of your church. Take care to help them understand that your new (or expanding) single-parent ministry is being promoted because they need support, not because they are not capable parents.

b. Asking the Lord to provide this special group of parents with strength and encouragement will go a long way.

> Give proper recognition to those widows [mothers] who are really in need. But if a widow has children or grandchildren, these should learn first of all to put their religion into practice by caring for their own family and so repaying their parents and grandparents, for this is pleasing to God. . . .
>
> No widow [mother] may be put on the list of widows [mothers] unless she is over sixty, has been faithful to her husband, *and is well known for her good deeds, such as bringing up children*, showing hospitality, washing the feet of the saints, helping those in trouble and devoting herself to all kinds of good deeds. (1 Timothy 5:1-5,9-11, emphasis added)

Although this passage speaks to widows, I believe you can substitute the term "single mothers" into each spot you find the word "widows" and understand God's

151

message. We, as a body of believers, are required to help single mothers and fathers who are raising their children to love the Lord.

2. The Statistics Point Out That Single-Parent Families Are Critically in Need of Support

There's a divorce in the United States every twenty-seven seconds, and each year two million kids under eighteen will be caught in the middle of their parents' divorce.

- Since 1971, single-parent families have increased by about one million each year.[1]
- There's a divorce in the United States every twenty-seven seconds, and each year two million kids under eighteen will be caught in the middle of their parents' divorce.[2]
- Single-person households have grown by nearly five million since 1980 and now account for 24 percent of all American households.[3]
- Fifty-nine percent of all children born last year will spend some time growing up in a single parent home.[4]
- The number of single-parent family members in the U.S. who attend church is estimated to be at least fifty million.[5]
- The single-parent survey concluded that children from single-parent families are more likely to have problems than children from two-parent families.

The survey of 1,000 teens and children in counseling and in treatment centers revealed that 64 percent were from single-parent families. The survey concluded these kids were more prone to have problems with:

- Drugs
- Alcohol
- School grades
- Behavior
- Teen pregnancy
- Anger
- Sleep disorders
- Running away
- Defiance
- Self-esteem
- Suicidal thoughts
- Depression
- Eating disorders

3. The Church Needs to Get Involved

a. The church must sense its responsibility to the increasing number of single-parent families within the church and the surrounding community.

b. This responsibility includes a sense of obligation to the Word of God to help parents train up children in the way of the Lord.

c. There is really no support available in the secular world for single-parent families.

d. Our churches should be the most appropriately equipped organizations, in terms of resources and willingness, to take on this challenge.

e. Churches must have a vision for helping to reverse the out-of-control divorce cycle.

4. The Church Must Be Willing to Find Ways to Help Single-Parent Families

Let your congregation know that your church will soon be starting (or expanding) single-parent family support groups, which are comprised of: (1) adult single-parent support groups, (2) single-parent family teen support groups (ages thirteen and up), and (3) single-parent family children's support groups (ages six through twelve). Each group will offer a curriculum that covers relevant issues for single-parent families today. For instance, one of the best parts of this program is that the single parents will be in their support group learning about drug and alcohol use and abuse while the single-parent family teens and children are hearing a similar message tailored for them. This format is designed to generate positive conversations about these important topics not only at church, but at home as well.

a. The single-parent support group. Explain to your congregation that once a week for a six-month period of time the single parents from your church will have an opportunity to get together for an hour of fellowship, mutual support, and sharing of information.

The single-parent support group will work in the following manner: For the first three weeks of the month, the group will get together for a one-hour round-table discussion of current issues in their families. This will be an opportunity for them to share ideas, helpful hints, and problems, as well as to offer support and encouragement to one another. The fourth week will feature a thirty-minute discussion guide on specific relevant issues from the book *Helping Single Parents with Troubled Kids* and will be followed by a thirty-minute discussion period. The discussion guide should be presented by one of the church staff members or a lay leader, who will also lead the discussion.

The single-parent support group discussion guides (found in chapter 9) are designed to cover a one-year period, or two six-month sessions. After the year is up, an additional year's supply of lectures are available. If you wish to continue your groups, contact me at the address listed in the back of this book.

b. The single-parent family teen support group (ages thirteen and above). The same evening that the single moms and dads are in their support groups, the church will also be sponsoring a teen support group for single-parent family teenagers. Like the support group for their parents, the teens will get together for the first three weeks of the month for a time of fellowship, fun, encouragement, and the exchanging of ideas. The fourth week will also feature a specially designed thirty-minute discussion for teens from the book *Helping Single Parents with Troubled Kids* and will be followed by a thirty-minute discussion period. The discussion guide should be presented by one of the church's youth ministers or other staff members.

c. The single-parent family children's support group (ages six through twelve). Again, on the same evening that the single-parent family moms, dads, and teens are in their support groups, the kids from single-parent families will also get together. Like the teen support group, the children will get together for the first three weeks of the month for a time of fun, fellowship, and encouragement. The fourth week will also include a specially designed thirty-minute discussion for kids from the book *Helping Single Parents with Troubled Kids* and will be followed by a thirty-minute discussion period. The discussion guide should also be presented by one of the church's children's ministers or other staff members.

SUPPORT GROUP DISCUSSION GUIDES FOR SINGLE PARENTS

As we discussed earlier, it is an imperative part of the recovery process for single parents and their children to participate in the weekly support groups at your church. It is equally important that the material you present is fresh, stimulating, and above all, helpful. This chapter contains twelve discussion guides for single parents.

These discussion guides correspond with those in chapter 10, which are designed for teens' and children's support groups. Thus, while the single parents are in one room discussing problems related to drugs and alcohol, the teens and children are in their rooms discussing the same subject. The benefit of coordinating these lectures is to foster ongoing discussion between parent and child. Used correctly, these discussions will also provide a solid foundation of communication between parent and child that can be built upon.

Discussion suggestions for each session are set in italics throughout this chapter and chapter 10.

GROUP SESSION 1

YOUR FAMILY AND YOUR PARAPARENT

1. Why ParaParenting Is Important
A widely recognized issue facing single parents raising children is the lack of a role model who is the opposite sex from the custodial parent. Boys being raised by their single moms particularly need to identify with male role models. This identification process can be as simple as learning how to throw a baseball or as complex as discussing girls or dating. It is not a criticism of any mom to acknowledge that there are just some subjects her son would feel more comfortable talking over with another male.

It is equally important for daughters to identify with a healthy and consistent male role model. When girls grow up in a family where the father is absent, they have no firsthand knowledge of how moms and dads are supposed to act

IN THIS CHAPTER

● *Twelve sessions to use in your single parents' support group.*

155

around each other. By introducing ParaParents into the single-parent family unit, sons and daughters are able to observe and be a part of some of the dynamics that go on between husbands and wives, men and women, as well as sons and daughters.

2. What Types of Things ParaParents Do

The two most important connections to establish between the single-parent family and ParaParents are support and encouragement. Encouragement is vitally important when things seem to be overwhelming for the single parent. A phone call or a conversation over a cup of coffee is often all it takes to keep life in perspective.

Support is also important to single parents. ParaParents can help single moms and dads learn how to do things that used to be taken care of by the other parent. These things can include learning how to oversee a child's homework, do home repairs, or buy major items like cars.

ParaParents can also support single-parent families by just being there for the parent and child. I encourage single moms and dads to include ParaParents in school activities, church functions, and other social events.

3. Other Things ParaParents Can Do

- Attend church with their single-parent family members.
- Participate in home Bible studies with them.
- Get together with them for lunch or dinner.
- Baby-sit (occasionally).
- Provide friendship and companionship.
- Plan regular outings to the park or other recreational areas.

Ask group for input regarding how they can envision ParaParents helping out.

4. What ParaParents Aren't

- Financial support
- An "anytime" baby-sitter
- Someone to take your anger out on
- Someone to do the work you can't do
- A replacement for you as your child's parent (or for your ex-spouse as the absent parent)

5. Maintaining a Good Relationship Between ParaParents and Single Parents

Single parents should be responsibly involved in keeping the relationship with the ParaParents healthy. You can do this by:

1. Showing your appreciation regularly.
2. Not abusing the relationship.
3. Not being jealous if your children compare you to the ParaParents.
4. Being sure both you and the ParaParents talk about and understand your separate roles.

GROUP SESSION 2

HELPING CHILDREN UNDERSTAND DIVORCE

1. What Children Do and Don't Need to Know About the Divorce

Children are not blind to problems in the home. All children, even very young ones (ages two through five), know when things aren't quite right. They sense trouble even if they aren't old enough to comprehend what is happening. As a result of their sensitivity to their parents' conflict or turmoil, children may develop behavioral problems as their way of reacting to what they don't understand and what they fear.

Most experts agree that it is a mistake to shelter children over four years old from the fact that Mom and Dad aren't getting along very well. You need to be honest; the child will perceive you to be lying if your words say everything is okay, while your actions indicate otherwise.

Most parents have found it safe to limit the discussion to these facts: (1) Mom and Dad are having problems, and (2) sometimes married people simply need space between them. You must reassure children that they are going to be okay and that this is a problem between Mom and Dad. Make sure children know that the need for space applies only to husbands and wives and not to parents and kids. Clearly communicate that, even though they are not together, both parents still love the children.

Ask how some of the parents in your group have talked with their children about the divorce.

There is a limit to what children need to know. Be cautious not to transfer your angry or vengeful feelings to your child. Often, when a husband or wife feels violated or mistreated in a marriage, the natural reaction is to look for support for their feelings. This equates to choosing sides, and it is potentially very destructive to children. For instance, it serves no healthy purpose for a child to hear about a parent's extramarital affair.

Ask for examples of choosing sides.

2. Making Sure Kids Know the Divorce Wasn't Their Fault

Children, especially between the ages of three and ten, have a natural tendency to see things as being all good or all bad. There is very little room in their minds for variations or compromises. Subsequently, it is common for a child to take personal responsibility for a divorce.

Interviews with children of single-parent families who participated in the survey commonly produced statements such as, "If I hadn't made Dad (or Mom) yell at me, they would have stayed together," or "If I had just done better in school, my parents wouldn't have argued as much." It is a parent's responsibility to make sure the child does not feel responsible in any way for the divorce.

Ask for personal experiences from parents whose children felt they caused the divorce. Ask them to discuss how they handled the situation.

3. Dad Is Still Dad, and Mom Is Still Mom

During the divorce and for up to two years afterward, children need as much consistency as possible. They need to know that, even though Mom and Dad are not together, they haven't stopped being Mom and Dad.

A common pattern among older children and teens is to play (or manipulate) one parent against the other. In order to maintain healthy relationships between the children and both parents, moms and dads need to work together to set limits and boundaries on the child's behavior.

Ask for examples of when and how their children became manipulative following the divorce.

Single dads (and moms) need to avoid trying to compensate their guilty feelings for the divorce by becoming a Disneyland parent. A Disneyland dad (or mom) is a parent who will buy or do anything the child wants during visitation.

Ask for examples of how any of the parents or their ex-spouses have fallen into the mold of becoming a Disneyland dad or mom. How did they handle the problem?

4. Explaining Visitation

Most of the time, older children and teens know that Dad (or Mom) has a legal right to visitation. Often there is squabbling between parents about dates, times, and other conditions of visitation. These disagreements can make a child feel like a piece of property. With older children and teens, take the time to explain what visitation laws and agreements are all about. Consult your attorney if you have questions regarding problems that arise in regard to visitation.

Ask if any parents in your group can share how they talked to their children about visitation. Have parents take special note of how visitation problems were discussed.

5. Unfortunately, You're Not Alone: Divorce Is Common

There is comfort and security in numbers. Let your children know that somewhere around 50 percent of their friends are from single-parent or blended families. Let them know that there is a good chance some of their friends at school are also from divorced families. Indicate to them that it might be helpful to talk to these friends about how they managed to get through the divorce.

Ask your group how many of their friends or family members are divorced.

GROUP SESSION 3

DEALING EFFECTIVELY WITH ANGER

1. The Laws of Recovery

There are essentially four choices you can make as to how you cope with anger:

- You can keep your anger inside, which will eventually result in an ulcer or nervous breakdown (neither of which is a fun option).
- You can choose to withdraw and vegetate. (This is known as the "eat worms and die" method and is even less fun.)
- You can take your anger out on everyone around you. (This will make you a candidate for assassination.)
- You can decide to resolve your hurt and anger in a healthy way.

Ask the group members to discuss the reality of these four options. Ask if they know of any other ways of dealing with anger and how they can learn to feel differently.

2. The Three Elements of Resolving Anger

Remember: The longer you wait to start resolving your anger, the harder it is going to be. The recovery process includes three necessary attitudes:

a. Honesty

The heart is deceitful above all things and beyond cure. Who can understand it? (Jeremiah 17:9)

To recover, you must work your way out of your denial. Come to terms with the fact that you shared (at least to some extent) some responsibility for the divorce. Bear in mind that recovery is nearly an impossible feat to accomplish when you are consumed by the role of being the victim. The faster you stop pointing the finger or blaming your ex-spouse, the faster you can move forward with your life.

Ask your group members if any of them found themselves in the role of victim and how they got free of that role.

b. Forgiveness

Be kind to one another, tender-hearted, forgiving one another, even as God in Christ forgave you. (Ephesians 4:32, NASB)

Forgiveness starts with the understanding that God made each and every one of us. Since the fall of Adam and Eve, we as the human race have been imperfect and ultimately fallible.

Come to terms with the fact that divorce is, unfortunately, a human byproduct of our imperfect selves. But it is not for us to condemn ourselves or others for what is right or wrong, good or bad. Our Lord, and only He, is in a position to judge our actions. As Matthew 7:1 says, "Do not judge, or you too will be judged."

Forgiveness is tied directly to recovery. Finger-pointing or feeling victimized is counterproductive to forgiveness.

Ask the members of your group what types of things they are trying to forgive themselves or their spouses for.

c. Patience

When the way is rough, your patience has a chance to grow.
(James 1:4, TLB)

Anger is unresolved hurt feelings. It is not an emotion that can be stuffed down inside, as it will always surface and resurface. Anger does not pass quickly or easily; a process must be followed.

Ask for examples of how long it has taken some of the parents in your group to resolve their angry feelings. This should demonstrate that there is no right or wrong answer regarding recovery time.

Don't assume that you can work through your feelings of anger and hurt in a week, two weeks, or even months. People process these feelings at their own pace. You will find that time is directly proportionate to your honesty and forgiveness. In Ephesians 5:15-16, Paul wrote, "See then that you walk circumspectly, not as fools but as wise, redeeming the time, because the days are evil" (KJV). Learn to be patient with yourself and with others as God works through the circumstances of your lives.

Ask a few parents in your group how they have handled anger in their lives. Suggest that some who have been divorced a longer period of time share their coping mechanisms.

GROUP SESSION 4

YOU DON'T HAVE TO BE A SUPER-PARENT

Read Luke 2:41-50. This is the story of how Joseph and Mary went with Jesus to Jerusalem when He was twelve years old. On the way home, they discovered that Jesus was not with them, but had remained behind in Jerusalem. The message to parents in this scripture is rich. If Joseph and Mary, the parents chosen by God to give birth to and to raise Jesus, were human and fallible enough to leave the Messiah behind, how can we expect to be perfect parents ourselves? Discuss what this scripture means to various parents in your group. The valuable message in this and other Scriptures is simply to be the best parents we can be.

1. Admitting and Owning Your Mistakes

As role models, we as parents must learn to admit our human frailties to our children. Our kids need to know that we are just as capable of messing up as they are. When we make a mistake that impacts our children, it is incumbent on us to ask them for forgiveness. This is a sign of strength and maturity, not weakness.

Your willingness to admit and take responsibility for your mistakes will provide a positive model for your children. How can we expect our children to come to us when they have made mistakes if we have not created an environment where they feel comfortable being human? It is in these families where human mistakes are not acceptable that sons and daughters cannot come home and tell parents of drug or alcohol experiences, problems at school, or pregnancy.

Ask for examples from any parents in the group who have recently asked their children for forgiveness (or from those who may need to do so).

2. Serving One Father

Matthew 23:8 cautions us against calling anyone on earth our father: "For One is your Father, He who is in heaven" (NASB). We need to be clear with our children that they (as we) serve only one perfect Father and that the rest of us are normal, flawed people.

3. Correcting Mistakes

It should be of some consolation that there is really little you can do to your kids that will mess them up for life. Sure, divorce is a sad thing for everyone involved, but you each will get through it. Your ability to work through this and to help your kids cope will ultimately provide you with a tremendous sense of accomplishment.

Initiate a group discussion about the worst thing that each parent can remember doing to his or her child. Make a point of illustrating that the child got through it okay.

GROUP SESSION 5

RECOGNIZING AND UNDERSTANDING CRISIS
(PART ONE)

1. The Three Elements of Crisis

a. Potentially precipitating events. Some circumstances or events can precipitate a crisis and should be labeled "potentially hazardous" to the health of a single-parent family. These can be either internal problems, such as physical ailments, or external struggles, such as a death in the family or a divorce. Other examples are relocating to a different area, witnessing a traumatic event, being involved in a car accident, or experiencing an illness or injury.

b. Reacting strongly to events and circumstances. When such events or circumstances occur, they often produce strong emotional reactions or feelings of:

- Anxiety
- Depression
- Sadness
- Terror
- Anger
- Paranoia
- Isolation
- Persecution

c. A decreasing ability to function. A decrease in functioning is usually apparent in children and teens when the following problems occur:

- Poor or failing school grades
- Attendance problems at school
- Poor concentration level
- Acting out
- Sleeplessness
- Poor communication
- Depression
- Avoidance (isolation)
- Sickness
- Inability to get along with others
- Withdrawal

Ask the parents in your group to examine these three elements of a crisis to determine if their children may be having problems.

2. How a Crisis Differs from a Problem

a. Problem. A problem is generally defined as a situation that is difficult to deal with. Problems usually are not extremely difficult to work through; don't evoke feelings of high anxiety, fear, depression, or oppression; and don't cause other significant decreases in functioning.

b. Crisis. The following points indicate a crisis rather than a problem:

- A crisis can be brought on by one or more problems.
- A crisis evokes a reaction rather than a response.
- A crisis is generated by significant events and evokes moderate to major emotional tensions and anxiety.
- Crisis generally occurs when we are unable to understand or cope with a problem or event.

3. Recognizing and Responding to Crisis

- Identify the significant event that could lead to a crisis.
- Look for an emotional reaction to a crisis. This is an initial reaction in most cases, but it can be delayed up to six months.
- Look for a decrease in functioning (depression, change in sleep patterns or appetite, etc.).
- Try to increase and improve communication. Talk openly and honestly with your child about his or her needs and wishes.
- Be alert for further change.
- Consider counseling options.

Discuss with your group how they have handled crises in their lives and how they have helped their children manage a crisis.

GROUP SESSION 6

THE TWENTY-ONE WARNING SIGNS OF CRISIS
(PART TWO)

O Lord, do not Thine eyes look for truth? (Jeremiah 5:3, NASB)

Discuss with the group how Helping Single Parents with Troubled Kids *focused on the twenty-one most significant warning signs of crisis in teens and children who had been through a divorce. The importance of knowing and being able to recognize these warning signs is that it can help single parents move from a reactive to a proactive position to avert crisis.*

1. Inevitability of Changes in a Child's Behavior Following Divorce

It should be noted that changes in behavior are normal and are to be expected in children and teens as problems between parents increase. These problems generally intensify as the divorce nears and will generally continue on during the post-divorce period (usually for at least six months to a year). Normal reactions can vary widely but certainly include all signs listed in figure 9.1.

Be very cautious of children who do not emote or verbalize their feelings or distress over the divorce.

FIGURE 9.1
TWENTY-ONE WARNING SIGNS OF CRISIS

1   My child became lonely, quiet, or moody.
2   My child just seemed depressed.
3   My child's self-esteem was very low.
4   My child began having difficulty sleeping.
5   My child seemed so negative about everything.
6   My child began to isolate.
7   My child was often very angry and abusive.
8   My child's eating habits changed.
9   My child became argumentative and lied to me.
10 My child began fighting at school and at home.
11 My child's school grades began to fall.
12 My child began violating curfew times.
13 My child was arrested for shoplifting.
14 My child dropped out of once-loved activities.
15 I caught my child drinking (or taking drugs).
16 My child refused to go to church anymore.
17 My child became lazy and procrastinated regularly.
18 My child dated/befriended kids against my wishes.
19 My child became sexually active.
20 My child's appearance really changed.
21 My child stopped making eye contact.

Ask the parents in your group what types of behavior changes they noticed in their children during and after their divorce. Look for and point out similarities between their stories.

2. Recognizing the Twenty-One Warning Signs of Crisis

Parents should watch their children for warning signs that might indicate they are having problems coping with the divorce.

Be prepared to present and discuss the Twenty-One Warning Signs. After all the signs are presented, encourage the parents in your group to discuss them individually and to offer their personal experiences in dealing with children who manifested these signs.

GROUP SESSION 7

PARENTING STYLES

1. The Need for Discipline

In 1946, Dr. Benjamin Spock wrote a book entitled *The Common Sense Book of Baby and Child Care*. This book produced great controversy and misunderstanding about permissiveness in raising children.

In 1976 Dr. Spock wrote an article entitled "How Not to Bring Up a Bratty Child." In this article he stated, "The way to get a child to do what must be done is to be clear and definite each time. I'm not recommending the overbearing manner of a drill sergeant that would rub anyone the wrong way. The manner can be and should be friendly. A firm, calm approach makes the child much more likely to cooperate."[1]

Dr. Spock, whose influence promoted permissiveness in raising children, has been quoted as saying that he believes his approach of the late forties to be wrong. In fact, children do need discipline.

Ask your group if they recall how their parents raised them. Most group members were children during the Dr. Spock generation.

2. The Four Most Common Parenting Styles

a. The "let's be buddies" parent. "Let's be buddies" parents are most easily recognized by the following traits:

- They treat their children more like friends than children.
- They have a hard time being firm with their children, and/or they feel unwilling or unable to discipline their children.
- They feel slighted when their children prefer to spend time with a friend or with the other parent rather than with them.
- Their children tend to act disrespectful to them.
- Other parents tell them their children are taking advantage of them.
- Their children do not respect the limits and boundaries these parents set for them.

Ask the parents in your group if they can relate to any of the above characteristics.

b. The controlling parent. Controlling parents are most easily recognized by the following traits:

- They rely on threats to get their children to comply with their wishes.
- They keep increasing the consequences to make sure their children will comply.
- They feel personally assaulted or minimized when their children don't do exactly as they are told.
- They often consider their spouse to be too lax.
- They have children who do not feel comfortable coming to them with problems.
- Their children may cry easily or retreat when the parent is angry.
- They often see their children as too passive and unable to make independent decisions.

Ask the parents in your group if they can relate to any of the above characteristics.

c. The passive parent. Passive parents are most easily recognized by the following characteristics:

- They tend to overlook when their children bend or break the rules, even if they were told there would be consequences.
- They feel guilty when they have angry feelings toward their children.
- Their children manipulate them easily.
- They have difficulty saying no to their children.
- Their children often ignore directions or requests from them.
- They are often inconsistent in their rules, limits, and boundaries.

Ask the parents in your group if they can relate to any of the above characteristics and if they can provide examples.

d. The balanced parent. Balanced parents are most easily recognized by the following traits:

- They demonstrate unconditional love and acceptance. Because of the attitude of the parent, the child understands that it is human to make mistakes or to do bad things at times. Even during these times the child knows that he or she is loved. In other words, the balanced parent disciplines the situation, not the child.
- They establish firm and fair boundaries. Balanced parents establish reasonable expectations and boundaries in advance. They communicate these boundaries to their children and make sure they are clearly understood and agreed upon. They listen to their child's input when appropriate. Consequences for violating a boundary are discussed in advance and are followed through.

- They are consistent. Balanced parents respond to situations or problems the same way day after day, week after week.
- They are flexible. Balanced parents are flexible rather than rigid. They encourage conversation in conflict and are able to change their minds if it is fair and appropriate to do so. Children feel they have a voice in decisions that affect them.
- They communicate fairness. Balanced parents are fair. They allow for communication that goes both ways and allows the child to feel valued in the relationship. Balanced parents ask children for their opinions and validate their feelings.

Ask the parents in your group if they can relate to any of the above characteristics. Determine how many in your group feel they are balanced parents or were children of balanced parents.

GROUP SESSION 8

TALKING WITH OUR KIDS ABOUT ALCOHOL
(PART ONE)

1. Alcohol as a Drug

Alcohol is often the first level of escape for teens and children, just as it is for adults who would prefer to avoid the pain of reality. A secondary problem with alcohol use is that it is a depressant. When consumed by young people who may already be depressed from the breakup of the family, it can compound and intensify their depression. Many scenarios involving teen suicide include the use of alcohol.

An April 1991 study, released by Surgeon General Antonia Coello Novello, revealed that eight million teenagers—or more than a third of the nation's teenage student population—drank alcohol weekly and nearly a half-million are "binge" drinkers who consume an average of fifteen drinks each week.[2]

Ask parents in your group to share how they have found their children drinking or why they have reason to believe their children may be drinking.

2. The Rights of Parents

In rating parents, no points are taken off for good detective work. Often during interviews with parents, I learned that they became aware of their children's activities with alcohol by looking in their rooms. Sometimes these discoveries were innocent while at other times the parent was searching the room. I feel it is well within parents' rights to look through their children's rooms whenever they detect that something going on merits their attention.

Ask if there are any parents in the group who have found alcohol in their children's rooms. Ask them how they handled the situation.

3. An Education Plan for Parents and Children

Kids know more than you think they do about alcohol, so don't be afraid to bring up the subject. Even children as young as four years old have heard about alcohol abuse from playmates, at preschool, or on television.

With young children it is effective to sit down and begin talking casually with them about alcohol abuse. You may start by saying, "Does your teacher at school talk to the class about drugs and alcohol?" From that point you can ask them what they know about the subject. Determine if they know that alcohol is bad for them and if they know what happens when kids drink. You should also let them know that you want them to come home and tell you if they have been offered drugs or alcohol at school or other places.

Ask the parents in your group how they have discussed this subject with their younger children.

With older children and teens you can be more direct. Let them know that you are concerned about alcohol and all the peer pressure they may be receiving. Ask them what they have learned about drugs and alcohol from school or from friends, and ask if any of the kids they know from school use drugs or alcohol. It is important for you to know just how much they know. You should also tell them that it is okay to call you if they ever find themselves in a compromising position—either having drunk too much to drive or being stranded where there is drinking going on.

> **FACT:** Drunk driving accounts for 50 to 55 percent of all traffic deaths among fifteen- to seventeen-year-olds.[3]

4. Warning Signs of the Use of Alcohol

- Decreased function
- Fighting/aggressiveness
- Change in sleeping patterns
- Staying away from home
- Moodiness
- Lack of eye contact
- School problems
- Decreased appetite
- Odor of alcohol
- Change in friends
- Use of breath mints to cover odor of alcohol

Ask the parents in your group if any of their children have displayed some of these symptoms.

GROUP SESSION 9

TALKING TO OUR KIDS ABOUT DRUGS
(PART TWO)

Recap some of the items that were contained in group session 9 prior to moving on to the warning signs of drug use.

Statistics from the single-parent family survey include (1) that 43 percent of the adolescents stated they had used drugs other than marijuana, and (2) that 18 percent of the children stated they had done so.

1. Cocaine

a. Description. Cocaine is a derivative of the coca plant grown primarily in South America. It is processed into a white, powdery substance that can be "snorted" through the nostrils, smoked in water pipes, injected, or rolled and smoked like a cigarette. Cocaine is most commonly packaged in small amber vials, in small zip-lock baggies, or in folded pages of magazines or notebook paper. Cocaine is generally regarded to be the toughest drug to give up.

b. Warning signs of use. Warning signs of cocaine use include the following symptoms:

- Flushed appearance
- Constant sniffing
- Irritated mucous membranes
- Dilated pupils (during four-hour period after use)
- Paranoia
- Need for more money
- Mood swings
- Anxiety/panic attacks
- Hyperactivity often followed by a depressed mood
- Avoidance of family, church, and/or friends

Ask for discussion from parents in your group whose children have displayed any of these symptoms.

c. Equipment used. Paraphernalia used in taking cocaine may include the following items:

- Straws
- Razor blades
- Mirrors
- Vials
- Small spoons

2. Marijuana

Statistics from the single-parent family survey include (1) that 69 percent of the teenagers stated they had smoked marijuana, and (2) that 38 percent of the children stated they had smoked marijuana.

FACT:
1. One marijuana cigarette does the same damage to the lungs as fourteen tobacco cigarettes.
2. Because of processing advances, marijuana today is ten times stronger than it was in the sixties.
3. Marijuana can remain in the fatty tissues of the system for thirty days or longer.
4. Marijuana is psychologically as well as physically addictive.[4]

---

a. Description. Marijuana is a plant that is grown primarily in South America, although it is also grown in Hawaii and the Far East. In its most common form, it is a green leafy substance that is often ground into fine particles. It may also be processed into a form called hashish, which is a brownish-green substance resembling the color of a dirt clod. Marijuana is most often rolled into cigarettes and smoked, while hashish is smoked in various kinds of pipes. Marijuana is most commonly packaged in zip-lock plastic baggies.

b. Warning signs of marijuana use. Users of marijuana will usually manifest at least one of the following symptoms: decreased motivation, changes in appetite, and memory lapses. Medical and psychological profiles of marijuana users also document resulting hormonal imbalances and personality imbalances. In addition, other physical consequences that result from the use of marijuana include (1) reproductive dysfunctions such as impotence and (2) the destruction of brain cells.

GROUP SESSION 10

TALKING WITH OUR KIDS ABOUT SEX

1. The Scope of the Problem of Sexual Activity Among Teens and Children

A 1990 survey conducted as research for the Centers for Disease Control revealed that 54 percent of all high school students have had sexual intercourse.[5] Among ninth grade students, 40 percent have had sex. By tenth grade, the figure has reached 48 percent; by eleventh, 57 percent; and by twelfth, 72 percent. Increasing the concern, the single-parent family survey revealed that children and teens (especially girls) who have limited exposure to their fathers are more likely to engage in premarital sex. Three conditions contribute to making single-parent children and teens, particularly girls, a high-risk group.

- They may be searching for love, acceptance, relationship, and attachment. This search often begins when the father (or another significant male role model) leaves the home.
- They may be angry and view a sexual relationship as a means of expressing their anger toward their parents.

- The relationship loss that occurred during the divorce has created a desire to find relationship. Young people from divorced families often do not know how to relate to the opposite sex due to the lack of role-modeling. As a result, they may see a sexual relationship as appropriate.

> **FACT:** More than one million teenage girls become pregnant each year. Four out of five of them are unmarried, and 30,000 are under the age of fifteen.[6]

2. The Need for Dialogue

Don't shy away from talking to your children about sex. Let them know that sexual feelings are a normal part of the maturing process. Let them know that along with these increased sexual feelings come increased responsibilities, such as abstinence.

It is sometimes a good idea for a single mother to ask a close friend, family member, family doctor, or youth pastor to discuss sex with a male child if the mother feels particularly uncomfortable doing so. This male-to-male approach can sometimes be far less stressful for both the child and the mother.

Ask how some of the parents in your group went about addressing this topic with their children. Ask them to discuss how they approached the topic, how they conducted the conversation, and at what age they felt it appropriate to begin these talks.

3. Recommended Reading

Some good reading materials on this subject are *Handling Your Hormones* by J. Burnes (Harvest House, 1986), and *Why Wait?* and *The Teenage Q & A Book*, both by Josh McDowell (Here's Life, 1987; Word, Inc., 1990).

GROUP SESSION 11

ESTABLISHING AND MAINTAINING BOUNDARIES

1. Defining Boundaries

Ask the parents in your group for their definition of boundaries.

Boundaries can be defined by envisioning them as our property lines. We are responsible for everything within our property (or control), and we have no right to set boundaries in areas outside of our control. Boundaries are our way of communicating:

- Who we are
- Who we are not
- What we want
- What we don't want

- What is acceptable to us
- What is not acceptable to us

2. Qualities of Boundaries

Reasonable boundaries consist of the following three qualities:

- They must be fair and appropriate.
- They must be consistent.
- They must be firm but not necessarily rigid.

3. Scriptural Examples

Two of the best illustrations of God's boundaries are found in Job 38 and Genesis 18.

a. Firm boundaries. In the book of Job, the Lord says to Job, "Where were you when I laid the earth's foundation? Tell me, if you understand. Who marked off its dimensions? Surely you know! Who stretched a measuring line across it?" (Job 38:4-5). The Lord continues making His limits known to Job by asking him, "Who shut up the sea behind doors when it burst forth from the womb, when I made the clouds its garment and wrapped it in thick darkness, *when I fixed limits for it and set its doors and bars in place, when I said, 'This far you may come and no farther; here is where your proud waves halt'*" (Job 38:8-11, emphasis added).

The book of Job offers an illustration of God's firm boundaries. In the passage above, God is describing how He set boundaries on His creation, specifically the ocean in this case. This is an example of a firm boundary set by God, and God used these words to assure Job of His sovereignty.

b. Flexible boundaries. Conversely, in Genesis 18, God provides us with an illustration of how He can be flexible in His boundaries:

> The men turned away and went toward Sodom, but Abraham remained standing before the LORD. Then Abraham approached him and said: "Will you sweep away the righteous with the wicked? What if there are fifty righteous people in the city? Will you really sweep it away and not spare the place for the sake of the fifty righteous people in it? Far be it from you to do such a thing—to kill the righteous with the wicked, treating the righteous and the wicked alike. Far be it from you! Will not the Judge of all the earth do right?"
>
> The LORD said, "If I find fifty righteous people in the city of Sodom, I will spare the whole place for their sake." (Genesis 18:22-25)

You may recall the entire story, in which a bold yet humble Abraham negotiated with God until He agreed that He would even spare the city of Sodom if there had been ten righteous people. This is a great example of how the Lord, who is a perfect and loving Father, can be flexible in His boundaries.

Discuss these two passages of Scripture that describe boundaries. Talk about how boundaries can serve as a strong and necessary wall when they need to stand against the invasion of others. Talk about how at other times our boundaries can be less rigid and solid and more open and flexible—more like a chain-link fence than a concrete wall.

Also discuss the three qualities of boundaries and how they relate to Scripture.

4. Communicating Boundaries to Your Children

- Make your boundaries known to your children.
- Be clear where the boundaries are.
- Let your children know why the boundary is there.
- Let your children negotiate with you about your boundaries when appropriate.
- Let your children establish their own boundaries.
- Honor the boundaries of others and they will honor yours.

Close by discussing these points about boundaries. Challenge parents in your group to go home and begin setting boundaries immediately. Ask if any of the parents in your group would like to commit to setting a boundary this week and then reporting back next session about how it went.

5. Recommended Reading

A book to read for help in continuing to work on setting boundaries is *Changes That Heal*, by Dr. Henry Cloud (Zondervan, 1992).

GROUP SESSION 12

VITAL CONCEPTS FOR IMPROVING SELF-ESTEEM IN CHILDREN AND TEENS

1. Perfect (??) Role Models

Ask your group members if they can remember any good role models from television when they were growing up. (Some examples you can use are Ozzie and Harriet from "The Ozzie and Harriet Show," Jim and Margaret from "Father Knows Best," and Ward and June from "Leave It to Beaver." Ask the group, "Who are the parental role models today, and where do we find them?"

These seemingly well-adjusted television role models gave many of us the illusion that parents ought to be perfect. Not surprisingly, when home life didn't turn out to be the way it appeared during thirty-minute sitcoms, parents often felt depressed and inadequate. Unfortunately, in the real world we are asked to do our best twenty-four hours a day for 365 days a year.

2. Barbie Dolls and Nintendo Games

No matter how trite the saying, there is merit in quality versus quantity of time spent with children and teens. One of the hardest things for single parents to do is to have fun playing with their children of the opposite sex, doing the things they like to do. Single dads need to understand the importance of meeting children and teens on their levels. During visitations, if daughters like to play with Barbies, dads need to play with Barbies, too, and at least give the illusion of enjoying it. Conversely, if sons enjoy Nintendo, moms should try to enjoy a game of Super Mario Brothers.

Remember, expecting a child or teen to meet you on your level is unreasonable and will undermine your relationship with your children.

3. Children—on Loan from God

We as parents should always remember that God has entrusted His children to our care for a very specific period of time. Our offspring are His children, just as we are His children.

If you were to draw a graph illustrating what the task of parenting—and specifically discipline—looks like, you would probably draw a sharp incline from the child's birth through age ten. From ages ten to fourteen, the line levels off gradually and then begins declining slowly as the child approaches upper adolescence and adulthood. It is this "de-parenting" model that allows children to develop the inner dependence and self-esteem that prepare them to go out on their own.

4. Active Listening

Some techniques of active listening will go a long way in helping you to be a more successful parent. First, always make eye contact with your children when they are talking to you, or when you are talking with them.

Second, respond; don't react. Responding is a process, while reacting is a reflex. Responses require thought, self-control, feeling, and consideration of ramifications and consequences. Reactions involve impulse. They are short and sometimes hurtful. Reactions are often reflexes of hurt and/or anger.

5. Positive Reinforcement

If you can gain compliance from your kids through positive reinforcement, you are doing a good job. Positive reinforcement techniques include:

- Praising your children often.
- Letting them know they do things well.
- Talking to them about their spiritual gifts.
- Catching them doing things right and then immediately telling them so.
- Praising the child and disciplining the action.
- Finishing off all punishment with a compliment or other indication that you still love and accept the child.

⊰ 10 ⊱
Support Group Discussion Guides for Children and Teenagers of Single-Parent Families

As in chapter 9, discussion suggestions for each session are set in italics.

YOUR FAMILY AND YOUR PARAPARENT

Ask the kids in your group if they ever feel as if they would enjoy having a man around to talk to when their dads aren't around. Ask those who live with their dads if they ever miss talking to their moms about "mom stuff." Pose the question of what types of things they wish they could talk about but don't with their parents.

Ask your group of children and teens whom they think of as role models for how married people are supposed to act together, since their parents are separated.

Ask your group of children and teens the following question: "If there was a way to bring a married couple or a single adult who cared a lot about you into your lives to do stuff with you, would you be interested?"

Let them know there are people who care about them and want to help. They are called ParaParents.

1. What ParaParents Are and What They Do

- ParaParents can be friends or family members, a married couple or a single person.
- ParaParents are people who will be there for you to provide support and guidance.
- ParaParents are adults you can talk to when you can't or prefer not to talk to your mom or dad.
- ParaParents are volunteers to help you and your mom or dad cope with some of the emotional stuff that happens after parents divorce.
- ParaParents go on outings with you, to school plays, to ball games, and to other activities where you would like an adult friend to come along.

IN THIS CHAPTER

- *Twelve sessions to use in your children's and teenagers' support group.*

175

2. What ParaParents Aren't

- They aren't there to tell you what to do.
- They aren't baby-sitters.
- They aren't there for you to take your anger out on them.
- They aren't a replacement for your real father or mother.
- They aren't foster parents.
- They aren't there to get mad at you.
- They aren't there to buy you things or spend money on you.

Ask the children and teens to discuss other ways they can see ParaParents as being nice to have around.

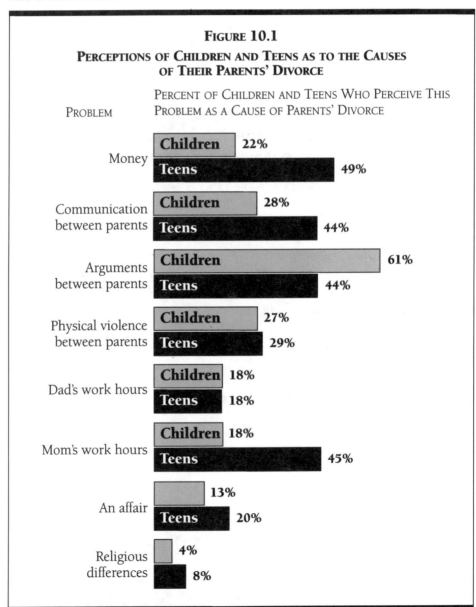

Figure 10.1

Perceptions of Children and Teens as to the Causes of Their Parents' Divorce

Problem	Percent of Children and Teens Who Perceive This Problem as a Cause of Parents' Divorce
Money	Children 22% / Teens 49%
Communication between parents	Children 28% / Teens 44%
Arguments between parents	Children 61% / Teens 44%
Physical violence between parents	Children 27% / Teens 29%
Dad's work hours	Children 18% / Teens 18%
Mom's work hours	Children 18% / Teens 45%
An affair	13% / Teens 20%
Religious differences	4% / 8%

GROUP SESSION 2

UNDERSTANDING AND EXPLAINING DIVORCE

Ask your group what they feel were the main factors that caused their parents' divorce.

1. Understanding the Divorce

In the single-parent family survey, the results listed in figure 10.1 (on page 176) indicate the perceptions of teens and children as to the primary causes of their parents' divorce.

Discuss these eight primary issues and ask how many of the kids in your group observed similar problems in their homes. The idea is to get them to focus on situations that were totally out of their control as factors of the divorce.

2. No Fault Divorce

Ask children and teens in your group to specify who they thought was most responsible for the divorce (see figure 10.2 on the next page). The purpose is to get them to see that placing blame or responsibility does not have to be part of the recovery process.

Again, it's important to focus their attention away from themselves as the cause of the divorce. Talk to them about how no single person, especially a child or teenager, could have that much power and influence.

3. Choosing Sides

Start by asking for their ideas of what choosing sides means after a divorce.

Choosing sides is a common occurrence following a divorce. It is common for parents to try to get children to side with them during and after the divorce. It is also common for children to feel as if they need to choose between parents after a divorce.

Begin a round-table discussion about how each member of the group felt pressure from one or both parents to take that parent's side. Ask them to share some of these experiences and talk about how they handled the situations. Encourage them to share how difficult it was to feel pulled apart from both parents.

GROUP SESSION 3

DEALING WITH ANGRY FEELINGS

1. Anger and the Laws of Recovery

There are essentially four choices you can make as to how you cope with your anger:

- You can keep your anger inside, which will eventually result in causing you physical problems (e.g., stress, stomach problems, headaches).

- You can choose to withdraw (e.g., vegetate, keep to yourself, isolate).
- You can take your anger out on everyone around you.
- You can decide to resolve your hurt and anger in a more healthy and productive manner.

Ask your group members if they can think of some ways of resolving their feelings (e.g., talking to someone or exercising) without doing self-destructive things.

2. The Three Elements of Resolving Anger

Remember: The longer you wait to start resolving your angry feelings, the harder it is going to be.

a. Honesty

We are all sons of one man; we are honest men. (Genesis 42:11, NASB)

The heart is deceitful above all things and beyond cure. Who can understand it? (Jeremiah 17:9)

To recover, you must work your way out of your denial. That means that you have to come to terms with the facts of the divorce.

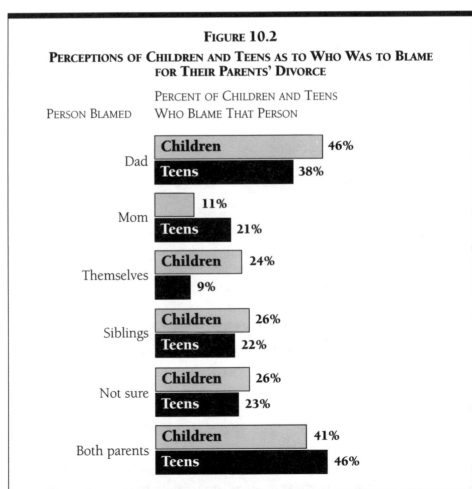

FIGURE 10.2

PERCEPTIONS OF CHILDREN AND TEENS AS TO WHO WAS TO BLAME FOR THEIR PARENTS' DIVORCE

PERCENT OF CHILDREN AND TEENS
PERSON BLAMED — WHO BLAME THAT PERSON

Person Blamed	Children	Teens
Dad	46%	38%
Mom	11%	21%
Themselves	24%	9%
Siblings	26%	22%
Not sure	26%	23%
Both parents	41%	46%

Talk with your group about reasons for divorce and the necessity of looking at these reasons honestly. Often we don't want to admit that our parents are imperfect and may have done bad things to each other that led to the divorce.

b. Forgiveness

Be kind to one another, tender-hearted, forgiving one another, even as God in Christ forgave you. (Ephesians 4:32, NASB)

Discuss how forgiveness starts with understanding that we are all imperfect and fallible. Help your group to understand that divorce is an unfortunate byproduct of our human, imperfect selves. Remind children and teens that it is not for us to condemn ourselves or others for what is right or wrong, good or bad. Our Lord, and only He, is in a position to judge our actions. As Matthew 7:1 directs us, "Do not judge, or you too will be judged."

Discuss with the group that forgiveness is tied directly to their ability to recover from the divorce. Finger-pointing, blaming, and feeling like a victim all hinder forgiveness. Ask some of the members of your group for examples of how they have forgiven or are trying to forgive their parents for the divorce.

c. Patience

When the way is rough, your patience has a chance to grow. (James 1:4, TLB)

Anger is unresolved hurt feelings. It is not an emotion that can be stuffed inside, as it will always surface and resurface again. Anger does not pass quickly or easily; a process must be followed.

Ask the children and teens in your group for examples of how long it has taken them to resolve their feelings of anger and how some of them have accomplished this. This should demonstrate that there is no right or wrong answer regarding recovery time.

Don't assume that you can work through your feelings of anger and hurt in a week, two weeks, or even months. People process these feelings at their own pace. You will find that time is directly proportionate to your honesty and forgiveness. In Ephesians 5:15-16, Paul writes, "See then that you walk circumspectly, not as fools but as wise, redeeming the time, because the days are evil" (KJV). Learn to be patient with yourself and with others as God works through the circumstances of your lives.

Ask for examples from children and teens whose parents have been divorced longer to share how they worked through angry feelings.

GROUP SESSION 4

GOD GAVE US FEELINGS FOR A REASON

1. Getting in Touch with Your Feelings

The word *feelings* (or a derivative of the word) appears twenty-seven times in the *New International Version* of the Bible. Throughout the Bible, God gives us messages of how we are supposed to share our feelings with others.

Talk to your group about feelings. Start out with an explanation of the term. Share Webster's Dictionary definition of feelings as: "a state of mind: emotion or a general emotional condition."1

2. Facing Your Feelings

As a general rule, our feelings typically cause us problems under certain conditions. They cause us problems:

a. When we're not in touch with our feelings. Even though we may not be in touch with what we are feeling, those feelings will cause us problems anyway. Often, our own denial (or our fear of facing the truth) will block our feelings in our subconscious (the part of our mind where thoughts and feelings take place that we aren't aware of).

Rest assured, feelings blocked in the subconscious will always surface. They may show up in physical problems (stomach ulcers, hypertension, stress) or in our relationships with ourselves, with others, and with God.

b. When we don't understand our feelings. Often when we don't understand our feelings, we believe we must keep them inside. The steps to understanding your feelings are: (1) give thought to them, (2) pray about them, and (3) if they are not clear, talk to others who can help you understand them.

c. When we have nobody to talk to about our feelings. Sometimes when we are troubled by various thoughts and feelings, we feel we have nobody to turn to. The truth is that many people would love to help. Pastors, youth leaders, ParaParents, friends, and relatives can often offer solutions if you simply give them a chance.

d. When we believe our feelings are so bad that we can't share them. Sometimes we forget what God is telling us throughout the Bible in His messages of forgiveness. For instance, Romans 5:8-9 gives us a powerful picture of God's love and forgiveness: "God demonstrates his own love for us in this: While we were still sinners, Christ died for us. Since we have now been justified by his blood, how much more shall we be saved from God's wrath through him!"

Talk to the children and teens in your group about the fact that they are not alone in their feelings. They have not thought, felt, or done anything that countless others before haven't done. Remind them that Christ died for all of their sins.

e. When we don't want to take responsibility for our feelings. We all need to take responsibility for our own feelings. This doesn't mean you should feel responsible for anyone else's feelings or for the feelings of others that caused the divorce. However, it does mean that you should be responsible for your feelings and that only you are responsible for resolving them. No one else can do that for you.

GROUP SESSION 5

WORKING THROUGH THE TOUGH TIMES

1. Problems Versus Crises

There are problems and there are crises, but there is a difference between the two. A problem is defined as a situation that is difficult to deal with. Problems are usually easier to deal with and don't evoke strong feelings of anxiety or depression.

A crisis, on the other hand, can produce feelings of being overwhelmed, hopeless, and helpless. A crisis can bring about a decrease in your ability to function, while a problem usually doesn't.

Ask your group members for examples of some problems and crises they have gone through in their lives. Help them distinguish between the problems and the crises by examining them in light of the elements of a crisis, which are suggested in the section that follows.

2. The Three Elements of a Crisis

a. A potentially precipitating event. Events that tend to bring about crises can be either internal problems, such as a physical ailment, or an external struggle, such as a death or divorce in the family. Some other examples of crisis-producing circumstances can include relocating (moving to new schools, neighborhoods, etc.), being involved in a serious car accident, witnessing a traumatic event (gang shootings), or experiencing a severe illness or injury (personally or in the family).

b. Strong emotional responses. Such events as those above or other comparable circumstances can produce a significant emotional reaction such as:

- Anxiety
- Depression
- Sadness
- Terror
- Paranoia
- Isolation
- Persecution

c. A decrease in functioning. These signs may be indications that you are not functioning as well as you did prior to your parents' divorce. In fact, these may be signs that you are having problems and should talk to someone who can help you deal with your feelings about the divorce.

- Poor or failing grades or poor attendance at school
- Inability to concentrate

- Acting out
- Sleeplessness
- Poor communication with others
- Depression
- Sickness
- Avoidance or isolation
- Inability to get along with others
- Antisocial behavior (shoplifting, stealing, cutting classes, drinking or using drugs, etc.)

Ask the children and teens in the group if they have ever experienced any of these decreased abilities to function. Ask them to explain what was it like to feel the way they did and how they worked through those feelings.

3. Handling a Crisis

- Don't isolate. Resist the depression you are feeling that makes you prefer to be alone.
- Talk to others (your mom and/or dad, your youth pastor or pastor, your ParaParents, or a counselor) about your problems.
- If you start to feel worse, don't be afraid to ask someone for help.

GROUP SESSION 6

DEALING WITH CHANGES

1. Common Physical Changes That Follow Divorce

- One parent moves out.
- You have to relocate (to a different house, apartment, town, or state).
- You have new friends and schools due to a change in residence.
- Family finances often become more strained.
- You may have fewer things (cars, vacations, clothes, etc.).

Talk to children and teens about these changes. The most valuable experience for this group is for them to share some of their personal stories regarding how they learned to cope with changes in their lives. Ask them how they felt and acted during these times and what adjustments they had to make.

2. Common Emotional Changes That Follow Divorce
a. A sense of loss.
Discuss that the obvious loss is one parent being gone. Discuss also that probably the most devastating loss is that both parents are no longer together and the family unit has been severed. Encourage children and teens to talk about how they learned to handle that grief.

b. A wide array of feelings, the most notable of which are depression, anxiety, and stress.

Again, solicit personal stories from teens and children about how these three emotions entered into the post-divorce period and how they may have worked through some of those feelings.

c. The stigma of being from a single-parent family.

Sadly, kids from single-parent families often feel they will never be accepted into the same circle of friends they had before the divorce. Your words will not mean nearly as much to them as will some of the stories from the members of the group. They need to hear from other teens and children that they were not treated any differently by their peers after the divorce.

3. Common Changes in the Family

Even though it may feel like the divorce had the hardest impact on you, it is necessary to remember that your parents and your brothers and sisters were also impacted by the divorce.

Remind the children and teens in the group that it is not their responsibility to take care of the rest of the family. Children with codependent traits (taking care of others and being more concerned for the feelings of others than themselves) will naturally try to make everyone else feel better at the expense of their own feelings. Identify kids in your group who fit this pattern and help them to take responsibility only for their own feelings.

One of the hardest things for young people to understand after a divorce is that some parents don't seem interested in them any longer. You may even have gone through periods following your parents' divorce when one of your parents didn't seem interested in visiting with you. Divorced parents go through many changes too, and they also have to make a number of difficult adjustments in their own lives.

Ask the children and teens for their perspective on this kind of situation and how they felt during that time.

It is also appropriate to talk to them about the stress, confusion, and sometimes anger that parents can experience during and after the divorce.

Make sure the children in your group don't associate the lack of visitation with the divorce being their fault or with their not being good or important enough to the parent. It is okay to suggest that moms and dads can "lose their way" during divorce and that sometimes it takes time for them to restore order to the family. Nonetheless, be careful not to criticize either parent for a lack of visitation.

GROUP SESSION 7

MOVING ON AND MAKING GOOD DECISIONS

We have already discussed how divorce can cause trauma in young people's lives. The message in this session is how to pick yourself up, dust yourself off, and move forward.

1. No More Victims of Divorce

The divorce was not the responsibility of teens or children in this group. However, when we look at the circumstances of the divorce of your parents, it is easy to see how many of you can begin feeling like victims in the divorce.

The role of a victim is unique. It is a feeling of powerlessness and hopelessness.

Use the analogy of the tide flowing in and out at the beach. The seaweed comes in and then back out without independence or power.

2. No More Bad Decisions

"Victim" thinking often produces other problems or even further crisis. Sometimes children and teens like you feel they are victims and have no ability to think for themselves. If this happens, you can find yourselves making bad decisions—decisions of whether or not you should drink, if you should hang around with a different crowd, if you could get by with cutting school or experimenting with drugs, and other choices like these. Wrong decisions can often lead to a rapid downhill slide after divorce.

Ask your group if any of them have ever felt themselves slipping into the victim's role after their parents were divorced. Ask them if they have made bad decisions that caused them even more problems later.

3. No More Martyrs

Children and teens who feel as if they are the ones who suffer because of the divorce and who accept the role of the victim following their parents' divorce can become martyrs. Martyrs are people who feel good when other people feel sorry for them. Martyrs enjoy sympathy and attention, and sometimes they continue to act out the roles of being victims and martyrs so that they can continue getting attention.

Discuss how this kind of attention may look and feel important to children and teens who have been through divorce. Explain that this attention is misdirected and unhealthy in the long run. Explain that they can get trapped in these roles and that the longer they remain in them, the harder it is to regain control of their lives. Encourage them to decide not to be victims or martyrs any longer.

4. Freeing Yourself from the Victim/Martyr Role

a. Don't be lazy. The victim/martyr role requires that you be as helpless as possible. This is a lazy personality to be trapped in. If you want to feel better about your life and begin regaining control of it, the first step is not being lazy. Learn to identify when you are slipping into your victim/martyr role, and commit not to do it any longer.

These phrases are some things you may say when you are feeling like a victim or a martyr. Use them as warning signs of when you need to change your attitude:

- "I can't change."
- "There's nothing I can do about it."
- "I guess it's just my fate."
- "I don't deserve to have it any better anyway."

b. Confront people and stand up for yourself. When you find yourself in one of these patterns of feeling powerless and you are thinking that there is nothing you can do, consider confronting the behavior (and the person) that is causing you to feel like a victim. For instance, if you want to see your father more often but you feel the amount of his visitation is only his decision, consider some other options. You can call your dad and let him know your feelings. You can ask him to call or visit more often. You must realize that the situation may not change; however, you have at least taken a step in regaining control of your own happiness.

Try to find and be with people who won't allow you to feel like a victim/martyr anymore. While this won't feel like much fun for a while, you will be disciplining yourself in a way that will help you to become a happier person. As Hebrews 12:11 tells us, "No discipline seems pleasant at the time, but painful. Later on, however, it produces a harvest of righteousness and peace for those who have been trained by it."

Ask the children and teens in the group to make a commitment to each other. Ask them to watch the others in the group for this tendency, and then teach them how gently to confront each other when they see someone acting out the victim/martyr role.

GROUP SESSION 8

TALKING HONESTLY ABOUT ALCOHOL

Talk to the children and teens in your group about their perceptions of alcohol and its use. Ask them how widespread they think the use of alcohol is at their school or other places they frequent.

1. Alcohol as an Escape Mechanism
Alcohol is often the first level of escape for teenagers and children just as it is for adults. Alcohol is commonly used by people who do not want to face their feelings and problems.

2. Alcohol as a Drug
Don't be fooled into thinking that just because alcohol is legal it is okay. Alcohol is a depressant. This means that alcohol (just like other drugs) can make you feel depressed. That is even more important to think about if you are already feeling depressed about things in your life (e.g., divorce, moving, school, etc.).

3. Some Statistics About Alcohol and Young People

An April 1991 study, released by Surgeon General Antonia Coello Novello, revealed that eight million teenagers—or more than a third of the nation's teenage student population—drank alcohol weekly and nearly a half-million are "binge" drinkers who consume an average of fifteen drinks each week.[2] This means that if this were an average group and you were all juniors and seniors in high school, at least one out of every two of you has had something to drink during the past year.

Ask the children and teens in the group how widespread they think the problem of alcohol abuse is among their peers. Share the following fact with them:

Fact: Drunk driving accounts for 50 to 55 percent of all traffic deaths among fifteen- to seventeen-year-olds.[3]

Ask the kids how they might handle the situation of being at a party where friends started drinking. You can use this question as a foundation to talk about what they would do if they were offered alcohol at a party. Ask them to consider whether or not they would call their parents if they needed a ride home after drinking.

4. The Effects of Alcohol

The use of alcohol can cause many physical, psychological, and emotional problems, such as:

- A decrease in ability to carry out daily functions and activities
- A change in sleeping patterns (Use of alcohol may make it harder to get to sleep or stay asleep. It may change the hours you sleep; or it may cause you to sleep excessively.)
- Moodiness
- School problems (even if you don't get caught)
- An increased likelihood that you will get into fights with friends and family (The result is that drinking cripples your relationships.)
- A decrease in appetite
- Internal problems with your body (e.g., liver, kidneys, heart, brain cells)

5. Alcoholism and Heredity

Although a few recent studies conclude that alcoholism can be attributed to (or at least linked to) heredity, most experts would agree that heredity is approximately 40 percent of a factor in a person becoming an alcoholic. Another significant, if not greater, influence in the use of alcohol is example. Parental examples are found to play a major role in whether or not their children drink (or abuse) alcohol. Parents who do not drink or drink only in moderation are less likely to have children who abuse alcohol. I base this conclusion on the families I have interviewed over the past fifteen years.

As a final note of encouragment, remind the members of your group that they are the only ones who can decide if, when, or how much they will drink. They might be surprised by the number of peers who are proud of the fact that they don't drink. Teach them to take control of their own lives and make good choices.

GROUP SESSION 9

TALKING HONESTLY ABOUT DRUGS

Talk about the single-parent family survey, which revealed that 43 percent of the teens and 18 percent of the children stated they had taken drugs other than marijuana. As your group discussed the dangers of alcohol abuse, let them know the same applies for drug abuse. Encourage them to confront their problems head on rather than burying them behind drugs.

There are literally thousands of legal and illegal drugs. The most common illegal drugs used by teens and children today (other than nicotine) are:

1. Alcohol
2. Marijuana
3. Cocaine
4. Methamphetamine (crystal, speed, uppers)
5. Acid (popularized again in the late eighties)
6. Inhalants (paint, white-out, glue, thinners)
7. Phencyclidine, also known as PCP (angel dust)[4]

Ask your group if they know of any other drugs that are currently being used by friends or acquaintances.

1. Cocaine
   a. Description. Cocaine is a derivative of the coca plant, which grows primarily in South America. Cocaine is processed into a white, powdery substance that is often "snorted" through the nostrils, smoked in water pipes (called bongs), infrequently injected, or smoked like a cigarette. Cocaine is gaining recognition as being one of the toughest drugs to give up.
   Cocaine is most commonly packaged in small amber vials, in small zip-lock baggies, or in folded pages of magazines or notebook paper.
   b. Problems related to cocaine use.

● Hyperactivity
● Sleeplessness
● Paranoia
● Heart failure
● High blood pressure and strokes
● Mood swings
● Nasal and facial deterioration

- Social problems
- Brain damage
- Depression

2. Marijuana

FACT:
1. One marijuana cigarette does the same damage to the lungs as fourteen tobacco cigarettes.
2. Because of processing advances, marijuana today is ten times stronger than it was in the sixties.
3. Marijuana can remain in the human system for thirty days or longer.
4. Marijuana is both psychologically and physically addictive.[5]

Tell the children and teens in the group the results of the single-parent family survey, which revealed that 69 percent of the teens and 38 percent of the children who were surveyed had smoked marijuana. Share the following facts about marijuana with the children and teens in your group.

Problems related to marijuana use.

- Decreased motivation
- Decreased appetite
- Reduction of brain cells
- Personality imbalances
- Reproductive failure or dysfunction
- Increased use and increased likelihood of graduation to use of other drugs
- Hormonal imbalances

GROUP SESSION 10

TALKING HONESTLY ABOUT DATING AND SEX

1. The Scope of the Problem

A 1991 survey from the Centers for Disease Control revealed that 54 percent of all high school students have had sexual intercourse.[6] Among ninth grade students, 40 percent have had sex. By tenth grade, the figure has reached 48 percent; by eleventh, 57 percent; and by twelfth, 72 percent. In addition to these statistics, the single-parent family survey taken from families like yours and kids like you revealed that children and teens (especially girls) who have limited relationships with their fathers are more likely to engage in premarital sex. Three conditions contribute to making single-parent children and teens like you, particularly girls, a high-risk group. They are:

- You may be searching for love, acceptance, relationship, and attachment that is missing in your lives. This search often begins when the father (or another significant male role model) leaves the home.
- You may be angry with your parents and you may, at least subconsciously, view a sexual relationship as a means of expressing your anger toward your parents.
- The relationship loss that occurred during the divorce has created a desire in you to find relationship. Young people from divorced families often do not know how to relate to the opposite sex due to the lack of role models. As a result, you may feel a sexual relationship is normal and acceptable.

Talk with children and teens in your group about their views of sexual relationships. Ask them if they feel pressure from other kids their age to experiment sexually. Share with the group the following fact and discuss it.

> **FACT:** More than one million teenage girls become pregnant each year. Four out of five of them are unmarried, and 30,000 are under the age of fifteen.[7]

2. Reasons to Wait Until Marriage

a. Stress, guilt, and fear. Premarital sex can cause great emotional stress. You all know the difference between right and wrong in relationships. Giving in to sexual pressures can sometimes feel like the right thing to do at the time; however, dealing with your feelings afterward can be devastating. For you girls, in addition to feeling guilty, sexual activity causes a tremendous fear of becoming pregnant. For boys, you should naturally be afraid of fathering a child and being ultimately responsible for the child emotionally, physically, and financially for the rest of your life.

b. AIDS and other sexually transmitted diseases. Consider the increasing spread of AIDS in the United States. All children and teens like you think at your age that life will last forever. For that reason, young people like you today don't seem to be as concerned about acquiring this deadly disease as perhaps you should be. One of the most important reasons to wait until marriage before engaging in sexual activity is to feel safe in your relationship with your chosen partner once you do decide to marry.

Although AIDS has received most of the headlines, you also need to know that there are several other sexually transmitted diseases, such as chlamydia, genital herpes, gonorrhea, trichomoniasis, syphilis, and pelvic-inflammatory disease. Many of these diseases, like AIDS, have no known cure.

3. Avoid High-Risk Dating Situations

- Date in groups or with other couples.
- Avoid dark, secluded, and intimate locations.
- Avoid parties or other situations where drugs and/or alcohol can add to sexual temptations.
- Choose dating locations and activities that are least likely to lead to intimate conditions.
- Talk to your date about your feelings about waiting and ask him or her to honor your standards.

Discuss the suggestions above with the children and teens in your group.

GROUP SESSION 1

EXPRESSING YOUR EMOTIONS

1. Love-Hate Relationships

Love-hate relationships are often a part of the single-parent family. Even though you love both parents, you still can feel a conflict over your anger about the divorce and your feelings of being abandoned by one parent. This may be even more true for you if you feel cut off from one parent due to visitation requirements or other conditions.

Ask your group to talk about any love/hate relationships they may have felt since their parents separated or divorced.

2. Facing Your Fears and Other Feelings

> For I am convinced that neither death nor life, neither angels nor demons, neither the present nor the future, nor any powers, neither height nor depth, nor anything else in all creation, will be able to separate us from the love of God that is in Christ Jesus our Lord. (Romans 8:38-39)

The best way of dealing with your feelings is to break out of your denial and confront them. You can accomplish this task in many ways.

a. Writing. Write a letter to the person you feel is connected to (notice I didn't say responsible for) your feelings. The letter should talk honestly, from your heart, about *all* of your feelings. You may want to include what you feel you need from this person in order to feel better about the situation. You don't necessarily have to even send the letter; sometimes just writing it is enough.

Ask if any of the kids in your group have ever written a letter like this to a parent.

b. Confront others. If you are troubled about a relationship, confront the person with the truth. Often, a loving confrontation is very helpful in resolving your feelings. This means that if you are feeling hurt or violated by someone, you should talk openly to them about your feelings.

The most important element in this process is that you tell them how *you* are feeling. It isn't necessary that they apologize or even respond. The important part is that you get your feelings out into the open.

Ask the kids in your group if they have ever been in the position of confronting a parent with the truth about their feelings and what the response was.

3. Having Reasonable Expectations

One of the sad realities about divorce is that your life will never be quite the same again. This is not to say that life won't be great, or hopefully even better. But your life will be different. Sometimes you have to learn to look at life reasonably and with the proper perspective in order to get on with it. It is easy to get caught up in the feeling that your parents' divorce is the end of the world.

4. Practicing Forgiveness

Be kind and compassionate to one another, forgiving each other, just as in Christ God forgave you. (Ephesians 4:32)

Talk to the group about forgiveness. Although they may be angry at everyone, including God, for their parents' divorce, at some point children and teens must learn to be able to forgive their parents. This is generally the final and most important step toward moving on with their lives.

GROUP SESSION 12

A HEALTHY SELF-IMAGE AND HAVING FRIENDS

1. The Real Self Versus the Ideal Self

Since you are from a divorced family, you may have the misconception that you are:

- Different and unacceptable because of the divorce.
- Unlovable.
- Unworthy of having good relationships and friendships.

Talk to your group about these three feelings. Ask group members if they have experienced any of them; ask how they felt during those times; and ask how they may have gotten free of those feelings.

Discuss how a lowered self-esteem can be a result of their feeling that the loss of a parent somehow changes who and what they are. Reinforce that the divorce had no impact whatsoever on what kind of people they are.

Consider this list of feelings (from figure 10.3) that you have probably experienced at some time during the divorce. This information is adapted from *The Teenage Q & A Book*[8] and presents feelings along with specific Scriptures that will help you maintain an honest and positive self-image.

2. Spiritual Gifts

You may want to focus your attention on a passage from Romans 12, which tells you that you are a unique and special person:

> God has given each of us the ability to do certain things well. So if God has given you the ability to prophesy, then prophesy whenever you can—as often as your faith is strong enough to receive a message from God. If your gift is that of serving others, serve them well. If you are a teacher, do a good job of teaching. If you are a preacher, see to it that your sermons are strong and helpful. If God has given you money, be generous in helping others with it. If God has given you administrative ability and put you in charge of the work of others, take the responsibility seriously. Those who offer comfort to the sorrowing should do so with Christian cheer. (Romans 12:6-8, TLB)

It is important for all the children and teens in your group to see themselves as individuals, specially created by God, in His image. Talk to them about their spiritual gifts and remind them that each of them has special God-given gifts and talents. It is up to each of them to determine which of these talents they possess and then to use them to serve the Lord. This concept is crucial in helping children and teens improve their self-image.

Figure 10.3
Balancing Feelings in Light of Scripture

How I Feel	Scripture	The Real Truth
Unacceptable	Romans 15:7	I am accepted.
Inadequate	Philippians 4:13	I can do all things.
Fearful	Isaiah 41:10	I am supported by God.
Insecure	Proverbs 3:25-26	I can be confident.
Unloved	Ephesians 3:17-19	I am loved.

APPENDIX A:
SINGLE-PARENT FAMILY
WELLNESS CHECKUP

Conditional permission is given to copy pages 194-195, 207-212 for use with your ministry to single-parent families. No pages in any other part of this book may be copied, nor may the following pages be copied for any reason other than actual use in your single-parent family ministry.

Instructions: The Single-Parent Family Wellness Checkup is designed to be completed on a regular basis. Children and teens whom you consider to be at high risk should be monitored weekly. Monthly checkups should suffice for those who seem to be adapting well to their new family system.

Whenever someone you are monitoring answers yes to any of the questions that follow, refer immediately to the corresponding warning signs in chapter 6 for additional help. You should also document additional responses to any warning signs at the bottom of the checkup form.

After you have completed the form, start a file on the teens and children whom you are monitoring and make a note on your monthly or quarterly planner as to when the next checkup is due.

To be on the safe side, discuss all potential warning signs with other staff members who see or work with the child or teen. You should also consider the validity of other options, such as: (1) meeting with the parent(s), (2) counseling with the child or teenager yourself, or (3) referring the child or teen to another professional.

SINGLE-PARENT FAMILY WELLNESS CHECKUP

Family name _____

ABOUT THE CHILD OR TEEN

Name _____

Age _____ Phone _____

Address _____

City _____ State _____ Zip _____

Closest friend(s) _____

Lives with: ❑ mom   ❑ dad   ❑ other _____

Joint custody: ❑ yes   ❑ no

How often is visitation with non-custodial parent? _____

Date of parents' separation or divorce _____

Months since divorce (as of this checkup) _____

ABOUT THE CUSTODIAL PARENT

Name _____

Address _____

City _____ State _____ Zip _____

Phone (home) _____ (work) _____

ABOUT THE NON-CUSTODIAL PARENT

Name _____

Address _____

City _____ State _____ Zip _____

Phone (home) _____ (work) _____

ABOUT THE PARAPARENT

Name _____

Address _____

City _____ State _____ Zip _____

Phone _____ ParaParent since (date) _____

CHILD AND TEEN CHECKUP FORM

Date of this checkup _____

Date of last checkup _____

Date of next checkup _____

Does the child or teen appear to be:	Yes	No	Where to find further help in this book:
1. Lonely, quiet, or moody?			page 104
2. Depressed? (low energy, poor concentration, low motivation)			page 106
3. Suffering from low self-esteem?			page 109
4. Having difficulty sleeping?			page 110
5. Negative about everything and everybody?			page 112
6. Isolating himself or herself?			page 115
7. Angry or abusive to others?			page 117
8. Exhibiting changed eating habits?			page 120
9. Argumentative and deceitful?			page 122
10. Fighting at school and at home?			page 123
11. Doing poorly at school?			page 125
12. Violating curfew?			page 127
13. Shoplifting or stealing?			page 130
14. Dropping out of school or church activities?			page 131
15. Using alcohol or drugs?			page 132
16. Refusing to come to church or church functions?			page 135
17. Lazy or inclined to procrastinate?			page 136
18. Dating or befriending kids against the parents' wishes?			page 137
19. Pregnant or sexually active?			page 138
20. Changed in appearance?			page 140
21. Unwilling to make eye contact?			page 142

Comments or action taken _____

_____

_____

Completed by _____

In consultation with _____

APPENDIX B:
THE PARENT SURVEY

Below is a sample of the survey used to measure the responses from the 288 parents who participated in the single-parent family survey. The finding number following each question indicates where additional information related to the question is found in this text. A summary of responses also follows each survey question.

1. Are you the mother or father of the patient?
   Mother: 77%
   Father: 23%
   See chapter 4 - findings 1 & 6

2. What is the patient's sex?
   Male: 68%
   Female: 32%
   See chapter 4 - findings 2 & 3

3. What is the patient's age?
   Adolescents:
   17: 28%
   16: 25%
   15: 22%
   14: 16%
   13: 9%
   Children:
   12: 31%
   11: 25%
   10: 19%
   9: 14%
   8: 11%
   See chapter 4 - findings 4 & 5

4. Does the patient live with you?
   Yes: 82%
   No. Patient lives with father (or not with person responding to survey): 6%
   No. Patient lives with other relative: 12%
   See chapter 4 - finding 6

5. If the patient resides with you, how often does he/she see the other parent?
   Daily: 2%
   Weekly: 16%
   Twice a month (usually every other weekend): 28%
   Monthly (usually due to geographic constraints): 31%
   Less frequently: 23%
   See chapter 4 - finding 7

6. How many children do you have living with you?
   (This question was asked in an attempt to discern any correlation between children and teens in treatment and the number of siblings in a family. However, no significant information was derived from this statistic due to its general conformity to national averages.)
   0: 6%
   1: 57%
   2 or more: 37%

7. Is this the first time your child has been in counseling or treatment?
   Results from inpatient hospital settings:
   Yes: 81%
   No: 19%
   Results from outpatient counseling centers:
   Yes: 48%
   No: 52%
   If your response was yes, how old was the child when he or she first received psychological counseling or treatment?
   13 or older: 68%
   Under 13: 32%
   See chapter 4 - findings 4, 5, & 10

8. Has your child been in trouble with the police or school authorities?
   Yes: 69%
   No: 31%
   See chapter 4 - finding 9

9. For what type of problem(s) did you bring him or her in?
   Results from inpatient hospital settings:
   Conduct disorder: 36%
   Alcohol and/or drugs: 27%
   Depression: 26%

Eating disorder: 9%
Other psychological problem: 2%
Dual diagnosis: 56%
Results from outpatient counseling centers:
Depression: 35%
School problems: 27%
Conduct disorder: 25%
Alcohol and/or drugs: 11%
Other psychological problems: 2%
Dual diagnosis: 31%
See chapter 4 - findings 9 & 10

10. At what age did he or she begin having trouble in this area?
    (This question was intended to be correlated with question 3 concerning the patient's age. The anticipated benefit to knowing at what the age the patient began experiencing trouble was to factor it against the actual age of the patient at the time of admission. The results from this question indicated that the parents had an average of six months after the first warning sign before the problem became a crisis.)
    See chapter 4 - findings 4, 5, & 8

11. Do you come from a single-parent home?
    Yes: 56%
    No: 44%
    See chapter 4 - finding 11

12. What age was the patient when the other parent left home?
    (No independent findings were listed for this question because, in and of itself, it had little significance. This question was designed to be related to the age of the child or teen at the time of crisis. The combined result of these questions provided the Windows of Opportunity theory.)
    See chapter 4 - findings 4, 5, 8, & 12

13. Do you feel he or she would be in treatment or counseling now if you and your spouse were still together?
    Yes: 26%
    No: 74%
    See chapter 4 - finding 13

14. Were there any changes in your child during the divorce or separation?
    Yes: 78%
    No: 22%
    See chapter 4 - findings 2, 3, 8, & 14

15. Do you attend church?
    Yes: 72%
    No: 28%

If yes, approximately how often?
Weekly: 34%
Twice a month: 38%
Once a month: 19%
Less often: 9%
See chapter 4 - findings 15 & 16

16. Do your children attend church?
Yes: 66%
No: 34%
If yes, how often?
Weekly: 22%
Twice a month: 42%
Once a month: 22%
Less often: 14%
See chapter 4 - findings 15 & 16

17. Were there any warning signs of his or her problems prior to the crisis? If yes, please explain.
(The data collected in response to this question was combined with the corresponding answers from the children's and teens' survey. The results of these two areas comprised the majority of the Twenty-One Warning Signs of Crisis.)
See chapter 4 - finding 14

18. Do you have any advice for other single parents?
(The answers to this question along with data from interviews as well as information from the teens' and children's surveys provided the information contained in the Twenty-One Warning Signs of Crisis.)
See chapter 4 - finding 14 - pages 62-63

19. Was he or she able to talk to you or anyone else about problems?
The child or teen had no one to talk to other than me (responses from moms and dads): 45%
The child or teen talked to me (responses from moms): 13%
The child or teen talked to a youth pastor at church (no response from dads): 5%
The child or teen talked to the pastor at church (responses from moms and dads): 2%
The child or teen talked to a counselor (no responses from dads): 3%
The child or teen talked to a male relative (responses from moms and dads): 6%
The child or teen talked to my ex-spouse (responses from moms): 13%
The child or teen talked to other people: 3%
I don't know: 5%
See chapter 4 - finding 16

20. Whom (if anyone) did you turn to for support in raising him or her?
No one: 62%
See chapter 4 - findings 15 & 16

APPENDIX C:
THE CHILDREN'S AND TEENS' SURVEY

Below is a sample of the survey used to measure the responses from the 352 children and teens (including 61 children and 291 teens) who participated in the single-parent family survey. The finding number following each question indicates where additional information relating to the question is found in this text. A summary of responses also follows each survey question.

1. Whom do you live with?
   My mother: 82%
   My father: 12%
   Another relative or guardian: 6%
   See chapter 4 - finding 6

2. How old were you when your parents separated?
   (This question was designed to be correlated with the parents' answers and other data to formulate the Windows of Opportunity theory.) (See appendix B.)
   See chapter 5 - finding 1

3. My parents used to argue:
   Responses from adolescents:
   All the time: 56%
   Often: 22%
   Once in a while: 6%
   Never: 16%
   Responses from children:
   All the time: 62%
   Pretty often: 8%
   Once in a while: 2%
   Never: 28%
   See chapter 5 - finding 2

4. My parents used to get violent sometimes with each other only, me, my brothers/ sisters, my parents never hit us.

Responses from adolescents:
Each other: 57%
Me: 69%
My brothers/sisters: 64%
My parents never hit us: 31%
Responses from children:
Each other: 61%
Me: 45%
My brothers/sisters: 51%
My parents never hit us: 55%
See chapter 5 - finding 3

5. Did you know that your parents were not getting along well?
Responses from adolescents:
Yes: 87%
No: 13%
Responses from children:
Yes: 68%
No: 32%
See chapter 5 - finding 4

6. On a scale from 1 to 10 (10 being the most stressful), how stressful was it for you during the divorce?
Responses from adolescents:
Average response from females: 8
Average response from males: 6
Responses from children:
Average response from females: 9
Average response from males: 8
See chapter 5 - finding 5

7. Other than your parent at home, was there anybody around for you to talk to about the divorce or other problems you were going through?
Responses from adolescents:
No: 68%
Yes: 32% (Responses included relatives, friends, teachers, school counselors, and church youth leaders.)
Responses from children:
No: 62%
Yes: 38% (In addition to the responses given by the adolescents, these responses included girlfriends or boyfriends.)
See chapter 5 - findings 4, 6, & 20

8. If you attend church, was there anybody there you were able to talk to? If yes, whom?
Responses from adolescents:

No: 94%
Yes: 6% (Pastor, youth leader)
Responses from children:
No: 98%
Yes: 2% (Pastor, youth leader)
See chapter 5 - findings 6 & 20

9. Do you think you would be in counseling or treatment now if your parents had stayed together?
    Responses from adolescents:
    No: 61%
    Yes: 39%
    Responses from children:
    No: 64%
    Yes: 36%
    See chapter 5 - finding 7

10. Understanding that your answers are confidential and no one will know you answered these questions, have you ever:

    Shoplifted   Stolen from others
    Smoked marijuana   Cut school often
    Taken other drugs   Used alcohol
    Run away from home   Had a sexual relationship
    Gotten into fights   Hurt animals
    Had suicidal thoughts   Just hated everyone
    Had trouble sleeping   Wanted to hurt others physically
    Had an eating disorder (compulsive overeating, anorexia, bulimia)

    Adolescents and children who responded yes to each category.
    Shoplifted:
    Adolescents: 76%
    Children: 68%
    Stolen from others:
    Adolescents: 66%
    Children: 41%
    Smoked marijuana:
    Adolescents: 69%
    Children: 38%
    Cut school often:
    Adolescents: 78%
    Children: 12%
    Taken other drugs:
    Adolescents: 43%
    Children: 18%
    Used alcohol:
    Adolescents: 82%

Children: 48%
Run away from home:
Adolescents: 21%
Children: 8%
Had a sexual relationship:
Adolescents: 67%
Children: 18%
Gotten into fights:
Adolescents: 61%
Children: 18%
Hurt animals:
Adolescents: 5%
Children: 2%
Had suicidal thoughts:
Adolescents: 69%
Children: 38%
Just hated everyone:
Adolescents: 66%
Children: 62%
Had trouble sleeping:
Adolescents: 76%
Children: 83%
Wanted to hurt others physically:
Adolescents: 62%
Children: 37%
Had an eating disorder (compulsive overeating, anorexia, bulimia):
Adolescents: 11%
Children: 4%
See chapter 5 - findings 7-11, 13-19, & 21

11. How did your family find out you were having problems?
Responses from adolescents:
I told them: 12%
I was arrested: 19%
My school teacher or principal told my parent(s): 8%
My pastor/my youth leader/somebody at church told my parent(s): 1%
I was failing school or classes: 49%
It was obvious I was having trouble: 44%
Responses from children:
I told them: 5%
I was arrested: 11%
My school teacher or principal told my parent(s): 8%
My pastor/my youth leader/somebody at church told my parent(s): 1%
I was failing school or classes: 34%
It was obvious I was having trouble: 41%
See chapter 5 - findings 22, 23, & 24

12. Who do you think was responsible for the breakup of your family? (Choose one or more of the following:)

Responses from adolescents:

My mom: 21%

My dad: 38%

Me: 19%

My brother(s) or sister(s): 22%

Not sure: 23%

Both parents: 46%

Responses from children:

My mom: 11%

My dad: 46%

Me: 24%

My brother(s) or sister(s): 26%

Not sure: 26%

Both parents: 41%

See chapter 5 - findings 3, 7, 12, 25, & 26

13. What do you think were the main reason(s) for the divorce? (You may select more than one answer.)

Responses from adolescents:

Money: 49%

Communication between Mom and Dad: 44%

Arguing: 44%

Physical violence between my parents: 29%

My dad's work hours: 18%

My mom's work hours: 4%

An affair: 20%

Religious differences: 8%

Responses from children:

Money: 22%

Communication between Mom and Dad: 28%

Arguing: 61%

Physical violence between my parents: 27%

My dad's work hours: 18%

My mom's work hours: 1%

An affair: 13%

Religious differences: 4%

See chapter 5 - finding 27

14. Do you have any advice for other kids who are going through a divorce or separation with their parents?

(This question was intended to extract information from the teens and children that could prove helpful to others in similar situations. The answers from this question also appear throughout the book.)

See chapter 5 - pages 98-100

APPENDIX D:
ParaParenting Forms

Form D.1

PARAPARENTING INFORMATION AND AGREEMENT

Instructions: Please complete the following information and agreement cards that will help us to match you with a single-parent family within our church. The church is acting solely as a resource for getting you together with a single-parent family and is not involved in or responsible for the ongoing process or outcome. Thanks for your willingness to help. This card will remain on file in the church office.

Name _____ Date _____

Age _____ Phone number _____

Address _____

City _____ State _____ Zip _____

Married: Yes ❑   No ❑   If yes, how long? _____

Ages of children _____

I could spend _____ hours each week with the family and/or child.

I feel I relate better with kids between the ages of:

     2-5 ❑   6-9 ❑   10-13 ❑   14 and older ❑

I feel I relate better to: boys ❑   girls ❑

My interests and hobbies are _____

_____

_____

_____

Form D.2

UNDERSTANDING YOUR ROLE AS A PARAPARENT

1. I am volunteering my time to be a ParaParent with a single-parent family.
2. I understand that I have no legal obligation to this single-parent family.
3. I am in good physical and mental health.
4. I understand that intimate physical contact with any member of the single-parent family is unacceptable.
5. I am committing to work with the single-parent family for a minimum of six months. There is no minimum or maximum amount of time that I am expected to spend with the single-parent family each week. This amount of time will be discussed and agreed upon with the parent or guardian of the single-parent family.
6. If a conflict arises and I am unable to continue in my role as a ParaParent, I will do everything in my power to make the transition smooth for the single-parent family.
7. If for any reason the parent or guardian of the single-parent family or an administrator of the church believes I should step away from my role as a ParaParent, I will agree to do so without recourse.

_____

ParaParent Signature   Date

_____

ParaParent Signature   Date

Form D.3

SINGLE-PARENT FAMILY CARD

Instructions: Please complete the following information card that will help us to match you with volunteer ParaParents within our church. The church is acting solely as a resource for getting you together with the ParaParents and is not involved in or responsible for the ongoing process. This card will remain on file in the church office.

Parent's name _____ Date _____

Phone number (work) _____ (home) _____

Address _____

City _____ State _____ Zip _____

Number of children _____

Information about my children:

1. Name _____ Age _____ Sex: Male ❏ Female ❏

   Hobbies and interests _____

   _____

2. Name _____ Age _____ Sex: Male ❏ Female ❏

   Hobbies and interests _____

   _____

3. Name _____ Age _____ Sex: Male ❏ Female ❏

   Hobbies and interests _____

   _____

4. Name _____ Age _____ Sex: Male ❏ Female ❏

   Hobbies and interests _____

   _____

5. Name _____ Age _____ Sex: Male ❏ Female ❏

   Hobbies and interests _____

   _____

Form D.4

UNDERSTANDING YOUR ROLE AND RELATIONSHIP
WITH THE PARAPARENTS
(Information and Agreement)

1. I understand that the ParaParent(s) is volunteering time to be with my family.
2. I understand that I have no legal or financial obligation to the ParaParent(s).
3. I understand that intimate physical contact between the ParaParent(s) and myself or any member of my family is unacceptable.
4. If an unresolvable conflict arises between myself or my family and the ParaParent, I will immediately ask that the relationship be terminated. I will contact the church administration if the situation is not resolved.
5. I will not ask nor expect monetary assistance from the ParaParent(s).
6. I will treat the ParaParents(s) with kindness and respect and will in no way take advantage of the relationship.

_____

Signature of Parent or Guardian   Date

Form D.5

SAMPLE BULLETIN ANNOUNCEMENT

INTRODUCING OUR SINGLE-PARENT FAMILY MINISTRY

Did You Know?
- Nearly half of today's children will live in a single-parent family at some point during their childhood.
- U.S. Government surveys state that in 1992 nearly one in four children were living in single-parent families, and that number is increasing.

What We Are Doing
We realize and respect that a significant portion of our church membership is comprised of single-parent families. It is our belief that we must do everything within our power to reach out to these single-parent families by offering them this new and exciting ministry program.

Features of Our Single-Parent Family Ministry
- Weekly single-parenting support groups
- Weekly single-parent family, teens', and children's support groups
- A special once-a-month training session, presented by our staff, for single parents and their families
- An innovative ParaParenting program that matches volunteers with single-parent families

How You Can Get Involved
If you are feeling led to help us with our exciting single-parent family ministry, please contact the administration office for more details.

Form D.6

SINGLE-PARENT FAMILY CARECARD

Name of family _____ Date _____

Children live with: mom ❑   dad ❑   grandparents ❑   other ❑

_____

Frequency of visitation: weekly ❑   monthly ❑   less often ❑   other ❑

Approximate date of divorce: _____

Primary custodial parent or guardian _____

Phone number (work) _____ (home) _____

Address _____

City _____ State _____ Zip _____

Noncustodial parent or guardian _____

Phone number (work) _____ (home) _____

Address _____

City _____ State _____ Zip _____

Children's names and ages

1. Name _____ Age _____ Sex: Male ❑ Female ❑

2. Name _____ Age _____ Sex: Male ❑ Female ❑

3. Name _____ Age _____ Sex: Male ❑ Female ❑

4. Name _____ Age _____ Sex: Male ❑ Female ❑

5. Name _____ Age _____ Sex: Male ❑ Female ❑

ParaParent: yes ❑   no ❑   Name _____

Phone number (work) _____ (home) _____

Address _____

City _____ State _____ Zip _____

Potential problems _____

Consultation with other staff: yes ❑   no ❑

Has the family been encouraged to attend single-parenting groups

or seminars? yes ❑   no ❑

Use reverse side for notes and special instructions.

NOTES

Chapter 1—The Single-Parent Family Epidemic

1. "Kids Count Data Book, 1991," Center for the Study of Social Policy, Washington, D.C.

2. U.S. National Center for Health Statistics, U.S. Department of Health and Human Services, 1989.

3. Living Arrangements of Children, U.S. Bureau of the Census, 1991.

4. *Single Adult Ministries Journal*, January 1992, issue 89, page 4.

5. *Newsweek*, June 8, 1992, page 21.

6. *Focus on the Family* magazine, April 1992, page 11.

7. *Focus on the Family* magazine.

Chapter 2—Observing the Single-Parent Family

1. William Reid and M. Wise, *Diagnostic and Statistical Manual of Mental Disorders*, DSM-III-R (New York: Brunner and Mazell, 1989), pages 33, 54-58.

2. DSM-III-R, pages 141-143.

3. Judith Wallerstein, *Second Chances: Men, Women and Children a Decade After Divorce* (Boston, MA: Ticknor and Fields/T.I.S. Enterprises, 1989), pages 44-46, 112-115.

4. U.S. Bureau of Census, 1989.

Chapter 4—Sixteen Significant Findings About Single-Parent Families

1. U.S. Bureau of Census, 1989.

2. William Reid and M. Wise, *Diagnostic and Statistical Manual of Mental Disorders*, DSM-III-R (New York: Brunner and Mazell, 1989), pages 198-199.

3. DSM-III-R, pages 53-54.

4. DSM-III-R, pages 58-61.

5. DSM-III-R, pages 59-60.

6. Frank Minirth and Paul Meier, *Love Hunger* (Nashville, TN: Thomas Nelson, 1990), pages 14-21.

7. DSM-III-R, pages 130-131.

8. Jane E.Broody, *The New York Times*, June 21, 1992, 6-H2.

9. As quoted by Josh McDowell and Dick Day in *Why Wait?* (San Bernardino, CA: Here's Life, 1987), page 60.

10. N. Gregory Hamilton, *Self and Others* (Northvale, NJ: Aronson and Jason, 1990), pages 6-19.

11. George Barna, *What Americans Believe* (Ventura, CA: Regal Books, 1991), pages 235-236.

12. Living Arrangements of Children Report, U.S. Bureau of the Census, 1989.

Chapter 5—What You Need to Know About Children and Teens of Divorce

1. National Institute on Drug Abuse, University of Michigan Institute for Social Research, 1989.

2. From the U.S. Centers for Disease Control, as published in *The Orange County Register*, June 21, 1992, page H-2.

3. Josh McDowell, *The Dad Difference* (San Bernardino, CA: Here's Life, 1989), page 11.

Chapter 6—The Twenty-One Warning Signs of Crisis

1. Wendy Baldwin, "Adolescent Pregnancy and Childbearing—Rates, Trends and Research Findings." From the CPR-NICHD (Bethesda, MD: Demographic and Behavioral Science Branch, NICHD, 1985).

Chapter 7—Helping Change Lives Through a ParaParenting Ministry

1. *Webster's New World Dictionary* (Springfield, MA: G. and C. Merriam, 1989).

Chapter 8—Introducing the Single-Parent Family Ministry to Your Congregation

1. *The World Almanac*, "Bureau of U.S. Census Report" (New York: World Almanac Publishing, 1989), page 834.

2. *Special Report* magazine, August-October issue, 1990, page 7.

3. *Special Report* magazine, August-October issue, 1990, page 7.

4. The Bureau of Labor Statistics, 1984, and Demography, 21, pages 71-82.

5. "1990 Yearbook of American and Canadian Churches," as published in *The World Almanac* (New York: World Almanac Publishing, 1991), page 608.

Chapter 9—Support Group Discussion Guides for Single-Parents

1. Benjamin Spock, "How Not to Bring Up a Bratty Child," *Redbook* magazine, February 1974, pages 29-31.

2. 1991 Department of Health and Human Services, report by Richard P. Kusserow, released by U.S. Surgeon General Antonia Coello Novello.

3. National Highway Traffic Safety Administration, "Morbidity and Mortality Weekly Report," number 40 (11), March 22, 1991, page 56.

4. S. Van Cleave, M.D., *Counseling for Substance Abuse and Addiction* (Waco, TX: Word, Inc., 1987), page 47.

5. 1990 U.S. Centers for Disease Control study, as reported in *The Orange County Register,* January 4, 1992, pages A1 and A21.

6. Josh McDowell, *How to Help Your Child to Say "No" to Sexual Pressure* (Waco, TX: Word, Inc., 1987), pages 10-11.

Chapter 10—Support Group Discussion Guides for Children and Teenagers of Single-Parent Families

1. *Webster's Intermediate Dictionary* (Springfield, MA: G. and C. Merriam, 1989).

2. 1991 Department of Health and Human Services, report by Richard P. Kusserow, released by U.S. Surgeon General Antonia Coello Novello.

3. National Highway Traffic Safety Administration, "Morbidity and Mortality Weekly Report," number 40 (11), March 22, 1991, page 56.

4. S. Van Cleave, M.D., *Counseling for Substance Abuse and Addiction* (Waco, TX: Word, Inc., 1987), page 185.

5. Van Cleave, page 47.

6. 1991 U.S. Center for Disease Control Study, as reported in *The Orange County Register*, January 4, 1992, pages A1 and A21.

7. Josh McDowell, *How to Help Your Child to Say "No" to Sexual Pressure* (Waco, TX: Word, Inc., 1987), pages 10-11.

8. Josh McDowell, *The Teenage Q & A Book* (Waco, TX: Word, Inc., 1990), page 61.

AUTHOR

Greg S. Cynaumon, Ph.D. is a family therapist with the Minirth-Meier New Life Clinic in Orange, California. Greg is also the host of the syndicated radio show, "Southern California Live," heard daily on radio station KBRT, AM 740, which focuses on issues of life from a Christian perspective.

Greg holds a master's degree and a Ph.D. in psychology from Sierra University.

Greg, his wife, Jan, and his two children, Tracy and Matt, reside in Orange County, California, Greg is on staff at Rose Drive Friends Church.

For more information regarding tapes, speaking engagements, or staff training sessions, write or call:

Dr. Greg Cynaumon
260 Newport Center Drive #430
Newport Beach, CA 92660
1-800-877-HOPE

SINGLES
Ministry Resources

Materials available from Singles Ministry Resources:

Foundational Books
- *Starting a Single Adult Ministry*
- *Giving the Ministry Away:* Empowering Single Adults for Effective Leadership
- *Growing Your Single Adult Ministry*
- *Developing a Divorce Recovery Ministry:* A How-to Manual
- *Helping Single Parents with Troubled Kids:* A Ministry Resource for Pastors & Youth Workers

Idea Books
- *The Idea Catalog*
- *Creative Weekends:* 291/2 Ready-to-Use Ideas for Your Single Adult Ministry (available 1995)
- *Building Your Leadership Team:* Practical Ideas for Single Adult Ministry (available 1995)

Program Materials
- *Just Me & the Kids:* Building Healthy Parent Families
- *Vacations with a Purpose:* A Planning Handbook for Your Short-Term Missions Team (Leader's Manual and Member's Handbook)

Newsletter
- Single Adult Ministries (SAM) Journal

To receive more information about these and other quality singles ministry resources or to order, contact your local Christian bookstore

OR

SINGLES MINISTRY RESOURCES
P.O. Box 60430
Colorado Springs, Colorado 80960-0430

Or call (800) 323-7543
Canada (800) 387-5856
or (719) 635-6020

SINGLES MINISTRY RESOURCES is a division of Cook Communications Ministries